Embodying
Colonial Memories

•   •   •

Embodying
Colonial Memories

• • •

Spirit Possession,
Power and the Hauka
in West Africa

Paul Stoller

Routledge
New York and London

Published in 1995 by

Routledge
29 West 35 Street
New York, NY 10001

Published in Great Britain in 1995 by

Routledge
11 New Fetter Lane
London EC4P 4EE

Copyright © 1995 by Routledge

Printed in the United States of America

Library of Congress Cataloging-in-Publications Data

Stoller, Paul.
    Embodying colonial memories : spirit possession, power, and the Hauka in West Africa /
        Paul Stoller.
            p.   cm.
    Includes bibliographical references (P.   ) and index.
    ISBN 0 – 415 – 90876 –0   —   ISBN 0 – 415 – 90877–9 (pbk.)
        1. Songhai (African people) — Rites and ceremonies. 2. Songhai (African people) — Religion.
    3. Songhai (African people) — Psychology. 4. Spirit possession — Niger — Niamey (Dept.) —
    History. 5. Cults — Niger — Niamey (Dept.) 6. Niamey (Niger : Dept.) — Religious life and
    customs. 7. Niamey (Niger : Dept.)—Politics and government. I. Title.

    DT547.45.S65S74 1995
    306.6'9965—dc20   94–41690
                                                                              CIP

In Memory of Nicole Echard
(1937 – 1994)

Contents

• ◆ •

Acknowledgments

•   •   •

The Hauka, Songhay spirits that mimic Nigerien colonial culture, "commissioned" this book in Tillaberi, Niger in June of 1987. I thank them for the invitation to tell their story. It has taken me a long time to bring my "commission" to this end, and I have many people and institutions to thank who helped me along the way. I first and foremost thank the Government of the Republic of Niger for granting me authorizations to conduct ongoing ethnographic research in the western regions of the country since 1976. I am grateful for funds, from the National Endowment for the Humanities, the National Science Foundation, the Wenner-Gren Foundation for Anthropological Research, the American Philosophical Society, and West Chester University, that have financed various stages of the field research on which this book is based. Funds from the John Simon Guggenheim Memorial Foundation and the National Endowment for the Humanities have provided time for reflection and writing.

The idea for this project was planted and fertilized on the magnificent grounds of the School of American Research (SAR) in Santa Fe, New Mexico. I thank Douglas Schwartz, President of SAR, for inviting me to be a Resident Scholar in 1992-93. I also thank the SAR staff for making my happy tenure in Santa Fe so intellectually productive.

There are many people who helped to shape the contours of this book, and I am immeasurably grateful to them. In Niger, the scholarship and friendship of Dioulde Laya, director of the Organization of African Unity's (OAU) Center for Oral, Linguistic and Historical Tradition, has been an ongoing source of inspiration. I am also much indebted to Chaibou Dan Inna, Professor of Literature at the University of Niamey, for finding many of the photos used in this book as well as for his encouragement and friendship. The friendships of Thomas Price and Hadiza Djibo of Niamey have been a great source of support. They have helped me in more ways than they will ever know.

In France, I have learned a great deal from the wisdom, energy and creativity of Jean Rouch. His monumental film, *Les maitres fous* (The Crazy Masters) inspired much in this book. There is also a great deal in this book that was inspired by my late friend, Jean-Marie Gibbal, whose lyrical reflections on spirit possession are presented in the recently translated *Genii of the River Niger* (1994). The examples of other Africanist colleagues in France (Marc Piault, Jean-Pierre Olivier de Sardan, Suzanne Lallemand, Laurent Vidal, Alice Sindzingre, Edmond Bernus, and the late Suzanne Bernus) have also taught me much about ethnographic research in and textual representation of Africa.

Many colleagues in North America took time to read all or parts of the manuscript. For the critical quality of their talk I thank John Chernoff, Herbert Cole, Alma Gottlieb, Laura Graham, John Homiak, Michael Lambek, Achille Mbembe, Jasmin Tahmiseb McConatha, David Napier, Kirin Narayan, and Marina Roseman. Richard Waller read the entire manuscript with an historian's eye for detail. His thoroughness clarified and gave depth to the historical sections of the text. I also thank Michael Taussig for writing *Mimesis and Alterity*, the work that provided a fruitful theoretical direction for *Embodying Colonial Memories*. The creative force generated through reading *Mimesis and Alterity* was sustained during long conversations with Rosemary Coombe. Her critical insight and her breadth of knowledge have given shape to the theoretical dimensions of this book. For that, I am deeply grateful.

T. David Brent got me started in the book-writing business. At a time when no one wanted or understood what I had written, David had the capacity to sense what others couldn't or wouldn't grasp. Like a champion, he fought and won the battle to publish *In Sorcery's Shadow*, my first book. His faith in my capacities gave me the confidence to continue on the writer's path. That is why his spirit is ever-present in my prose, no matter the form, no matter the context.

Embodying Colonial Memories is dedicated to the memory of Nicole Echard who died in Paris in June of 1994. Nicole was a scholar who approached the subject of spirit possession with great rigor and profound humanity. Her work on the Hausa *bori* cult is without equal. Nicole was also a dedicated and loyal friend. Although she was ill, she managed to read and comment on portions of *Embodying Colonial Memories*. Nicole had much to tell the field of anthropology about spirit possession and religion. Alas, death is most cruel when it silences a brilliant voice that hasn't yet said all that it wishes to say. My hope is that *Embodying Colonial Memories* will, in a small way, pay hommage to the clarity of Nicole's vision, the precision of her voice, and the depth of her character.

Diplomacy On A Dune

♦   ♦   ♦

The acrid smell of burning resins infuses Adamu Jenitongo's compound, preparing it for the spirits (*holle* in the Songhay language). It is late afternoon in Tillaberi, a small Songhay town in Republic of Niger, and the sounds of a Songhay spirit possession ceremony crackle through the dusty air: the high pitched "cries" of the monochord violin; the resonant clacks of bamboo drumsticks striking gourd drums; the melodious contours of the praise-singer's "old words;" the patter of dancing feet on dune sand.

It is a white hot day in June of 1987 and the mix of sounds and smells has brought spirits to Adamu Jenitongo's egg-shaped dunetop compound. Four mudbrick houses shimmer in the languorous heat. From under a thatched canopy at the compound entrance, the orchestra continues to play spirit music. Spirits like this place. Drawn by the pungent smells, they visit it day and night. On this day the *Gengi Bi*, or spirits of the earth, have already come to the compound to bless members of the audience, giving them the courage to confront their hunger and sickness. These spirits sing rather than talk, and their melodies have lingered and dissipated into the dusky air.

They are not the only visitors on this day: Clustered in front of the musician's canopy are three *Hauka* spirits—spirits that mimic European

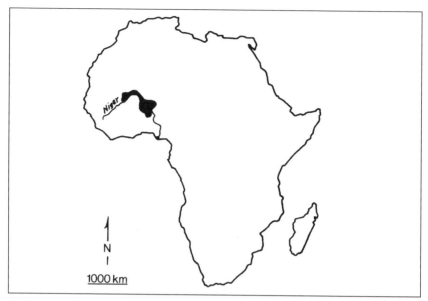

Songhay Country in West Africa.

figures. They groan, bellow and thump their chests with clenched fists as they stamp across the sand. Saliva bubbles from their mouths. They babble. Their eyes blaze.

Istambula, the leader of the Hauka, is there, as is Zeneral Malia, the General of the Red Sea. These "military" officers are well-served by Bambara-Mossi, a Hauka-conscripted foot soldier who is exceedingly crass. "Hauk'ize," Istambula shouts. "Hauk'ize of Tillaberi, present yourselves for our Roundtable," he says in Songhay. Slowly the non-possessed men and women who carry Hauka spirits form a loose circle around the deities. Bambara-Mossi makes sure that the mediums stand at "attention" in the presence of Istambula and Zeneral Malia.

Adamu Jenitongo and the anthropologist are seated under the shade of a tall eucalyptus, whose unquenchable thirst has withered the other trees in the compound. They sit silently on palm-frond mats and swat flies. The Hauka Roundtable is about to convene. Suddenly, Istambula breaks through the circle of mediums and runs stiff-legged in their direction. He leaves his feet like a swan diver and belly flops just in front of Jenitongo and the anthropologist.

"I swear to *Bonji* (God). I swear to Bonji," he mutters in pidgin French, "that . . . that you go come wit' us." Standing in the shadows of the canopy, the Hauka mediums look toward Jenitongo and the anthropologist. "You must join us," Istambula says, switching to Songhay. "We need your words."

Although Istambula's glowing eyes peer into the anthropologist's, he must be talking about the anthropologist's mentor, Adamu Jenitongo, the wisest and most powerful man in the region.

"We need your words," Istambula repeats in Songhay. "In the name of Bonji."

Adamu Jenitongo says nothing.

Mounkaila, a tall, wiry man, waves to the anthropologist from the canopy. "Hey, *Anasaara* (European) hey," he states in Songhay. "He wants you. Come!"

"Me?" the anthropologist asks.

Mounkaila beckons him to join the circle.

Meanwhile Istambula's inert body, stinking of sweat and dirt, is jolted with what seem to be electroshocks. His face crinkles like burning paper as he pushes himself up on one knee and lifts his right hand toward the anthropologist. "We go jus' now," he says in pidgin. "We need your words," he says in Songhay.

"Why me?" the anthropologist asks in Songhay.

"I European. You European. We European." he says in pidgin. "You hear me?"

Adamu Jenitongo tells the anthropologist to stand up. The anthropologist extends his hand to Istambula, who grabs it and pulls himself up. Braced against the anthropologist's shoulder, Istambula staggers over to the canopy to resume his place at the center of the group. Mounkaila puts his hand on the anthropologist's shoulder.

"Thank you for coming to our discussion. It is only correct that all the Europeans in Tillaberi attend the meeting. That, of course, includes you."

"Thanks," the anthropologist says nervously.

The Zeneral braces himself against one of the non-possessed Hauka mediums. He breathes heavily. His limbs move stiffly, robotically. "We must listen, now. There is talk that one of you must be straightened out. Who is on trial here?"

Mounkaila answers in pidgin. "He no de, Mon Zeneral."

The Zeneral erupts. "Why didn't he come?"

"He is ashamed," answers another of the Hauka mediums.

"Anasaara," the Zeneral says to the anthropologist in Songhay, "what do you think? Should he be here to account for what he has done?"

The anthropologist, of course, doesn't know the identity of the offender. But, having played this game many times before, he answers. "Of course, he should be here."

Istambula chimes in. "Hauk'ize. You know that we demand an oath," he begins in Songhay. "You mus' waka wit' Bonji," he follows in pidgin. "You must obey the rules," he says switching back to Songhay. "When we choose you, we give you force, and you must not abuse your power." He pounds his chest. "I Istambula. Istambula, do you hear? You go hear me, Hauk'ize?"

Bracing himself against Mounkaila, Istambula brings his contorted visage a few inches from the anthropologist's and sprays saliva in his face. "One of the Hauka'ize has had relations with his friend's wife," he says in Songhay. "Do you hear, Anasaara? Do you hear?" He swings away from the anthroplogist and Mounkaila, twirling in the center of our circle. "Do you hear, Hauk'ize. Relations with his friend's wife. No discipline. What is to be done with him?"

Bambara-Mossi slaps his massive chest with a hardwood baton. "I go cut

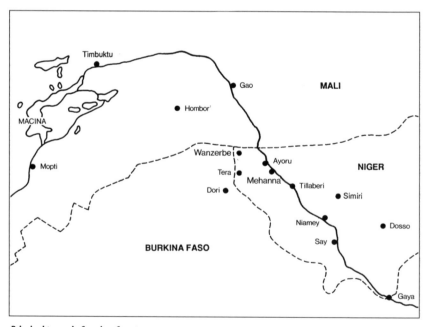

Principal towns in Songhay Country.

off, dangela," he says in pidgin French. "I go get knife. I go cut 'im fas' fas.'"

Laughter explodes at the Roundtable. "Non," says Zeneral Malia in pidgin. "He go tek white chicken an' kill 'im fo' bus.'"

Isambula nods. "Hauk'ize," he shouts. "Hauk'ize. I testify to Bonji and to Dongo, father of us all. The Zeneral has a good idea. You must go to this man's house and tell him. You must tell him to take a white chicken and go to my altar in the bush."

Mounkaila, who has become Istambula's spokesperson, repeats the deity's words.

"This particular person must go there," says Istambula, "do you hear me . . . he must go there on Saturday. And all the Hauk'ize must go with him." Istambula switches into pidgin. "I Istambula. I go bak Malia now. I go bak."

In response to Istambula's statements, the musicians increase the tempo. The pulsations ripple like waves through Istambula's body. He extends his arms and spins around like a top. He grunts and howls. Saliva flows like lava from his mouth. Bambara-Mossi and General Malia join him. The tempo is quite fast; the beat is intense. One by one the Hauka throw their bodies in the air, landing on their backs with thumps. They lay there on the dune like sacks of millet at market—heavy, motionless, and unconscious. Liberated from their Hauka, the mediums cough, slowly sit up and dust themselves off. Attendants bring them water.

The body of an African medium is possessed by a "European" deity who presides over a Roundtable discussion in which the views of Africans and other "Europeans" are expressed in a mixture of pidgin French and Songhay, an African language spoken by three million people in the Republics of Niger and Mali. The Roundtable is a remarkable public forum during which Istambula, the chief of the Hauka (Songhay spirits that burlesque European colonial personages), even invites the participation of the European "occupying" the body of an anthropologist. The problem under discussion—a Hauka medium's sexual transgression—is debated and resolved. The Hauka, who are curiously horrific, comedic and dignified, have come and gone. By resolving yet another social problem in Tillaberi, they have reinforced their authority. Like the French colonial army of many years past, the Hauka are seen as powerful political beings: they get things done quickly, efficiently. Most Songhay consider efficiency a European trait.

A medium possessed by Istambula.

Most people know the Hauka only through the shocking images of Jean Rouch's monumental film, *Les maitres fous*, in which possessed black men are portrayed as rabid "dogs" who shamelessly chomp on boiled dog meat. I have recently suggested that the images of *Les maitres fous* are the cinematic equivalent of Artaud's Theater of Cruelty, in which images move viewers beyond the anesthetizing influence of language to an uncompromising confrontation with the culturally repressed dimensions of their being.[1] But the existential power of these images doesn't give viewers much ethnographic information about the Hauka.[2] Viewers learn little about the history or the social context of the Hauka movement. They learn less still about the social power of the Hauka, a power which has grown with time. Jean Rouch has written about the Hauka in his untranslated *Migrations au Ghana*—but only tangentially.[3] Historians such as Finn Fugelstad have written essays that describe the early moments of the Hauka movement as a type of cultural resistance to French colonialism.[4] My own writing on the Hauka has included discussions of the history and evolution of the Hauka from colonial times to the present, considerations of the political power of the Hauka, particularly following Nigerien independence, and critical assessments of Jean Rouch's films, including, of course, *Les maitres fous*.[5]

The Hauka movement is a particularly compelling example of spirit possession, a subject with an extensive literature in anthropology, sociology, and religious studies. Like much of the scant previous writing on the phenomenon of spirit possession, many of the disquisitions on the Hauka have overlooked a fundamental point: that spirit possession is an embodied phenomenon. There can be little doubt that the body is the locus of possession phenomena. Whether writers call it trance or possession, the same dramatic process presents itself cross-culturally. Musicians, praise-singers, and priests use a variety of expressive media to entice spirits (external forces) to leave non-human realms and enter human bodies. In doing so, the spirit enters social space, transforming mediums both physically and symbolically. Much has been written about the medium's symbolic transformation and the "texts" she expresses.[6] Much less has been written about the bodily experience of possession.

In this book I argue that embodiment is not primarily textual. The human body is not principally a text; rather, the sentient body is culturally consumed by a world filled with forces, smells, textures, sights, sounds and tastes, all of which trigger social memories.[7] *Embodying Colonial Memories* will not only consider spirit possession, a typically anthropological subject, but also such subjects as the cultural sentience of the body and the dynamics of colonial and postcolonial movements of resistance and their discourses.

Hauka possessions are simultaneously frightening and funny. Elsewhere I have referred to Hauka spirit possession as "horrific comedy." The horrific/comedic embodiment of the Hauka and its mimetic connection to colonial memories evoke the past, manipulate the present, and provoke the future. Through the power of embodiment, the Hauka stutter-step over the border separating ritual from political practice. In the Republic of Niger, cultural diplomacy on the dune informs diplomacy in the Presidential Palace.

In *Embodying Colonial Memories* I use the compelling example of the Hauka to think about spirit possession as a set of embodied practices with serious social, cultural, and political consequences. In this way the study of spirit possession moves from the abstract consideration of how ahistorical, ritual texts constitute a discourse to the concrete analysis of how one set of embodied practices molds historical contexts to constitute power-in-the-world.

The book is organized into a prologue, four parts, and an epilogue. In Part One, "Sensing Spirit Possession," I argue for an embodied approach to the analysis of spirit possession. Chapter One, "Spirit Possession," considers the strengths and weaknesses of past approaches to this enticing phenomenon. In this chapter I suggest that the functionalist, psychoanalytic, and interpretive approaches to spirit possession have usually failed to tease out its embodied, historical and political dimensions. In Chapter Two, "Cultural Memory," I establish a link between spirit possession and cultural memory, which demonstrates how history is embodied in movements, postures, sounds and smells. In "Embodied Memories: Mimesis and Spirit Possession," Chapter Three, I extend Michael Taussig's recent analysis of mimesis and alterity to spirit possession, arguing that it is mimetic embodiment that accounts for the political power of Hauka deities in the Republic of Niger.

Having established the theoretical foundation of the book in Part One, I move on, in Part Two, "Confronting Colonialism in West Africa," to establish the historical and political context from which the Hauka movement emerged. Chapter Four, "From First Contacts to Military Partition," describes how West Africa came under the hegemony of France and Great Britain. In Chapter 5, "Colonizing West Africa," I map the contours of social relations during the colonial epoch in West Africa. Chapter Six, "Embodied Oppositions," tells the story of how West Africans defied colonial regimes through military and cultural resistance movements.

In Part Three, "Migrating with the Hauka," I focus specifically on how the French colonization of Niger resulted in the birth and migration of the Hauka movement. Chapter Seven, "Colonizing Niger," recounts the terror of the early military campaigns of the French and the social upheaval caused by the imposition of taxes and forced-work details. In Chapter Eight, "The Birth of the Hauka Movement," I analyze the emergence and political importance of the Hauka spirits in the 1920s. The political impact of the Hauka was so threatening to the French authorities that many

Hauka mediums were expelled from Niger. In this way, as detailed in Chapter Nine, "Transgressing to the Gold Coast," the Hauka migrated to what is now Ghana, where in the 1930s the movement flourished in what is now seen as its Golden Age.

Most literature on the Hauka fails to consider the survival of the movement in the postcolonial era. Although the Hauka usually mimic colonial identities, their power and influence grew exponentially following Nigerien independence in 1960. In Part Four, "Transforming State Power: The Hauka Movement in the Postcolony of Niger," I explore this paradox by probing how the Hauka have affected postcolonial national politics in the Republic of Niger. In Chapter Ten, "Independence and the Postcolony of Niger," I describe the political evolution of the Government of Niger, focusing explicitly on the socioeconomic impact of government policies on the lives of Songhay peasants. Given this political context, Chapter Eleven, "Peasant and Hauka in Niger's Postcolony," looks at local village life to consider how and why a movement that embodies colonial memories has expanded so dramatically during the past thirty years. In Chapter Twelve, "The Hauka and the Government General Seyni Kountche," my analysis suggests that the embodied aesthetics of Hauka spirit possession shaped state governance during the years of the Kountche regime. It is widely known in Niger that many members of the Supreme Military Council, including President Seyni Kountche himself, were Hauka mediums. I conclude the book with a short epilogue, "Memory, Power and Spirit Possession," which explores the theoretical importance of the relationship among memory, embodiment, power, and spirit possession.

The clang of cattle bells announces dusk in Tillaberi. The Haukas have come, settled their Roundtable business, and gone. No one leaves Adamu Jenitongo's compound, however, for one medium, the man who had been possessed by Bambara-Mossi, is thrashing about in the sand. The musicians play Hauka rhythms. A deep groan rolls through the air as yet another Hauka arrives in the social world. He is Chefferi, "the non-believer."

Chefferi sweeps up from the sand and squats like a wrestler. He tears at his trousers, ripping them off just above the knee. He yanks off his shirt and wraps it around his head like a woman's head scarf. He pounds his chest, pushes through the circle of onlookers, and struts over to Adamu Jenitongo.

"Albora. Albora."

"Yes," says Adamu Jenitongo in response to the respectful term used for wise old men.

"Albora," he repeats. "You must make *kusu* (magic cake) for the other Anasaara here."

"That's fine," says Adamu Jenitongo.

"Tell your wife to bring me the finest millet seeds. And then bring me the biggest and heaviest mortar and pestle here."

Adamu Jenitongo asks his senior wife for these things.

Chefferi runs his finger through a small bowl filled with golden millet seeds. "These are good." He picks up the pestle.

"Not big or heavy enough. Find me a proper pestle."

A young girl runs to the neighboring compound for a bigger pestle. Holding on to the dish, Chefferi bounds over to the hangar. "Play my music," he demands.

The musicians play Hauka rhythms. Dressed like a woman, Chefferi, big, thick, and frightening, stands at the center of a large crowd. Night has fallen, and the compound is illumined by the dim glow of kerosene lanterns that hang from the canopy's rafters. Like a circus performer, Chefferi waves at the crowd. "I, the Hauka non-believer, am going to give *kusu* to this Anasaara." He points at the anthropologist.

A young woman brings Chefferi two five-foot pestles carved from heavy hardwood. "These are good." He then lays on his back, and calls for two strong young women—millet pounders. One of the women places the heavy mortar on Chefferi's bare chest. "Put the millet in the mortar," he orders, "and pound it until it becomes a fine white flour. The women do as they are instructed and begin to pound. The pestles thump the mortar with great force. The sound of the thumps are in counterpoint to Chefferi's painful moans. The audience gapes at the wondrous spectacle.

The millet flour is soon as white and smooth as dune sand, and Chefferi triumphantly invites the audience to inspect the contents of the mortar. The young women lift the leaden mortar off his chest, and he leaps to an upright position. Chefferi grabs the anthropologist's arm roughly. "Anasaara. Anasaara. That," he says pointing at the millet flour, "is for you."

"I thank you, Chefferi."

Recitation of praise-poetry during a Hauka ceremony, Tillaberi, Niger (1981).

"Today, we had a Roundtable on this dune," Chefferi announces. "We Hauka solved our problems with grace, with dignity. Now I, Chefferi, the non-believer, give you this *kusu*. You are now my brother. May this *kusu* help you to solve your problems with grace and dignity. May it move you forward on your path. May your words be heard by many people. Do not forget the Hauka, Anasaara. Do not forget us!"

The women scoop the flour out of the mortar and put it into a wooden bowl. "Adamu Jenitongo, come here," Chefferi commands.

Slowly, the old man walks over to Chefferi.

"Albora, tomorrow prepare for this Anasaara, who is now my brother, this *kusu*. Prepare it so he may walk his path with grace and dignity, so that he will never forget us, never lose respect for us."

"This, I shall do," says Adamu Jenitongo.

"Good," says Chefferi. "It is time to return to Malia, to the Red Sea." The musicians hear this cue and begin to play Hauka music. Chefferi flies through the air and lands on his back.

Lying unconscious on the dune, Chefferi's being is momentarily lost between the worlds, between the Red Sea and Tillaberi, between the colonial past and the postcolonial present, between his presence and that of his medium. So it is when Hauka spirits encounter themselves and others in the netherworld between possession and consciousness.

Chefferi is neither European nor African; he is neither man nor woman, Christian nor Muslim. His unclassifiable body rocks with personal and political power. The Hauka embody difference, as I shall attempt to argue in this book, that generates power. They have the capacity to sicken or heal, read the past or predict the future, endanger or protect villages. The Hauka's powerful presence—their horrific/comedic embodiment—has been a model of and for political resistance, a model of and for governance in postcolonial Niger.

On that white hot day in 1987, Chefferi placed a heavy burden on the European who "occupied" the body of an anthropologist. He offered his chest as a platform on which to pulverize millet. He ordered Adamu Jenitongo to transform millet flour into magical *kusu*. When I, the anthropologist, ate that *kusu*, an embodied bond was sealed between the Hauka and me, a bond that demanded I write about them, as they would say, with remembrance and respect. This book, then, bears my burden. I humbly offer it to the Hauka with brotherly deference.

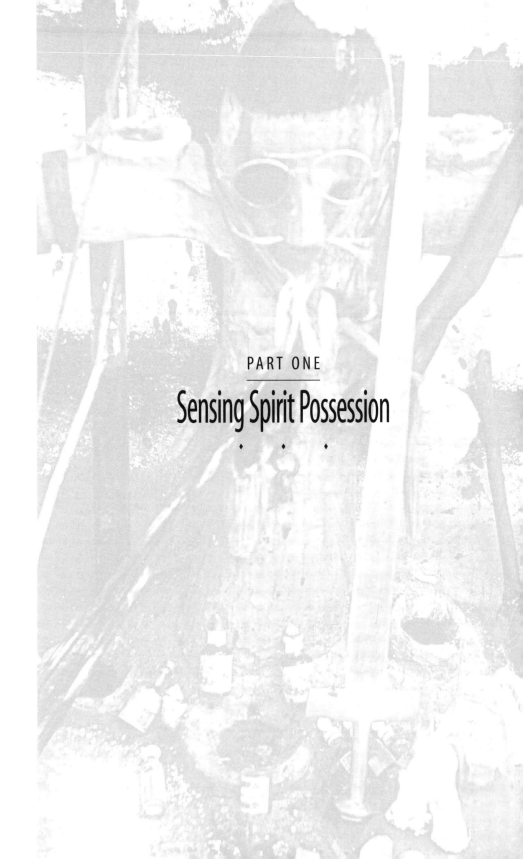

PART ONE

Sensing Spirit Possession

◆   ◆   ◆

Sensing Ethnography

•   •   •

Anthropologists who have lost their senses often write ethnographies that are disconnected from the worlds they seek to portray. For these anthropologists, tasteless theories are more important than the savory sauces of ethnographic life. That they have lost their senses of the smells, sounds, and tastes of the places they study is unfortunate for them, for their subjects, and for the discipline itself.

Vision has been the king of perception in the Western academy.[1] Accordingly, the guiding metaphors of the humanities and the social sciences have been visual ones: infrastructures and superstructures, systems and configurations, texts and metatexts. Throughout the history of anthropology, ethnographers have been participant *observers* who *reflect* on their *visual* experiences and then write *texts* that *represent* the Other's *pattern* of kinship, exchange or religion.

Recently a number of anthropologists and sociologists have challenged the interconnected paradigms of visualism and textualism. One of the most vocal critics, David Howes, has written " . . . that it is only by developing a rigorous awareness of the visual and textual biases of the Western episteme that we can hope to make sense of how life is lived in other cultural settings."[2] The epistemological issues raised by Howes and others are important for scholars to consider. Howes would replace visualism with a sensory anthropology that would flesh out the comparative analysis of societies. My own take on the question of sensing ethnography is less ambitious. For me, recognition of multisensorial perception leads to a more embodied, radically phenomenological approach to ethnographic fieldwork, a more sensorially evocative body of ethnographic writing, and a more rigorous framework for the analysis of culture-in-society.

The ethnographic study of spirit possession has also been a predominantly visualist practice. Theories of spirit possession spatialize the phenomenon in any number of ways. Possession is grafted to social structures or is *seen* as a set of texts that constitute a counterhegemonic discourse. In this part of *Embodying Colonial Memories,* I propose a sensorial alternative to these approaches, an orientation that considers spirit possession as a set of embodied practices.

CHAPTER ONE

Spirit Possession

• ◆ •

Anthropologists have long been enthralled by the specter of spirit possession. Numerous articles and books have been written on possession, and there are several memorable—if not controversial films—like Jean Rouch's *Les maitres fous*, that attempt to capture the carnivalesque nature of the phenomenon. Scholarly writing on spirit possession has not been limited to straightforward ethnographic description. Many anthropologists have used their materials on spirit possession to expound upon theories of society or of social meaning. Writers have employed one or several of the five dominant forms of explanation to analyze spirit possession: functionalist, psychoanalytic, physiological, symbolic (interpretive) and theatrical.

Functionalist writers, most notably I.M. Lewis, use spirit possession as a datum that putatively reveals underlying frictions in social structure. For Lewis and others, spirit possession exposes a "battle of the sexes." Most spirit mediums, Lewis and others argue, are women, an afflicted group in patrilineal societies. Women participate in spirit possession ceremonies to vent their frustrations, the argument goes, in order to enjoy fleeting moments of social prestige. Although functionalist writers pay careful attention to descriptive detail, they are invariably comparative analysts, considering the relation of mediumship, gender and social structure in a variety of societies.[1] The strength of a functionalist analysis is that it highlights spirit possession as a social process with social consequences.

Adamu Jenitongo attending to a spirit medium, Tillaberi Niger (1985).

However, the weaknesses of the model are three-fold: (1) it focuses entirely upon mediumship; (2) it fails to consider the social perspective of women's experience;[2] and (3) it overlooks the cultural and bodily dimensions of spirit possession.

Like the functionalist theorists, writers who use psychoanalytic models to explain spirit possession also focus attention on spirit mediums. Unlike the functionalists who concentrate on social structure, psychoanalytic writers like Jacqueline Monfouga-Nicholas and Andras Zempleni consider the psychodynamics of mediums.[3] Some of these writers consider pre-possession malady tantamount to a psychotic episode that society "treats" through initiation into the spirit possession cult.[4] The initiation, it follows, is cathartic. Following initiation, mediums perform useful social functions. Recent psychoanalytic studies are more nuanced. Writing on the Hausa *bori* in the Republic of Niger, Monfouga-Nicholas uses the Freudian notion of ambivalence to analyze spirit possession data.[5] The best known and most sophisticated psychoanalytic accounts are those of Gananath Obeysekere on Sinhalese spirit possession.[6] Although much useful historical information about the psychodynamic development of spirit mediums is provided, this kind of analysis usually fails to address the social, cultural (symbolic), or historical dimensions of spirit possession. Like the functionalists, psychoanalytic writers usually consider a complex local phenomenon in terms of Western categories. This tack usually results in studies that fail to address the importance of social meaning.

Scholars seeking biological explanations of spirit possession consider the physiology of the trance state. Many of them suggest that possession states alter brain waves.[7] Other scholars have probed the relation of music to the onset of trance.[8] Alfred Gell traces the onset of trance in India to disturbances of the inner ear brought on by rhythmic swaying.[9] Alice Kehoe and Dody Geletti argue that spirit possession is the biological result of food prohibitions. Using a wide array of cross-cultural data, they assert that mediumship devolves from calcium deficiencies.[10] It goes without saying that the physiology of the trance state is a fascinating subject. Assuming that contingent sociocultural phenomena can be explained by immutable biological principles, these scholars neglect the sociology and symbolism of spirit possession and reduce the body to its physio-chemical essentials.

While the functionalist, psychoanalytic, and biological models of spirit-possession analysis focus on aspects of the individual medium, writers taking a symbolic approach start from Georges Balandier's premise that possession is a form of intellectual communication.[11] Students of spirit possession's symbolism probe its cultural content—possession as a text that represents cultural knowledge, a text that transmits information about themes of cultural significance: the relation of men to women, of heaven to earth, of good to evil, of life to death. In these studies scholars analyze what the spirits say to their various audiences. The strength of such a theoretical model is that it explores the complexities of local expression and local ideas. The weakness of this kind of analysis, however, is that in considering the cultural content, analysts sometimes neglect the social and the psychological aspects. Some studies which employ this analytic model, moreover, place too much emphasis on possession's textuality, relying too much upon the assumption that images and other sensations (sound, smell, taste) are "texts." Generally, not even the best of these symbolic studies, which combine the symbolic, psychological and/or social aspects of the phenomenon, present holistic accounts of spirit possession.[12] An exception, of course, is Roger Bastide's monumental *The African Religions of Brazil* (1978), which

which was based upon the author's longstanding and intimate participation in *Candomble*, the major spirit possession cult in Brazil. And yet, even Bastide's work bypasses the notion of spirit possession as an embodied cultural practice.

The theatrical or performance approach to spirit possession was—and is—a French movement pioneered by Andre Schaeffner, Michel Leiris, Gilbert Rouget and extended by Jean-Marie Gibbal, all of whom suggest that possession is a form of cultural theater.[13] Priests become impresarios; mediums are actors; musicians form orchestras; spirit recitations become scripts that are central to the drama of the expression of culturally specific existential themes. An underlying assumption of this orientation is that the effectiveness of spirit possession is embedded in its performance. Many anthropologists have criticized performance analysts for ignoring the social and psychological dimensions of mediumship.[14] Others, like Valentin Mudimbe, criticize these writers for inscribing Western categories—metaphors of performance—onto non-Western cultural forms.[15]

Although the scholarship on possession is among the most sophisticated in anthropology, each of the various approaches is in its own way theoretically deficient. When I wrote *Fusion of the Worlds* (1989), I was much drawn to the performance model of possession, for I thought that it best captured spirit possession's sociocultural nuances. And yet, at the end of that volume I suggested that the metaphor of theater could take us only so far, for it provided merely a stage for the apprehension of spirit possession in Songhay—or anywhere else. In that book I proposed no solution to the theoretical quandaries of possession other than to suggest that it, like surrealism, is an attack on reality, an aesthetic reaction to the inadequacies of the world. I wrote:

> Possession in Songhay is a creative act, an aesthetic reaction to the inadequacies of the world. As Merleau-Ponty wrote, "It is by lending his body to the world that the artist changes the world into paintings."(1964) It is by lending her body to the world that the spirit medium renders meaningful a harsh Sahelien world filled with dissension, drought, famine and death.[16]

My argument in this book is that although the major theorists on spirit possession make significant contributions to social theory, they fail to consider adequately the centrality of the sentient body in possession, the relationship between bodily practices (spirit possession) and cultural memory, and the political power that devolves from embodiment. By concentrating our analytical gaze on the embodiment of spirit possession, I suggest, we are more likely to understand it as a phenomenological arena in which cultural memory is fashioned and refashioned.

Spirit Possession and the Body

There can be little doubt that the body is the locus of spirit-possession phenomena. I have already discussed how even the best studies of possession overlook the sensuousness of perception.[17] In doing so, scholars of spirit possession have written about "the body," but have usually ignored its sentience.

A spate of articles, anthologies and monographs have analyzed the centrality of the body in social theory. Feminist and poststructuralist scholars have suggested the social, cultural, and political consequences of maintaining the Cartesian split between mind and body. In anthropology, Emily Martin's study, *The Woman in the Body*, forcefully demonstrates the social, cultural, and medical consequences of an overtly sexist nosology based upon this Cartesian split. But Martin is by no means a single voice in the academy.[18] Seeking to avoid the representational and political pitfalls of disembodiment, a growing number of scholars have used the notion of the body—and embodiment—to criticize both Eurocentric and phallocentric predispositions in scholarly writing. As a result the body has emerged recently as a new site for analysis. Bourdieu writes:

> Taste, a class culture turned into nature, that is embodied helps to shape the class body. It is an incorporated principle of classification which governs all forms of incorporation, choosing and modifying everything that the body ingests and digests and assimilates, physiologically and psychologically. It follows that the body is the most indisputable materialization of class taste.[19]

As Bryan Turner points out, the body has a secret history in social theory, stemming from Nietzsche's Dionysian diversions into the erotics of the body, the sensuality of dance, and the rapture of ecstasy. But until recently, he argues, this secret history was hidden on a side road of social theory: "In recent developments of social theory there has been an important re-evaluation of the importance of the body, not simply in feminist social theory, but more generally in terms of the analysis of class, culture and consumption."[20]

Much of the emerging social science writing on the body therefore centers on Western conceptions. The essays in Mike Featherstone, Mike Hepworth and Bryan Turner's recent anthology, *The Body*, consider diet, appetite, consumer culture, martial arts, art, aging, Nietzsche, and human emotions. These are topics worthy of an embodied reformulation. The essays, however, do not take us much beyond the body-as-text, a metaphor that strips the body of its smells, tastes, textures, and pain.[21]

In anthropology it is especially important to consider these smells, tastes, textures and sensations, particularly in those societies in which the Eurocentric notion of text—and textual interpretations—are not important. I have noted elsewhere why it is representationally and analytically important to consider how perception in non-Western societies devolves not simply from vision (and the linked metaphors of reading and writing), but also from smell, taste, touch and hearing.[22] In many of these societies these "lower" senses are central to the metaphoric organization of experience; they also trigger cultural memory.

With very few exceptions, most writers on spirit possession have not discussed it as an embodied phenomenon. In Songhay, spirits must be enticed to their social bodies through music (sound), praise-poetry (sound), specific perfumes (smell), and dance (movement). What happens once the medium has abandoned her body to a deity? In a remarkable passage, Rouch describes the sentient embodiment that occurs in Songhay possession.

Following numerous indirect accounts [it is already indicated that the dancer must not remember the possession] the dancer sees the spirit [eventually the old initiates see it too] penetrate the dance circle and direct itself toward him or her; the spirit holds in its hands the skin of a freshly slaughtered animal and presents the bloody side of it to the dancer three times:

- the first time, tears flow from the dancer's eyes;
- the second time, mucus flows from the dancer's nose;
- the third time, the dancer cries out.[23]

On its fourth pass, the spirit places the bloody skin over the dancer's head. In this way the spirit captures the medium's double and enters the dancer's body. During spirit possession, the dancer's double is protected under the bloody skin. When the spirit leaves the body, it lifts off the bloody animal skin, liberating the dancer's double. The medium opens his or her eyes.

Sometimes mediums, like those in Tillaberi who carried Istambula, Zeneral Malia, and Bambara-Mossi, remain unconscious for several minutes. They always cough as if they had just left or were being suffocated.[24] Rouch's description ends without a local exegesis of the symbolism of the moment of possession.

Bori and Zar

Two recent studies of spirit possession, by Janice Boddy and Pamela Schmoll, take into consideration the centrality of the body. In Boddy's case, the body of the possessed medium is considered a site of struggle from which a subaltern discourse is derived; it is through the inscribed body that female self-awareness is triggered.

Boddy's Zar

In *Wombs and Alien Spirits* Janice Boddy extends and elaborates on I.M. Lewis' earlier work on the *zar* possession rites. In her rich and nuanced ethnography of the *zar* in Hofryiat, northern Sudan, Boddy has written a work that diverges from Lewis' purely functionalist account of this cult. Moving beyond the social, Boddy considers *zar* a universe of meaning in which metasocial and metacultural statements—not unlike Foucault's notion of the *énoncé* in his *Archaeology of Knowledge*—become the foundation of a cultural discourse. More specifically, the *zar* serves as a foil for northern Sudan's dominant discourse of Islam and as a site for the construction of what Boddy calls a subversive discourse.

> The presiding discourse in the village is a localized version of Islam ostensibly controlled by men, in which *zar* spirits play a legitimate though, from the men's perspective, tangential role. In this sense, women's amplification of *zar* beliefs into a possession cult can be seen as a kind of counterhegemonic process (cf. Williams 1977; Gramsci 1971; Sider 1980): a feminine response to hegemonic praxis, and the privileging of men that this ideologically entails, which ultimately escapes neither its categories nor its constraints. Thus, on the one hand, women tacitly reproduce the dominant system simply by participating in it, as they do. Yet this is only part of the story, for women's own system exists: accepted meanings reworked in the alternate discourse of possession are hardly less eloquent for being muted; they are merely inexplicit. Messages communicated by women to both male and female villagers via the *zar* often have subversive overtones as well as supportive ones; gender appropriate meanings emerge when individuals read these messages in light of their own experiences.[25]

As such, *zar* is not at all a cult of the afflicted; rather, it is central to cultural production in northern Sudan, a cultural production characterized by Bahktin's notion of heteroglossia. For Boddy, *zar* is a key component in the Gramscian process of producing and maintaining power relations and gender asymmetries—the construction of a powerful hegemonic discourse as well as the emergence of counterhegemonic discourses.

Boddy complements such abstract reflections on culture, power and discourse with concrete considerations of the place that individual mediums—women—occupy in the space of spirit possession. It is the medium's body that is invaded by alien spirits. During possession her body is and is not her own. In Boddy's view of *zar*, the body is the site of a text which is joined to other texts—other bodies, other objects, incenses and perfumes—that create a larger counterhegemonic discourse which is often ludic and parodic. In the end, Boddy considers the medium's body as a site of cultural and counterhegemonic production. Following the insights of the *écriture feminine* movement in France, Boddy asserts that the medium's body is inscribed onto the multidimensional cultural text of the society of northern Sudan. In this way, her work contributes to a growing literature on the body-as-text in the Islamic world. In this literature writers argue that the discourse of women, which is muted, is constructed through the body and body imagery.[26]

Schmoll's Bori

Like Boddy's *Wombs and Alien Spirits*, Schmoll's analysis of the *bori* cult among the Hausa of Niger is framed by the notion of discourse. For Schmoll, *bori* is a "complex discourse on power, empowerment in the face of subordination, as well as on the principle vehicle of that empowerment—knowledge."[27] It is here that Schmoll's analysis of spirit possession becomes a bit more philosophically explicit than Boddy's. Citing the work of Jean and John Comaroff, Schmoll decries the Western polarized notion of consciousness, which privileges the mind over the body, and which under-appreciates the importance of ambiguity in symbolic communication.[28] Taking the notion of consciousness a step further, Schmoll links it to experience: "We must play with the notion of 'knowing' as experience, all kinds of experience—thought, action, feeling, intuition—experience as sensations and perceptions, and not just experience as thought."[29] Schmoll says that anthropologists need to take into consideration the non-visual senses. "Taste, and sound and smells, the effect of music and rhythm on one's being, the tastes of herbs and plants . . . the odor of incense, of blood of putrefaction—are all part of one's experience, one's knowledge of the world, knowledge every bit as important—sometimes more so—than the facts one articulates mentally or verbally."[29]

For her part, Schmoll speaks to the importance of multisensory analysis. But she takes this multisensory analysis of spirit possession only so far. Like Boddy, she considers the female body a textual surface. In *Wombs and Alien Spirits,* for example, Boddy contrasts the symbolic roles of incense in marriage and in northern Sudanese *zar*. In marriage incense symbolically seals off the female body from the outside world. In *zar*, by contrast, incense is seen as opening the female body to outside penetration—by the spirits— which Boddy considers a "subversive discourse." In this way, incense is inscribed on the woman's body in northern Sudan, which, in effect, spatializes the body. Such spatialization steers Boddy away from a discussion of the relations between scent and meaning, odor and the social order.

Schmoll agrees with Boddy that the multivocality of spirit possession messages creates an arena of individual interpretation, but disagrees with Boddy's assertion that *zar*—possession—is a stage of consciousness-raising. "For it seems to me *bori* reflects a consciousness, an understanding, a multidimensional knowing that for most adepts is already there. . . I suggest that *bori* is less about women gaining insight into their own predicament than it is the active *practice* and transformation of that knowledge into tangible power—an exercise of empowerment—by restructuring both the social self and the relation between the self and the dominant Other(s)."[30]

In the Hausa context, empowerment is not consciousness-raising. Here it is worth quoting Schmoll at some length:

> Bori can thus be seen as a multitiered appropriation of power: intellectually through discussion and portrayal of it as well as through direct appropriation of it in the form of possession and humor. Here we again see not only the refusal of the Hausa to dichotomize experience into the conscious and unconscious, but the power derived from continually moving between playing with the various levels of awareness and modes of knowing. The girka (initiation) is, at one level negotiation with spirits—their sa'a (inner energy, power) exchanged for tribute and offerings and the periodic opportunity to `ride' the adept. At another it is the acquisition of sa'a by allowing one's body to be completely possessed by the spirit, and in so doing, possessed becomes possessor.[31]

Despite Schmoll's sensitive and faithful analysis of the *bori*, she, too, privileges the discursive. *Bori* is "seen" as social "disease," as a "discourse" on gender roles and relations, as a "discourse" on the *Anne* (the pre-Islamic ancestors), and as anti-colonialist "commentary." This analysis of *bori* as a complex discourse misses the opportunity to take the analysis of possession in other potentially fruitful directions. In the next chapter, I probe the connection between multisensorial embodiment and cultural memory.

CHAPTER TWO

Cultural Memory

◆　　◆　　◆

The overwhelming tendency to consider spirit possession ceremonies exclusively as discourse has two major theoretical consequences. The first is that many such studies of spirit possession fail to consider their relation to history. The second is that discursive analysis (possession as text) as opposed to sensory analysis (possession as bodily practice) unwittingly underscores the mind/body split in the academy.

In *How Societies Remember* (1989) Paul Connerton wonders how the collective memory of groups is expressed and sustained. He demonstrates that ceremonies like spirit possession, among others, are more than sites of consciousness-raising about gender relations, more than arenas in which anti-colonialist discourses are constructed.

> If there is such a thing as social memory . . . we are likely to find it in commemorative ceremonies; but commemorative ceremonies prove to be commemorative only in so far as they are performative; performativity cannot be thought without a concept of habit; and habit cannot be thought without a notion of bodily automatisms.[1]

Collective Memories

Connerton's essay is constructed upon a solid sociological foundation that derives from Durkheim and Halbwachs. In his monumental *The Elementary Forms of Religious Life*, Durkheim argues that it was the frame of the sacred in which collective consciousness—of society or the group—was established and reinforced. By separating the sacred from the profane, the individual from the group, Durkheim created static models of both individual and group consciousness that reified the social as an organic whole.

Halbwachs, who was a major figure in the second generation of French Durkheimians, refined Durkheim's theory by creating a more interactive model of collective representations and memory. Like Durkheim, he situated his analysis of collective memory in rituals. Unlike Durkheim, he considered the relationship between individual and group as dynamic and interpenetrating. He argued that landmarks (what Connerton calls commemorative rituals) prod our recollections and stimulate our thought. The individual-group dynamic, moreover, does not overlook the complexities of individual and/or group change.

> The frameworks of memory exist both within the passage of time and outside of it. External to the passage of time, they communicate to the images and concrete recollections of which they are made a bit of their stability and generality. But these frameworks are in part captivated by the course of time. They are like those wood floats that descend along a waterway so slowly that one can easily move from one to the other, but which nevertheless are not immobile and go forward. . . .[2]

For Halbwachs, social beliefs have a double character. They are collective traditions or recollections, but they are also ideas or conventions that result from a knowledge of the present.[3]

Social Memory

Connerton acknowledges Halbwachs's important contribution in his study of social memory, and distinguishes three types of memory: personal, cognitive, and habit. The first two types have been studied extensively. Psychoanalysts have focused upon the personal memory of one's life history. Psychologists have probed cognitive memory, which concerns our ability to recall certain external facts, stories, words, the meaning of a poem or short story—all of which is part of the attempt to delimit universal cognitive structures.[4] Little attention has been focused on Connerton's third category of memory, habit-memory, which he defines as "having the capacity to reproduce a certain performance."[5] Habit is something which does not lend itself to the visual bias that is central to discursive analysis. In their insistence on the discursive, scholars transform the figurative into language and text. And yet our memories are never purely personal, purely cognitive, or purely textual. Citing Halbwachs, Connerton argues that the analytical separation of individual and social memory is meaningless. To consider the formation of social memory, it follows, one must consider how those memories are constructed and conveyed through such commemorative ceremonies as spirit possession.

What is it about these commemorative ceremonies that triggers collective cultural memory? Connerton suggests a number of factors:

1. Ritual is performative in the sense of Austin's notion of the performative utterance (1962). That is, performatives constitute rather than reflect action; and
2. Ritual is formal in the sense that its structure and content are conservative, repetitive.

According to Connerton, both of these factors are mnemonic. In addition, performatives are not limited to verbal utterances; they are also "encoded in set postures, gestures and movements."[6] All rituals are constituted by performativity and formalism. But commemorative rituals have one additional feature that sets them apart; they "explicitly refer to mnemonic persons and events, whether these are understood to have a historical or a mythological existence . . .";[7] they are ritual re-enactments.

Up to this point, Connerton's argument is hardly innovative. Anthropologists taking the perspective championed by Victor Turner have long analyzed ritual in a similar manner. Two elements, however, distinguish Connerton's analysis of commemorative ritual. First, unlike most symbolic anthropologists, Connerton's focus is decidedly historical; and second, it is also embodied.

> A ritual is not a journal or memoir. Its master narrative is more than a story told and reflection on; it is a cult enacted. An image of the past, even in the form of a master narrative, is conveyed and sustained by ritual performances. And this means that what is remembered in commemorative ceremonies is something in addition to a collectively organized variant of personal or cognitive memory. For if ceremonies are to work for their participants, if they are to be persuasive to them, then those participants must not be simply cognitively competent to execute the performance; they must be habituated to those performances. This habituation is to be found . . . in the bodily substrate of the performance.[8]

In the last part of his book, Connerton demonstrates how bodily practices—the embodied substrate of performance—keys cultural memory. In cultural memory, "the past is, as it were, sedimented in the body."[9] The process of sedimentation occurs through two kinds of practices: inscription and incorporation. Inscribing practices refer to the storage and retrieval of texts in photographs, books, audio cassettes, video cassettes, and cinema. Incorporating practices refer to body postures, gestures, facial expressions, body movements, table manners.

As we have seen in the last chapter, the works of Boddy and Schmoll, among many other scholars, have privileged practices of inscription which can be analyzed discursively as texts, and which, as a metaphor, have even been extended to cultural markings on the body. Such is the focus of cultural hermeneutics from Schleiermacher to Ricoeur. "Inscriptions, and hence texts, were privileged objects of interpretation because the activity of interpretation itself became an object of reflection, rather than being simply practiced, in a particular context."[10] This is why hermeneutical analysis is so well suited to the study of Western culture—a culture of texts and textual analysis. Connerton is correct in asserting that scholars should pay more attention to incorporating practices, which in this book I term "embodiment." If we are to comprehend ritual in non-western settings, we need to juxtapose text and body. This point is especially important in the analysis of non-Western commemorative rituals in which scholars all too often transform body and bodily practices into texts. The body is inscribed. That the body is inscribed in these rituals is uncontestable, but to stop there is to make a serious epistemological error. For in its textualization the body is robbed of its movements, odors, tastes, sounds—its sensibilities, all of which are potent conveyors of meaning and memory.[11]

Considering embodiment, in fact, becomes central in the analysis of what George Lipsitz calls "counter-memory."[12] Counter-memory can be considered a subaltern discourse. Boddy refers to it as counterhegemonic and subversive discourse. Social scientists and literary critics approach counter-memory through the analysis of texts or events (like spirit possession) as texts. In anthropology, writers like Boddy, Schmoll, Comaroff, David Lan, and Lila Abu-Lughod take this textual approach, which, as I've argued, bypasses the localized significance of embodiment. In his consideration of counter-memory, Lipstiz looks to artistic rather than scholarly expression. More specifically, he looks to the novels of authors from the cultural margins: women and men from non-mainstream groups (Toni Morrison, Leslie Silko, John Okada) In these groups, memories are more likely to be stored in tales, objects and bodies than in texts. Toni Morrison articulates this point eloquently.

> You know, they straightened out the Mississippi River in places, to make room for houses and livable acreage. Occasionally the river floods these places. 'Floods' is the word they use, but in fact it is not flooding; it is remembering. Remembering where it used to be. All water has a perfect memory and is forever trying to get back where it was. Writers are like that: remembering where we were, what valley we ran through, what the banks were like, the light that was there and the route back to our original place. It is emotional memory—where the nerves and the skin remember how it appeared. And a rush of imagination is our 'flooding.'[13]

Writings like Morrison's *Beloved*, according to Lipsitz and others, mount a fundamental challenge to history's reliance upon inscription.

Gayl Jones' novel, *Corregidora*, is a case in point.[14] This haunting tale is about cultural memory, about the counter-memory of four generations of African-American women. Throughout the novel the protagonist's great grandmother repeats a refrain:

> The important thing is making generations. They can burn papers but they can't burn conscious, Ursa. And that's what makes the evidence. And that's what makes the verdict.[15]

In this tale, the evidence is sedimented in the bodies of four generations of black women, all of whom are haunted by the hulking presence of a Portuguese sailor who settled in Louisiana. Corregidora fed his lust by buying and possessing beautiful black women, including the women of Ursa's family. According to documents, Corregidora had legitimately employed these women. The documents, however, make no mention of his whoring, pimping and incestuous rages. But the heart of the story—the counter-memory—tells a different tale: one of sexual slavery, a story of the persistent memories of physical and emotional abuse and incest. Even Ursa and her mother—neither of whom had ever known Corregidora—were haunted by his presence. His hulking image torments their collective cultural memory, itself constituted by the invisible history of male sexual abuse. The following passage dramatically exemplifies cultural memory as a fundamentally embodied phenomenon.

> The two women in that house. The three of them at first and then when I was older, just the two of them, one sitting in a rocker, the other in a straight-back chair, telling me things. I'd always listen. I never saw my mama with a man,

never ever saw her with a man. But she wasn't a virgin because of me. And still she was heavy with virginity. Her swollen belly with no child inside. And still she never had a man. Or never let me see her with one. No, I think she never had one. . . . When I was real little, Great Gram rocking me and talking. And still it was as if my mother's whole body shook with that first birth and memories and she wouldn't make others and she wouldn't give those to me, though she passed the other ones down, the monstrous ones, but she wouldn't give her own terrible ones. Loneliness. I could feel it, like she was breathing it, like it was all in the air. Desire, too. I couldn't recognize it then. But now when I look back, that's all I see. Desire, and loneliness. A man that left her. Still she carried their evidence, screaming, fury in her eyes[16]

But the memories of abuse and abandonment extend well beyond those of Ursa's mother and her preordained fate with men. The fury and sadness also infused Ursa's voice, especially when she sang the blues at Happy's Club.

Sometimes I wonder about their desire. Grandma's and Great Gram's. Corregidora was theirs more than hers. Mama could only know, but they could feel. They were with him. What did they feel? You know how they talk about hate and desire. Two humps on the same camel? Yes. Hate and desire both riding them, that's what I was going to say. 'You carry more than his name, Ursa,' Mama would tell me. And I knew she had more than memories. Something behind her eyes. A knowing, a feeling of her own. But she'd speak only their life. What was their life then? Only a life spoken to the sounds of the Victrola . . . Still there was what they never spoke . . . what they wouldn't even tell me. How all but one of them had the same lover? Did they begrudge her that? Was that their resentment? There was something . . . They squeezed Corregidora into me, and I sung back in return.[17]

What Gayl Jones is telling us between the lines of her eloquent prose is that the power of collective memory does not merely emerge from textual inscriptions. It stems from stories (the oral tradition). It also emerges from somewhere behind the eyes. It is squeezed from the sound-pain of the blues. For Gayl Jones, collective memory is derived from sentiments so elemental that they are beyond words. When Ursa sings the blues, she is possessed by the spirit of cultural memory. Her singing is therefore body-felt, a fact her audience appreciates.

Connerton's theoretical designs fit spirit possession like a glove. Spirit possession is a commemorative ritual in which bodily practices (gestures, sounds, postures, and movements) are never minimized. For her part, Jones' literary evocation of collective memory brings us closer to a theory of spirit possession in which embodied practices—beyond the text—give us an opening to indigenous historiographic practice.

Embodiment, Cultural Memory, and Songhay Spirit Possession

Among the Songhay peoples of Niger and Mali, spirit possession has a long history. Jean-Pierre Olivier de Sardan traces the origin of possession to the late fifteenth century, a time when Islam was institutionalized during the reign of Askia Mohammed Toure.[18] Further, each spirit family in the Songhay pantheon—there are six families—represents a particular period in Songhay history. The *Tooru* represent the earliest and most powerful Songhay ancestors who founded the first Songhay dynasty—the Zas. The *Genji Kwaari* or white spirits are Muslim clerics who became important during the reign of Askia Mohammed. The *Genji Bi* or black spirits represent the first inhabitants of Songhay—the masters of the land. The *Doguwa* or Hausa spirits are of a much more recent vintage. They came into the Songhay pantheon around 1911 during a vast migration of Hausa-speaking peoples into Songhay. The *Hauka*, the subject of this book, are the spirits of colonization and date to 1925.

Based upon the parallel expansions of dominance, experience and spirit families, one could argue that Songhay spirit possession constitutes a "discourse" on history. That would be both facile and specious. There are three paths to the constitution and reconstitution of Songhay history; the written tradition, the oral tradition, and the performance of spirit possession ceremonies. The first path is that of written history. Unlike many groups in West Africa, there is a long textual tradition in Songhay. Two historical documents stand out: es-Sadi's *Tarikh es-Soudan,* collected and written in the seventeenth century, and Kati's *Tarikh al Fattach,* written in the sixteenth century.[19] Both of these books, which are principally histories of the Songhay Empire (1463-1591), were translated into French and published in France in 1900 and 1911, respectively. As scholarly treatises that document a sanitized (Islamized) history of the Songhay, they are virtually unknown in Mali and Niger.

The second path is that of the oral tradition. Like other groups in the Sahel, there is a longstanding epic tradition in Songhay.[20] The griot (bard) has long been the oral historian, the custodian of tales that speak to the greatness of Empire, the valor of past battles, the courage of past Kings. Whereas the *Tarikh* are whitewashed testaments to the Muslim purity of imperial Songhay, the oral tradition speaks to the non-Islamic magical capacities of Songhay kings.[21] But still, the *Epic of Askia Mohammed,* for example, is hardly what Lipsitz would call a literary vehicle for Songhay counter-memory. The epics have always been performed which means that their structures are invariable. Their content, however, varies with the social politics of the performance context. In addition, the epics are stories about the glories of the Songhay elite; they do not reflect the existential struggles of families of Songhay farmers.[22] Although elements of the epics are known to many people in Songhay, they trigger only flashes of Songhay cultural memory. They do not constitute a counter-memory. They do not speak to the elemental aspects of Songhay experience in the world. For that, we need to consider the third path to Songhay history: spirit possession.

The way of the text and the epic are decidedly disembodied paths to Songhay history. Such disembodiment constrains their messages. The text and the epic speak only to aspects of Songhay memory. Spirit possession ceremonies, however, spark Songhay counter-memories, which are, as we have seen, stored in movement, in posture, in gestures, in sound, odor, and tastes—in the flesh. Whereas the text and the epic speak to the consciousness of the nobility, the bodily practices of possession speak to what Ursa's Great Gram called "conscious."

Consciousness is discursive. "Conscious" is body-centered and figurative. Consciousness is derived from papers that can be burned. "You can't burn 'conscious'" says Ursa's Great Gram. "Conscious" is not logically articulated; it reverberates, to use Gaston Bachelard's poetic notion. "Conscious" is found "behind the eyes," in the fury of a glance, in a posture. It is found in the silence between the notes of Ali Farka Toure's *African Blues*. Pulverized into barely recognizable fragments, "conscious" travelled from Africa to North America in strips of cloth, in movement, in strange words, in bits of sound. When Ursa sang the blues, the sound of her voice embodied the haunting counter-memories of her past. But her past is one that cannot be excised from the counter-memories of African Americans. And the pasts of African Americans cannot be excised from the counter-memories of West Africans.

Songhay spirit possession is a sensory arena of counter-memory. The performance of spirit possession ceremonies *re-enacts,* to borrow Connerton's phrase, the experience of the Songhay. The Songhay say that the monochord violin "cries" (*heh*); its "cries" cut to the heart of Songhay. As the "cries" of the violin enter the bodies of both mediums and spectators, the music, according to Songhay teachers, resonates existential themes: the powerlessness of the human confrontation with nature; the utter contingency of life in the Sahel; the delicate balance between life and death; the unresolved tensions between men and women, old and young, friends and foes. These are themes of struggle, of perseverance in a hot, drought-plagued land, of resignation—even the nobles bear powerless witness to the ravages of nature in the Sahel. These themes, the very substance of counter-memory, are rarely found in historical texts or in epics.

But there is more to Songhay spirit possession than the "cries" of the monochord violin. There is a spirit language known only to specialists, a language that situates the spirits in remote time. The spirits also assume ritualized postures and vocalize in ways characteristic of their families, which marks their powerful otherness. The *sorko,* or praise-singer to spirits, recites "old words," the sounds of which beckon the deities from the spirit to the social domain. This recitation situates human beings and spirits in a client/master relationship which has life or death consequences.

Songhay spirit possession is also an arena of fragrance and movement. Particular kinds of pungent perfumes, like *Bint al Sudan,* are used by particular families of spirits. Incenses consisting of various aromatic roots and resins—the mixture shifts with the spirit family for which it is intended—are burned to attract and to please the spirits. Such fragrances may well remind the participants and audience of the opulence of the Empire. They may also trigger counter-memories of the sacrifices one (has) had to make to those who held power.

And finally there is movement. In a blur of movement, the various dance steps of Songhay possession recount the journey of the spirits from water to heavens and back to earth. There is more still, for spectators also see the faces of old women dancing, faces creased and folded by their gritty lives in the Sahel. The frail old women dance, their movements in sync with the quickening pace of the music. They dance and dance until one sees smiles so radiant that they wash away years of sun and hard work. These smiles speak to pride and power, for these women know—as do members of the audience—that without their bodies, which they lend to the spirits, there would be no spirit possession in Songhay. And without spirit possession Songhay would face the relentless world without the protection of the deities—all of this is contained in a beatific smile that embodies Songhay cultural memory.

CHAPTER THREE

Embodied Memories
• • •
Mimesis and Spirit Possession

So far, I've argued that spirit possession is an incontestably embodied phenomenon that triggers a myriad of cultural memories. Such a proposition, however, recounts only part of the tale. How can we explain the power of spirit possession to evoke the past, manipulate the present, and provoke the future? How can we explain the power of spirit possession to shape both local and state politics? My tentative answer, which I begin to articulate in this chapter, is that spirit possession is a site of mimetic production and reproduction, which makes it a stage for the production and reproduction of power.

Performing Possession

The putative link between theater and spirit possession is a long established one. I have already discussed—however briefly—the theatrical or performance approach to spirit possession. Indeed, the link between possession and performance can be traced to Aristotle, who, in his *The Politics*, analyzed Greek possession cults as a form of cultural theater. In France, a group of scholars (inspired partly by the clarity of Aristotle, partly by the histrionics of Marcel Griaule) analyzed spirit possession as a particularly compelling kind of ritual performance. The ethnomusicologist Andre Schaeffner, considered spirit possession a kind of pre-theater, a forerunner to the Greek chorus.[1] Michel Leiris, who, like Schaeffner,

Cultural memories embodied in movement.

accompanied Marcel Griaule on the infamous Dakar-Djibouti expedition (1931–33), also considered spirit possession in terms of theatrical metaphors.[2] The most comprehensive analysis of spirit possession from the performance vantage point is that of Gilbert Rouget, who in his *La Musique et La Transe*, traces how elements of Corybantes spirit possession evolved into classical Greek theater.

It is altogether tempting to employ performance theories to explain the complexities of spirit possession. One could say that the spirit possession cult is in fact a theatrical troupe organized like a repertory company. Spirit-possession priests become multifaceted impresarios who also work as stage directors and script doctors. Spirit mediums become actors, stage-hands and chorus dancers. There is also an orchestra whose music propels the "actors" to dance. From the spirit-possession stage, to push the point a bit farther, the troupe produces "plays" that evolve historical, social, and cultural themes.

The relation of performance and possession is sensitively explored by the late Jean-Marie Gibbal. For Gibbal spirit possession is a manifestation of the poetic imagination. Poet and anthropologist, Gibbal offers a more nuanced version of performing possession than many of his compatriots. For him, spirit possession is perhaps the inspiration for Artaud's renowned Theater of Cruelty. "The phenomenon of possession trance," Gibbal writes, "is part of the profound hallucinatory capacities of all humanity and escapes our total comprehension."[3] He adds:

> Lacking a grasp from inside the physical reality of the phenomenon of trance, of which possessions are expression, I have at least tried to translate the poetic vision of the Ghimbala priests, a vision poetic because it is strong, archaic, primordial, fracturing the real.[4]

Even at its poetic apogee, the metaphor of performance provides only a framework—a stage—for the apprehension of spirit possession. To reduce spirit possession to the threatricalization of cultural history, cultural resistance, or cultural texts is, to paraphrase Maurice Merleau-Ponty, to manipulate things and give up living in them.[5] When one refuses to give up living in things, following Merleau-Ponty's logic, one feels the texture of inner space in which "quality, light, color and depth . . . are there before us only because they awaken an echo in our bodies and because the body welcomes them."[6]

And yet, even Merleau-Ponty's embodied ruminations about art, spectacle and mind fail to explain the power of embodied practices like spirit possession. What is it about the poetics of the spirit medium, who, like the mime, presents an audience with a culturally stylized copy of social reality that affects us so compellingly? To answer this, we need to explore Michael Taussig's sensuous take on mimesis and alterity.

Mime, Mimesis, Alterity

Michael Taussig is one scholar who steadfastly refuses to give up living in things, for he believes that human perception is fundamentally sensuous.

> Like Adorno and Benjamin . . . my concern is to reinstate in and against the myth of Enlightenment, with its universal, context free reason, not merely the resistance of the concrete particular to abstraction, but what I deem crucial to thought that moves and moves us—namely its sensuousness, its mimeticity.[7]

In his most recent book, *Mimesis and Alterity*, Taussig applies his sensuous gaze to the power of mimesis and its relationship to alterity. Taussig takes as his problem the presence of curing figurines among the Cuna Indians of San Blas, Panama. Curiously, the figures depict colonial Europeans. Why would figurines of such intrinsic importance to Cuna healing rites take the form of colonial Europeans? From his vantage as a "European type" Taussig wonders: "What magic lies in this, my wooden self, sung to power in a language I cannot understand?"[8] This magic, in Taussig's analysis, cuts to the very heart of the anthropological enterprise:

> For if I take these figurines seriously, it seems that I am honor-bound to respond to the mimicry of my-self in ways other than the defensive maneuver of the powerful by subjecting it to scrutiny as yet another primitive artifact, grist to the analytic machinery of Euroamerican anthropology. The very mimicry corrodes the alterity by which my science is nourished. For now I too am part of the object of study. The Indians have made me alter to my self.[9]

The problem of the Cuna figurines leads Taussig into a wondrous maze of paradoxes. The Cuna say that the figurines consist of two aspects: inner and outer. It is from the intangible inner aspect that healing power is derived. This ethnographic fact compels Taussig to ask why the figurines take the form of Europeans. "Why bother carving forms at all if the magical power is invested in the spirit of the wood itself? And indeed, as our puzzling leads to more puzzling, why is embodiment itself necessary?"[10]

Walter Benjamin provides Taussig a provisional answer. "The ability to mime, and mime well . . . is the capacity to Other."[11] Through this capacity—what Taussig calls the "mimetic faculty"—one is able to grasp that which is strange—other—through resemblances, through copies of it. The power of the mimetic faculty devolves from its fundamental sensuality: miming something entails contact. Copying a thing, even a European type, is (electro)shocking; it creates a flash of sensation that engenders a sense of comprehension, mastery. For Benjamin and Taussig, knowing is corporeal. One mimes to understand. We copy the world to comprehend it through our bodies.[12]

Recognition, it follows, is an embodied phenomenon which is part and parcel of the mimetic faculty. Through the embodied displacement of the self, recognition strikes us in a flash. Here Taussig cites Benjamin: "the past can be seized only as an image which flashes up at an instant when it can be recognized and is never seen again."[13]

These sensuous mimetic processes, Taussig notes, are very much at work in magic. Sympathetic magic consists of copy and contact. Sorcerers make a copy of that which they want to affect. Through its magical power the copy acquires the properties of the original, which, in turn, implies the sorcerers' mastery and power over the object. Songhay sorcerers, for example, sometimes make copies of magic arrows and bows, which are associated with the arrows and bow of a particular spirit in the Songhay pantheon. On rare occasions they will speak to these replicas from their hearts, naming a victim. Then they take the bow and shoot the arrow in the direction of the victim's dwelling or village. The replica falls harmlessly on the ground in the sorcerer's compound, but the "inner" arrow flies through the night air. And if a sorcerer's aim is good—if the power pulsing in his veins is greater than that of his enemy/victim—the "inner" arrow strikes its victim. Victims will wake up in the middle of night, screaming, with pain shooting up their legs. Once struck, they become progressively weaker. And if they don't seek a cure, they will most certainly die from an invisible (inner) wound. This is an example of what Taussig and Benjamin mean by corporeal knowing.

First Contact/Second Contact and Songhay Possession

Taussig's disquisition on mimesis and alterity also—and importantly— considers the interpersonal dynamics of mimicry, especially during colonial encounters. Combing historical records, he demonstrates the central role of mimicry in various first contacts—first meetings between Europeans, like Charles Darwin on the *Beagle*, and primitive others, like the early nineteenth century Feugians. The latter are seen as great mimics. European first observers, by contrast, thought themselves poor mimics, a talent reserved for naturalized primitives. The apperceived role of mimesis, as demonstrated by Taussig's analysis, played a central role in the personal dynamics of these historic first encounters.

It is, however, the dynamics of what Taussig calls "second contact" that is of central concern in this book. In "second contact," a person sees himself or herself refracted in the images produced by alters. Taussig writes of the disarmingly ferocious shock of "second contact," which is often overtly political.[14]

One of the most illustrious cases of second contact is that of Igbo *Mbari* houses of southeastern Nigeria, in which sculpture depicting

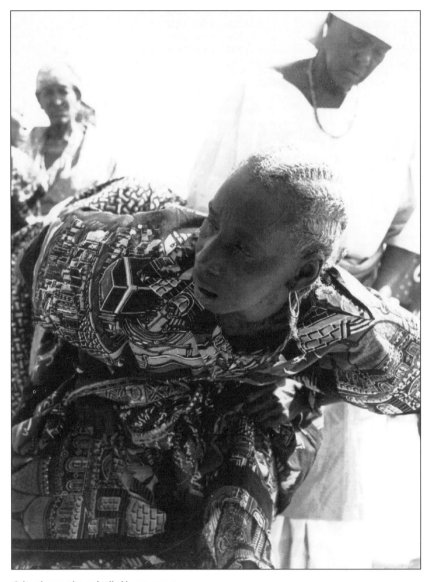

Cultural memories embodied in movement.

colonial white men are erected in isolated forest shrines: images of pith-helmeted, bespectacled white men emerging from the ground, of African white men, wearing coats and ties, speaking into a microphone (of this, more later).

Second contact, in fact, is a primary feature of spirit possession among the Songhay people of Niger and Mali. In the bodies of mediums many of the Songhay spirits become replicas of ancestors which embody the past, make contact with the present and determine the future.

The *Genji Bi* spirits, for example, embody the first occupiers of Songhay lands, the Kurumba and Gurmantche people who today live just to the west of the Songhay. The *Genji Bi* are spirits of soil fertility, beings who don clothing that exposes their legs and chests, who wash themselves with soil, and who sing rather than talk. These spirits are primitive alters to the civilized Songhay, who cover their legs and chests, who wash with water, and who sing only rarely. This Songhay reproduction of their neighbors' ancestors, the *Genji Bi*, is reminiscent of Darwin and Captain Fitzroy's naturalized, primitivist take on the Feugians.

First contact between the conquering Songhay and conquered Kurumba and Gurmantche peoples occurred in the fifteenth century. From a dispossessed Kurumba-Gurmantche perspective, second contact occurs at every *Gengi Bi* possession ceremony, for they see themselves through the culturally stylized embodiment of spirit possession. This kind of second contact would be similar to literate Feugians reading Charles Darwin or Captain Fitzroy or to an educated colonial Songhay reading about his primitiveness in a colonial report. Although this kind of second contact is usually from the vantage of the dispossessed, it is no less shocking than a white man seeing himself depicted in African or Cuna sculpture.

The same kind of dispossessed second contact occurs during Doguwa spirit ceremonies. The Doguwa, which are spirits from the Hausa-speaking eastern Niger, came into the Songhay pantheon early in the century, following a wave of Hausa migration into Songhay country. These spirits are mean, crass, mercurial; they drink blood, devour honey, and drive their victims insane before killing them. Among the Doguwa, men sometimes dress as women. Males and females use foul language and pay little attention to the filth that soils their bodies. Not a pretty portrait, and yet when these ceremonies are performed there are Hausa-speaking people in the audience who, like Taussig confronting the Cuna figurines, may experience the electroshock of "second contact."

Second Contact: The Hauka

Second contact, then, is usually a two-way street. The spirits of the Songhay pantheon, including the Hauka, are the embodiment of the Songhay imagination, which, lest we forget, incorporates African as well as European universes of experience and affects African as well as European audiences—yet in very different ways.

That "second contact" is a shocking disruption to the neat and tidy categories of European conceptual hegemony is incontestable. Taussig describes this disruption with eloquence:

> To become aware of the West in the eyes and handiwork of its Others, to wonder at the fascination with their fascination, is to abandon border logistics and enter into the 'second contact' era of the borderland where 'us' and 'them' lose their polarity and swim in and out of focus. This dissolution reconstellates the play of nature in mythic pasts of contractual truths. Stable identity formations auto-destruct into silence, gasps of unaccountable pleasure, or cartwheeling confusion gathered in a crescendo of what I call 'mimetic excess' spending itself in a riot of dialectical energy.[15]

For Taussig, the Hauka deities are a particularly compelling example of "second contact," for they mimic colonial personages. Like any deity in spirit possession, Hauka mediums are and are not the Europeans they so frighteningly and funnily depict. Taussig's second contact with the Hauka is through the "mechanical reproduction" of the film camera—Jean Rouch's classic ethnographic film, *Les maitres fous*. Taussig describes a magic moment in the film that, for him, encapsulates magical mimesis. It is a jump-cut from the sacrifice of an egg on the statue of the governor (of the colonial Gold Coast) to the military parade that celebrates the opening of the Colonial Assembly in Accra. One is teleported from watching a egg run over the governor's statue—a copy, after all—to the real governor.

> The film hurls us at the cascading yellow and white plumes of the white governor's gorgeous hat as he reviews the black troops passing. Those of us watching the film in a university lecture hall gasp. There is something immensely powerful released at this moment, begging for interpretation. The film with its ability to explore the optical unconscious, to come close and enlarge, to frame and to montage, creates in this sudden juxtaposition a suffusion of mimetic magic.[16]

Separated from the Hauka deities by screen and space, Taussig's analysis captures—for a Western audience—a magic moment of second contact; it is a telling example of the "Western rebirth of the mimetic faculty by means of modernity's mimetic machinery."[17]

For Songhay audiences as well as the European occupying the body of an anthropologist, the terrifying antics of the Hauka, however, are something other than Taussig's narrowly defined "second contact." Their presence is a shock to everyone, but Songhay observers, I would guess, are not so much concerned with the rebirth of mimesis in Euroamerica; rather, they continuously express their worries about their precarious fate in the world. There is something in the sensuous aesthetics of this Songhay mimicry of the military bearing of colonial personages that affects Nigeriens physiognomically.

What is it about the Hauka that compels a middle-aged Nigerien man with a doctorate in soil science to attend their ceremonies and keep in his house a "copy" of Commandant Bashiru's pith helmet? What is it about the Hauka that prompts the European occupying the body of an anthropologist to bear his Hauka burden? What is it about the Hauka that causes people who once controlled the Nigerien state to use Hauka aesthetics as a model of political action? These questions shape the discussion in the remainder of this book, for we shall be concerned with the sensuousness of Hauka embodiment, the potent cultural memories that the Hauka trigger, and the significance of Hauka aesthetics in past and present power relations in Niger. These disquisitions ultimately lead us to reflections on the centrality of the mimetic faculty in the production and reproduction of power relations.

But I fear that the Hauka would not be pleased with this progression. They would say readers/listeners should savor the Hauka story—bit by delicious bit. And so we shall dispense with direct theoretical exposition and submerge ourselves in historical and ethnographic specifics all to suggest that, as a set of embodied practices, spirit possession constitutes power-in-the-Songhay world.

PART TWO

Confronting Colonialism in West Africa

◆　◆　◆

Forms of Confrontation

◆   ◆   ◆

Recent work in colonial studies has focused on the contested and fragmented nature of (post)colonial discourses. In this emerging body of work, authors attempt to analyze colonialism and the discourse it produced from a cultural framework that is anti-essentialist. As Nicholas Dirks points out: "Colonialism not only has had cultural effects that have too often been either ignored or displaced into inexorable logics of modernization and world capitalism, it was itself a cultural product of control."[1] And, as Nicholas Thomas puts it: "Colonial cultures are not simple ideologies that mask, mystify, or rationalize forms of oppression that are external to them; they are also expressive and constitutive of colonial relationships in themselves."[2]

Much has been written about the nature of popular resistance to colonial domination. Colonial historians have long described campaigns of military resistance to the onset of colonial rule. Much less has been written, however, on the contemporary military resistance to oppressive rule in the postcolonial states. Current armed resistance movements in Mali, Niger, and Togo, for example, are cases in point. Resistance, of course, has never been limited to military revolt. Historians like E.P. Thompson and political scientists like James Scott have written eloquently on the dynamics of cultural resistance in England and Malaysia. Scott has termed the various media of cultural resistance "weapons of the weak."

There are two major problems associated with the literature on colonial and postcolonial resistance. The first is a lack of ethnographic specificity. Undifferentiated peasants or plebs employ symbolic weapons that "resist" the oppression of colonial rule.[3] Indeed, analysts of movements of resistance sometimes miss the sociocultural nuances embodied in parodic forms of cultural expression. All the more reason to ground analyses of resistance in West Africa and Niger in historical and ethnographic specifics. The second problem is brilliantly stated by Achille Mbembe whose argument applies both to colonial and postcolonial relations of power. He writes:

> To account for both the imagery and efficacy of postcolonial relations of power, we must go beyond the binary categories used in standard interpretations of domination (resistance/passivity, subjection/autonomy, state/civil society, hegemony/counterhegeomony, totalization/detotalization). These oppositions are not helpful; rather they cloud our understanding of postcolonial relations. In the postcolony the commandement seeks to institutionalize itself in order to achieve legitimation and hegemony, in the form of a fetish.[4]

To achieve this institution of power the state—or colonial administration—designs a set of evocative ideas developed from a mix of local cultural repertoires.[5] Using slightly different terms, Mbembe's argument echoes that of Dirks and Thomas. He is writing about the fractures and fissures of (post)colonial discourse from a decidedly cultural vantage.

In this part of the book, I attempt to take up Mbembe's challenge by describing from a multiperspectival cultural vantage the complexities of colonial culture in West Africa. By carefully situating the historical and social context of West African military and cultural opposition to European colonialism, the chapters in this part of the book will establish a regional framework from which we will consider, in Part Three, the establishment of and opposition to colonialism in Niger.[6]

This part of the book is divided into three chapters. In Chapter Four, I describe the forces that drove the nineteenth-century colonial powers (France and Britain) to partition West Africa. In Chapter Five, I consider the establishment of colonial rule, and describe the construction of an embodied hegemonic discourse.[7] And in Chapter Six, I demonstrate how West Africans defied colonial culture through embodied oppositions. Chapters Four, Five and Six are intended to give non-Africanist readers a very short course on the history of European-West African contact. Readers interested in more nuanced historical dispositions or in historiographic debate, of which there is a great deal, are urged to consult the notes.

CHAPTER FOUR

From First Contacts to Military Partition

· · ·

The story of the Hauka begins with first contacts between Europeans and West Africans; first contacts, however rare, brought on by the Atlantic slave trade which, along the Guinea and Upper Guinea coasts, dates to the late fifteenth century. It was not until the abolition of the slave trade in the nineteenth century that Europeans began their comprehensive economic exploitation of West African lands and peoples. For fear of what was then a mysterious and incurable "fever," few Europeans dared to leave the safety of their anchored ships; fewer still left the security of coastal enclaves to explore the "interior."

As long as the slave trade was profitable, there was little need or desire for Europeans to know their West African alters. Indeed, first contacts between Europeans and their West African alters were usually indirect—through intermediaries called *lancadoes.*[1]

From the late fifteenth through the early seventeenth century, few people were willing to undertake first voyages from Portugal or Britain to the "Fever Coast," as it was then known. Slave merchants might be willing to pay a ship's captain enough money to feed his wanderlust, but who could one hire to "man" ships destined for a danger zone? With entrepreneurial resourcefulness slave traders searched the debtors prisons in Portugal and Britain for able-bodied men. For many debtors a mission at sea was preferable to wasting away in a dank, disease-ridden prison cell. And so debtors constituted the early crews of most slave ships. Many of the debtors did not return to Europe. Fashioning a life on African soil was an existential choice preferable to a certain return to poverty and a probable return to prison. From the sixteenth to the turn of the eighteenth century scores of European debtors established themselves in what is now coastal Senegal, Guinea, Sierra Leone, Ghana and Nigeria. There they married local women, who were often of noble descent.[2]

Local rulers astutely exploited the presence of the foreigners. And why not? These former debtors, after all, spoke a version of the slaver's language (Portuguese, English). If they were married well (to borrow from Kristin Mann's book title)—to daughters of local rulers—and learned to speak one or more African languages, they might serve local princes and kings magnificently as intermediaries. Indeed, the economic fit was perfect, for few European slavers wished to confront the medical or military dangers of the seventeenth- or eighteenth-century West African "interior."

In conjunction with European slavers, these *lancadoes,* who spoke creole languages amongst themselves (Creoliou and Krio) established outposts on the West African coast from Senegal to Nigeria. They built slave pens and amassed small fleets of boats which they sailed up such rivers as the Senegal, the Gambia, and the Niger to purchase slaves from indigenous rulers. Many of the *lancadoe* traders became enormously rich, using the profits from the slave trade to eventually construct vast trading networks.[3]

Before 1800 there was virtually no European penetration into the West African hinterland. A few hardy Frenchmen had established a number of trading outposts several hundred miles up the Senegal River, but " . . . all in all the Europeans had established but forty-three fortified stations on the West Coast, of which thirty-one were situated along the two-hundred-mile coastline known as the Gold Coast."[4]

Prior to the "official abolition" of the slave trade in 1807, Europeans, mainly the French and the British, were not excessively interested in dominating West Africa. Given the profitability of the slave trade and the inhospitability of West African lands that bred fatal tropical diseases as well as hostile indigenous armies, this fact is hardly surprising. In eighteenth century European theory, West Africa was a land of primitive backwardness and savage insensibility. Eighteenth-century European practices, however, suggest a grudging, partially articulated respect for indigenous West African polities.[5]

The marriage of economics and politics profoundly changed the relationship between Europeans and West Africans in the nineteenth century. Pressured from strong and influential political movements, the slave trade was officially abolished during the first decade of the nineteenth century. That is not to say that the profitable slave trade ceased to exist, but the passage of ordinances in Denmark and Great Britain greatly reduced the number of slaves transported from Africa to the New World.[6]

Great Britain was quite serious about enforcing the Abolition on shipping and used naval power to prevent other nations from engaging in slave trading. But these activities, in the view of British humanitarians, were insufficient. As explained by Michael Crowder:

> The humanitarians believed that effectively to abolish the slave trade one would not only have to seize the carriers and blockade the ports of their supply, but cut the coastal middle-men off from their source of slaves. It was argued that if the Africans of the interior could be given alternative means of earning exchange with which to buy the European imports they desired, other than by selling their fellow men, then the slave trade could be remedied. Thus Africans were to be simultaneously converted to Christianity and encouraged to grow tropical agricultural produce such as cotton which Britain needed. This coincided with official British interest in promoting trade with Africa as well as the desire to ensure the complete cessation of the slave trade.[7]

Crowder and other colonial historians of West Africa, however, believe that economic forces—commercial interests—more than noble humanitarian desires, brought on the end of the slave trade.

It was industrial expansion that motivated Britain—and later France—to expand their trade with Africans. Great Britain needed to establish new loci for an increasing number of manufactured goods, and desired to import increased amounts of West African palm oil to lubricate industrial machines and produce candles and soap.[8] Following the abolition of the slave trade, then, trading interests in Liverpool and Marseilles actively sought trade outlets in West Africa. Among the commodities exported were groundnuts, gum, indigo and peppers. By 1830, however, it was apparent that palm oil would become the most important West African export.[9] While Britain concentrated on increasing the sale of manufactured goods in West Africa, France, still an agricultural nation, attempted to establish cash crop plantations in Senegal. These schemes proved to be disastrous and were abandoned by 1840. During the first part of the nineteenth century, then, European impact on West African peoples was minimal, except for certain populations living along the Guinea and Upper Guinea coasts, populations that began to participate directly in cash economies.

Mid-nineteenth-century European exploration of the West African interior had a mixed impact on West African societies. Exploration of the lower Niger, for example, initially eradicated the middlemen—often the ever-resilient descendants of the *lancadoes*—in Nigerian oil production. These economic advances prompted potentially lucrative trade contacts with the Hausa states in northern Nigeria. Early explorations of the Niger River, however, were exceedingly costly; many members of these expeditions died of "fever," which reinforced the image of Africa as the "white man's grave." Given these results, Europeans limited trading activities to coastal areas, and were forced to employ middlemen to contact peoples farther inland.[10]

Between 1850 and 1880, then, trade between Europe and West Africa was lackluster. Based upon the principal of laissez-faire, the trade had little impact on West African states, especially those of the interior. The trade constituted a classic case of what Walter Rodney called "underdevelopment." The European powers extracted important commodities that helped to fuel the fires of industrialization, which, in turn, propelled large-scale social change in Great Britain and France. However:

> The nature of the imports which paid for African produce did less. A few printing presses and cotton ginning machines, replacement parts for locally used steamships, the books imported by the missionaries and the tools imported by mission-trained African carpenters and coopers is a list which almost exhausts those imports which may be said to have had any effect in increasing productivity. The vast bulk of imports before 1870 consisted of a small number of items which were by their nature quickly consumed and contributed almost nothing to the quality of the economy or its development; alcoholic liquor, guns and ammunition, tobacco, beads and not a very large proportion of cotton cloth together formed the major import items.[11]

At mid-century the major European powers had limited economic and political dominion over West African lands. Great Britain's interests consisted of the Gold Coast forts, Freetown, and Bathurst, on St. Mary's Island at the mouth of the Gambia River. Under the aggressive expansionist policies of Faidherbe, the French had annexed by 1865 one-third of what today constitutes Senegal.[12] In exchange for military protection—against the Ashanti—the British also established official Bonds—treaties—with several African states along the Guinea Coast. The British annexed these states in 1874, which, in effect, created her first colony—the Gold Coast—in West Africa.[13]

And yet the British were quite reluctant colonizers before 1880. Colonial investments in the Gold Coast, Sierra Leone and southern Nigeria far exceeded economic returns. As a result British colonial policy was monolithic.[14] Why create a nuanced colonial policy for territories which prompted debilitating economic frustration rather than enhanced political power? Compared to the British, the French were quite expansionist on the eve of the scramble for West Africa. Interested in expanding the growing groundnut trade to the interior of the western Soudan, the French extended their control from coastal Senegal to the east, meeting some resistance from the likes of El Haji 'Umar (see Chapter Six). What is curious, however, is that the French, like the British, understood the economic folly of colonial investment. Crowder suggests that the French expanded their West African colonial influence in response to their humiliating defeat at the hands of the Prussians in 1871. The French navy and the army wanted glorious compensation for the infamy of their loss, and West Africa was a place where they could exercise their pride—for the glory of France.[15]

From the vantage of Europe, West Africa in 1880 was an unproductive wasteland, a white man's graveyard, that produced little if anything for the colonial powers. Why, then, did the European powers scramble to partition vast tracts of unproductive African lands between 1880 and 1900?

The Partition of West Africa

The partition of West Africa, it seems, resulted from both political as well as economic factors. As already noted, the French seemed more economically optimistic—perhaps more naive—than the British who bemoaned their economic burdens in West Africa. Crowder quotes Lord Salisbury's telling comment about the abrupt change in European attitudes toward West Africa. "When I left the Foreign Office in 1880 nobody thought about Africa. When I returned to it in 1885 the nations of Europe were almost quarrelling with each other as to the various portions of Africa they could obtain."[16]

Despite the economic pitfalls of investment in West Africa, any number of traders persisted in their belief that vast riches could be found in the West African interior. Would it not be better, they argued, to exploit the resources of these lands from within the relative safety of a colonial protectorate? In this way, they could render superfluous the influence of the ever-present African middlemen and eliminate the sometimes cut-throat competition between Europeans of different persuasions.

Such arguments, often ridiculed, were nonetheless resilient in Paris and London. In Europe there was widespread ignorance of West African social realities, which led people to harbor unrealistic expectations. Fed by the descriptive riches of the travel accounts of Caillé, Barth, and Stanley, traders and politicians reasoned that Africa was a land of rich potential interior markets that could be reached by way of the great rivers (the Niger, the Congo) or by way of railroads. Little attention was paid to the navigability of the rivers—a serious problem—or to the staggering investment costs of building a railroad.

More pragmatically, traders sought to exploit the interior markets because of increased competition along the coasts, which lowered their profit margins. In the interior, of course, Europeans had to confront once again the ever-present African middlemen who were none too keen about losing their economic power. Caught in potentially dangerous situations, traders sought the protection of their respective governments.

In the latter part of the nineteenth century the trading elements became bold and successfully exercised their influence for expansion—however foolhardy such expansion may have been considered. French traders in St. Louis, Senegal, successfully backed the appointment of Faidherbe as Governor of Senegal; they thought, correctly so, that he would take a hard line against their principal competition,the Moors. As we shall see in Chapter Six, Faidherbe was also an early expansionist whose policies and activities sparked African military opposition in Senegal. Taubman Goldie's political clout enabled him to secure from the British government a charter such that his company, U.A.C., could take up the administration of most of Nigeria.

Interest in the "colonies" was also growing among the educated middle classes. Although colonial commercial matters struck the fancy of educated people in France and Great Britain, Europeans were very much taken with so-called humanitarian issues. The Humanitarians of the early nine-teenth century focused their attentions almost exclusively on the abolition of the slave trade. In the late nineteenth century, "humanitarian" issues, tempered by ignorance and manifest racism, took on the tones of "the white man's burden" and "la renaissance culturelle."

These "humanitarian" motives put additional pressure on European governments to occupy West Africa. Crowder notes that "theories of the racial superiority of the white man coupled with the explorers' and mis-sionaries' tales of the backward condition of Africa, increased support for the occupation of Africa and its subjection to the 'benefit' of European rule."[17]

The increasing interest in Africa—whether for economic or "humani-tarian" reasons—promoted a sense of competition between European governments. As Great Britain and France began to consolidate their African holdings—especially the British annexation of Egypt—Germany, under Bismarck, entered the competition. African colonization in itself was an afterthought for Bismarck, but German colonization would, he reasoned, prevent French or British domination in Africa. And so the scramble for Africa was on.[18]

The Berlin Conference

In 1884-85 Bismarck called the African colonial powers (Britain, France, Portugal, and Germany) to the conference table. The Berlin Conference did not sanction the partition of Africa, which had already begun in earnest. The French had already initiated their march toward the east and had conquered Bamako in 1882. Germany had already annexed Togo and Cameroon. In Nigeria, Goldie had concluded treaties with the Sokoto caliphate.

The purpose of the Conference was to establish rules for the occupation of Africa, rules that would ostensibly ensure a peaceful partition of the continent. As Crowder notes, the central question of the Conference con-cerned the occupation of coastal Africa, but in practice the Act that result-ed from the deliberations provided the ground rules for the occupation of the interior as well as the coast. The Act had the following provisions:

1. If a power wanted to lay claim to African territory, it should inform the other signatory powers in case the latter wanted to make claims of their own;

2. If such claims and counter-claims were to be valid, they had to be supported by occupation;

3. Major rivers such as the Niger and Congo would be zones of free navigation;

4. Free trade would be maintained in the Congo basin. [19]

The Conference, then, established a legal basis for the "African Scramble." Crowder wryly notes:

> The rules agreed upon, the various participants began to play the game with differing degrees of enthusiasm, and for different stakes. As far as West Africa was concerned, it was rather like a game of Monopoly, with France and Britain the only two serious contestants, Britain relying for her success on Park Lane and Mayfair, Whitechapel and the Old Kent Road, whilst France bought up anything she could lay her hands on that hadn't been taken by Portugal or Germany.[20]

In this way, Africa was carved into bits and pieces, bits and pieces still reflected on contemporary maps.

If anything, the European powers were ill-prepared for the colonization of West Africa. They knew little about indigenous institutions, histories, conflicts, or economies. They knew less still about the ecological or political conditions that would affect investments and, ultimately, governance. But the political history of partition gives only a partial picture of the beginnings of European dominance in West Africa. J.L. Flint, an economic historian, suggests that the partition devolved from failure of "legitimate commerce," itself based upon the assumptions of theories of laissez-faire economics. Before the establishment of European administrations, the trade between West Africa and Europe had resulted in little, if any, social change on the continent.[21] In this climate of economic failure, European traders undoubtedly needed the support of their respective governments—a prime condition for increased formal European intervention in West Africa.

Perhaps the most compelling explanation for West Africa's partition comes from A.E. Hopkins, also an economic historian. In his *An Economic History of West Africa*, Hopkins anticipates the current trend toward global analysis in economics. He argues that what happened in West Africa resulted from the global confrontation between Europe and the rest of the world. Here it is worth quoting Hopkins' lucid argument at some length.

The economic expansion of Europe in the nineteenth century had a profound and destabilizing effect on West Africa because it changed the structure of export production and involved the region in the trade cycle of the new, industrial economy. The Afro-European alliance which had made the external slave trade possible and profitable started to dissolve early in the nineteenth century. A new generation of African producers and traders began to develop outside the limits of the old, foreign trade enclaves, but was unable to establish a completely satisfactory partnership with merchants on the European side of the frontier. In some cases difficulties arose because of obstruction from traditional rulers, but even where the indigenous authorities were willing to cooperate, and achieved a measure of success in doing so, there were limits to the concessions they were prepared to make.[22]

As long as legitimate commerce was successful, as it was during much of the nineteenth century, the stresses and strains of the Afro-European trade were manageable. In the last quarter of the nineteenth century, Europe experienced an economic depression which, according to Hopkins, caused "England, France and Germany to come into conflict with each other, as well as with African states."[23]

Whatever the explanation for partition, the European states took it upon themselves to establish colonial dominion over West Africa. One thing is clear: African peoples did not welcome the European colonizers. To quote Crowder:

But few African leaders desired that the political control of their countries should be alienated permanently to the newcomers. It is one of the fictions of colonialism that Africans accepted colonial rule willingly, and in some cases with relief. In fact at least two-thirds of the peoples of West Africa have a history of overt resistance to colonial penetration. In blunt terms, then, what took place between 1885 and 1906 was the military occupation and subjection of West Africans to an administration they did not want, and whose imposition they often resisted bitterly.[24]

The partition and occupation of West Africa set the stage for the imposition of colonial rule and the establishment of what Balandier and Crowder, among others, called the "colonial situation," the subjects of Chapter Five. Using a more contemporary framework, "colonial situation" translates to colonial discourse. Although this discourse was fissured, fractured, everalterable and profoundly cultural, its ideational foundation was rocksolid; it established the sociocultural order that triggered the birth of the Hauka Movement in Niger in 1925.

CHAPTER FIVE

Colonizing West Africa

Until the European partition of West Africa, the growth and ultimate failure of Euro-African trade had limited impact on West African economies, let alone West African social life. Even during the 20-year period of partition and conquest, the colonial powers were so preoccupied with their conquering stratagems—and with one another's territorial appetites—that even the maneuvers of European armies had little impact on the everyday routines of most West Africans. In most regions social and economic life remained virtually unchanged. Such stasis was short lived, however, for the sudden imposition of British and French colonial rule provoked widespread social and economic change in many regions of West Africa.

> The establishment of colonial administration over larger territorial units after the partition itself proved to be the catalyst of fundamental economic change. Colonial administrations needed officials, great and small, black and white, to administer the domains; these had to be paid in cash, housed, transported about the country. Cash revenues were, therefore, needed and a military force had to be there to insist in the last resort on the taxes being paid . . . A large and ever-expanding work force, salaried or wage-earning, therefore arose from the very fact of colonial administration.[1]

In this chapter, then, we shall explore the policies of British and French colonial administrations and attempt to describe the impact of these on the sociocultural life of West Africans.

Colonial Administrations and the Colonial Situation

Many writers have suggested that the subjugation of West African peoples was surprisingly swift—almost effortless. This suggestion led to the belief, which Crowder, among others, debunks, that West Africans warmly welcomed the British and French as the restorers of order to a world that had become chaotic. Nothing could be farther from the truth, for West Africans, as we shall see in Chapter Six, opposed European incursion from its outset and continued to oppose it until the end of the colonial epoch. At first, West Africans organized armed groups to oppose the military occupation of their lands, which, as they correctly perceived, threatened their sovereignty. In time, however, the Europeans quashed these revolts. West Africans had to adjust to the various policies and rules of colonial administrations. These rules and policies, which constituted the colonial situation, prompted widespread non-military opposition to European control. Immanuel Wallerstein defined the colonial situation in the following manner:

> By the term colonial situation we simply mean that someone imposes in a given area a new institution, the colonial administration, governed by outsiders who establish new rules which they enforce with a reasonable degree of success. It means that all those who act in the colony must take some account of these rules, and that indeed an increasing amount of each individual's action is oriented to this set of rules rather than to any other set, for example, the tribal set, to which he formerly paid full heed.[2]

What was it about the colonial culture that prompted widespread opposition? In this chapter we will describe the powerful impact of the colonial culture on the social lives of West Africans. In Chapter Six, we shall consider how West Africans opposed various aspects of the colonial situation. One thing is certain: "The impact of European administration led to change in all spheres of African life. . ."[3]

Colonialism and Domestic Slavery

Although the European naval patrols were able to reduce the flow of the trans-Atlantic slave trade to a trickle by the latter part of the nineteenth century, their military incursions into the West African interior had little effect on domestic slavery. In West Africa, domestic slavery had been a longstanding social institution in many societies. Domestic slaves, who were either prisoners of war or the prisoners' patrilineal descendants, were "attached" to or "members" of "free" families. Domestic slaves had rights as well as obligations. In some cases, they became important political personages. In the medieval West African Empires of Ghana, Mali, and Songhay, domestic slaves comprised the overwhelming majority of the imperial population. They were foot soldiers, bards, craftspeople, most of whom cultivated staple crops (corn, sorghum, millet, rice).

At the beginning of the colonial administration, domestic slavery constituted the bedrock of many, if not most, West African societies.[4] Imagine, then, the social disruption caused by its eradication.

In the French colonies, Governor-General William Ponty set out to abolish slavery in 1901, but it was not until 1905 that he put forward a decree that punished anyone who raided, traded, or kept slaves. The punishment was two to five years in prison and a steep fine. Such a decree went a long way toward abolishing open slave markets, but did little to undermine domestic slavery in French West Africa.

Crowder notes that there were good political reasons for the French to drag their feet on the question of domestic slavery. Although the "humanitarians" in France pushed hard for the abolition of domestic slavery, the French "paid" their African soldiers (who are represented in the Hauka pantheon as the spirit Bambara-Mossi), in domestic slaves. And so the French armies were seen initially as another group of slave raiders. Hardly a way to encourage the abolition of domestic slavery! The French also forced large numbers of West Africans to join labor brigades, a colonial form of slavery.[5]

However reticent it might have been, the French "official" abolition of slavery, in part, set into motion the massive migration of (former) domestic slaves. Colonial officials estimated that by 1908 some 200,000 domestic slaves in the Western Sudan had quit their masters. In 1911 Governor-General William Ponty suggested that 500,000 "captifs" had liberated themselves. In a colonial report circulated in 1912, French colonial officials estimated that one in every three slaves in the Western Sudan had fled from his or her master.[6] What motivated the flight of these domesticated slaves? Obviously, they were not content to be "attached" to or "members" of noble families. It is clear that most of the former "captifs" left the Western Sudan for Nigeria and the Gold Coast. Perhaps economic opportunity was better there than in the French administered coastal colonies. Perhaps they left the Sudan for fear of being conscripted into a forced labor gang. Clearly, they sought relief from oppressive and unremitted economic exploitation.[7]

Like the French, the British resorted to forced labor in their West African colonies, but the issue of slavery in Nigeria, the Gold Coast, Sierra Leone, and the Gambia seemed less central to the colonial mission. And yet, the

British feared the social changes that abolition would unleash. Colonial administrators therefore sought to discreetly subvert their anti-slavery proclamations.

The British officially abolished slavery at the outset of their colonial administrations. In northern Nigeria, Lord Lugard insisted that the enslaved apply for what he referred to as "permissive freedom."[8] Such a technicality, of course, significantly slowed the pace of abolition. In his anti-slavery proclamation, the governor of the Gold Coast was careful to point out that the colonial government had no intention of forcing slaves to leave their masters. In the Gambia, the 1906 Anti-Slavery Ordinance did not abolish slavery; slaves, however, could purchase their freedom for ten pounds at the death of their masters. The Ordinance of 1906 also forbade the transfer of slaves.[9]

From the indigenous perspective, the French and British came to conquer and to occupy. West African nobles—domestic slave owners—resented the occupation; it ended their sovereignty. From the domestic slave perspective, the French and British replaced one kind of slavery with another: forced labor, something to be avoided at all costs.[10]

Forced Labor and Taxation

The colonial administrations, as already noted, were ill-prepared to govern West African polities. Fed by the partial descriptions of the nineteenth-century explorers, the colonizers' limited knowledge of West African social realities provoked a variety of crises. To make matters even worse, London and Paris provided little financial support for colonial enterprises. This fact meant that the colonies had to more or less fend for themselves—in spaces of little ecologic or economic promise. What to do? Facing these circumstances, the various administrations began to tax their subjects and conscript able-bodied males into forced-labor gangs.

The forced-labor gang was among the most pernicious features of French colonialism in West Africa. "Slave labor for African masters was replaced by forced labor for the new French masters."[11] Some of the most egregious examples of forced labor occurred in what the French euphemistically called *villages de liberte*.

The invention of Gallieni, the *villages de liberte* were settled by slaves who had been liberated through the French occupation. In point of fact, the villages solved a great colonial need for labor. And so the *captifs* were gathered up and placed in these work camps. The French situated the villages near their administrative centers and organized them like prisons. Villagers who left a *village de liberte* would be tracked down—like runaway slaves in the American South—and thrown in prison for one month. Conditions in the villages were so deplorable that many villagers, if they managed to escape French posses, preferred to attach themselves to an African employer. Although many of the *villages de liberte* were abandoned by 1910, the attraction of forced labor remained. The French were not about to abandon the practice of forcing their *sujets* to labor on "public works." [12]

The French built the notion of forced labor into their system of colonial taxation. In addition to the labor of their *sujets*, French colonial administrations needed to raise funds. And so they created a "head tax."

> First there was the tax in labour known as *prestation*. Each adult was liable to 12 days' labour, redeemable at 1-3 francs a day. Then there was compulsory labour in return for payment. The most common form of labor was on roads and work on 'les champs administratifs' to increase agricultural production . . . In certain areas labour was requisitioned for commercial companies, as in the Ivory Coast, or for the construction of railways, and other public works.[13]

The French policy of direct taxation tied to conscripted forced labor altered agricultural practices and precipitated ongoing mass migration, most of it seasonal labor. Faced by the burden of excessively high direct taxes, many West Africans under French rule had to produce surpluses which they could sell off to pay the administration. Faced with high taxes and the threat of forced labor, young men migrated to wage-labor zones (Senegal, The Gold Coast, and Nigeria) to earn money to pay their taxes and/or to escape the cruel conditions of forced-labor camps. These policies instituted market economies in much of French West Africa. The French finally abolished forced labor in 1946.

The British West African policies on forced labor and taxation were more varied and less pernicious than in the French zone. As in the French case, the British sought to exploit resources to expand colonial market economies. Direct taxation and forced labor were means to this end. In Nigeria, Lord Lugard linked taxation to the burdens of civilization.[14] For Lugard, taxation supported the colonial administration, triggered economic production, and bolstered his policy of indirect rule. Having already had a long history in northern Nigeria, direct taxation was a policy rather easy to administer. In the Gold Coast and Sierra Leone, initial attempts to impose taxes triggered serious rebellions and had to be abandoned. Direct taxation was imposed in the Gold Coast in 1936, but it provided only a fraction of the colonial administration's revenues, most of which came from London and cocoa imports. There were also forced labor gangs conscripted by chiefs in British West Africa. The labor gangs worked on roads and railways, but most of the laborers were paid. Although forced labor and taxation were major components of British colonial policy in West Africa, they never took on the kind of social and political significance of similar practices in the French colonies. Unlike the French, the British administrations could profit from burgeoning local export economies.

The Decimation of Chiefs

The policies of taxation and forced labor in British and French West Africa had devastating social consequences. They rapidly and irrevocably transformed the West African economy from one primarily, though not exclusively, based on barter and local subsistence production to one based upon foreign money exchange and the production of export surpluses. In the French colonies, rural farmers now had to worry about how to acquire the francs to pay the hated head tax and how to avoid being conscripted into a forced-labor gang. Many cultivators left their families and lineages and sought wage labor in the British colonies. A way of living had been seriously altered.

The colonial policies of direct taxation, forced-labor gangs and the abolition of domestic slavery, however, can not be divorced from policies toward indigenous chiefs. In French West Africa the various colonial administrators faced many instances of direct and indirect resistance to their rule (see Chapter Six). One way of combatting resistance, they reasoned, was to weaken the role of traditional chiefs. Prior to colonization, chiefs governed over a variety of West African polities. Although the extent of their roles and their power varied from society to society, people respected their office, if not always the individual holding the office. Chiefs led armies, adjudicated disputes, made political decisions, and performed sacred rituals. In the early part of the colonial era, they often triggered various forms of opposition.

How to subvert the authority of chiefs? The French found a facile solution: make them into salaried tax collectors who conscript laborers for roads and railways. "These new functions were largely responsible for the changeover of the position of chief from the symbol of collective unity of his people to the most hated member of that community. The chiefs abused their traditional authority in raising taxes and labour not only for the French but for themselves."[15] In the French system, the *commandant de cercle* usually replaced the traditional chief. He answered to a regional commandant, who, in turn, answered to the colonial governor, who reported to the ultimate authority, the governor-general in Dakar. The French generally undermined the role of the local chief to subvert his power, though it would be specious to suggest that these changes were simply the results of colonial impositions; they also emerged from a complex of local responses to a myriad of sociopolitical and cultural changes.[16]

The story of chiefs in British West Africa is a complicated one, for it involves a kind of fetishism. It is far too easy to contrast unproblematically the direct rule of the French and the indirect rule of the British. The French policies were unabashedly pernicious, and yet there were elements in French colonial practice that could be classified as "indirect." By the same token one could agree with Crowder that British colonialism was "lighter in touch" than the French version, but it too had its pernicious "direct" aspects.[17] Although indirect rule preserved traditional political structures and upheld the role of the chief, no one believed that such a rule could be equated with pre-colonial sovereignty. In addition, it is clear that racism twisted its way into colonial policy—direct or indirect—becoming, ultimately, its guiding force.

The policy of indirect rule isolated the educated elite, a very real threat to British authority, and reinforced ethnic divisiveness. It was much easier to govern a colony that lacked political unity; and much easier to govern a colony in which the educated and commercial elite were marginalized. Indeed, indirect rule reinforced the reactionary character of many pre-colonial regimes, and despite the changes provoked by colonization, did little to develop—economically, socially or politically—the colonial territories.

In British West Africa, then, chiefs in most regions retained their positions in local structural hierarchies, but lost in varying degrees their autonomy.[18] Although they continued to perform their chiefly duties in local contexts, the ever-distant district officer became the ultimate authority. In French West Africa, by contrast, the *commandant de cercle* transformed the chief from a respected authority into a tax-collecting forced-labor overlord. Despite these differences of approach, the colonial policies toward chiefs decimated traditional authority, all to the administrative and political advantage of the colonial authorities.

Education and Colonialism in West Africa

In the past, scholars of the colonial period in West Africa presented it as a brutal epoch fraught with confrontation and loss. Clearly the colonial administrators designed and enforced policies on domestic slavery, taxation, forced labor, and traditional chiefs that appear to have devastated West African social, economic and political institutions. And yet, it was Western education that turned out to be the most transformative policy devised by the colonizers. While policies on slavery, labor, taxation, and chiefs dealt with the all important political and economic sphere of colonial life, education meandered its way in the streams of West African culture. Although Western education affected far more people in the British than French colonies, it had a widespread impact on West African conceptions of self and other.

The story of education in colonial West Africa begins, ironically enough, with European ignorance. Despite widely held beliefs in Europe that education was a concept foreign to West Africans, West African children were no strangers to the privations of "school," both formal and informal. In Muslim regions, formal education had a long history. "Primary" education for boys entailed the memorization of the Koran, a several-year process. When students did not apply themselves to their rote memorization, *marabouts* (Muslim clerics) routinely beat them. When *marabouts* recognized particularly promising students, they sent them to study with a master of Muslim medicine, theology or science. Sometimes West African students travelled as far as Cairo for their higher educations. In non-Muslim areas there were a wide range of formal/informal educations. Children learned how to farm, herd, hunt and gather. In some societies, boys and girls entered graded secret societies, which encompassed a great deal of learning, some of it secret, some of it metaphysical. This learning inevitably led to a series of initiations. Indeed, in most West African societies, "ritual" learning was a complex and lifelong pursuit.

The vast majority of the colonial authorities openly reviled the "uncivilized" nature of African education. Many of these men believed that African education was less than uncivilized; it did not exist at all. These kinds of attitudes set the parameters and the tone of the Western education policy in West Africa.

Both France and Britain wanted to educate Africans to bolster the colonial economy and staff the lower levels of the colonial administration. The French, for their part, sought to train a relatively small elite in French language and culture—black masters of French bureaucratic practices. The cultural values instilled through French education, the theorists argued, would ensure the elite's total loyalty to *le patri*. Although the graduates of this system would become "black Frenchmen," the French carefully designed colonial education to rigidly reinforce a racist colonial hierarchy. Crowder cites a text from an early French primer.

> It is always necessary to love those who deserve it and merit it. Difference in race makes little difference. Goodness has nothing to do with color. It is, on the one hand, an advantage for the native to work for the white man, because whites are better educated, more advanced in civilization than natives, and because, thanks to them, the natives will make more rapid progress, learn better and more quickly, know more things, and become one day really useful men. On the other hand, the blacks will render service to the white by bringing them the help of their arms, by cultivating the land which will permit them to grow crops for Europeans, and also by fighting for France in the ranks of native troops. Thus the two races will associate and work together in common prosperity and happiness of all. You who are intelligent and industrious, my children, always help the whites in their task. This is a duty.[19]

In this way the French intended colonial education as the means toward the end of a more productive colony in which the races were properly hierachized. On the philosophical plane, the French suggested that their colonial policy on education was one of "cultural renaissance." As Governor-General Jules Brevie stated in the 1930s, "However pressing may be the need for economic change and development of natural resources, our mission in Africa is to bring about a cultural renaissance, a piece of creative work in human material, an association of the two races which can be brought about only by a free and wholehearted acceptance of the African by the French."[20] Given the exceedingly small number of African students and the meager conditions in which they were educated, Brevie's lofty rhetoric masked the ultimate policy goal: to exploit West African lands and to destroy the savage cultural foundations of West African societies.

For the British, like the French, education was the means to render more efficient the colonial enterprise. Although the British engaged in less educational philosophizing, their system, in which missionary schools played a central role, emphasized individual industriousness and personal morality. They were also less insistent on the use of English as a colonial language than France was on the use of French. In British primary schools, teachers employed African languages in early forms; English never took on the colonial reverence of French in the Francophone colonies. For the British, the goal of education was as follows:

> To render the individual more efficient in his or her condition of life, what-ever it may be, and to promote the advancement of agriculture, the develop-ment of native industries, the training of people in the management of their own affairs, and the inculcation of true ideals of citizenship and service.[21]

Such a policy, it was reasoned, would enable the colonies to more or less run themselves—with the British colonial government being the ultimate, albeit distant authority. And yet the British, like the French, recognized the need to educate an elite to staff the lower posts in the colonial administra-tive structures.

European education propelled the emergence of elites in British and French West Africa. The French elite, small in number, were educated at institutions like the William Ponty School in Dakar. There, they received a rigorous French education and became colonial officials whose responsi-bilities and importance expanded with time. And yet, the elite in French West Africa posed little or no threat to French colonial rule. For the most part, these men, thoroughly trained in French language and culture, re-mained remarkably loyal to France. In the British colonies, by contrast, West Africans had many more educational opportunities. Qualified students could pursue their higher educations at Fourah Bay or at foreign institutions. This flexibility resulted in a fairly large educated elite, many of whom were unemployed. In the British administration there were many posts for "indirect rulers" and for West Africans with low-level technical skills. There were few if any posts for the highly trained, a fact that made the elite in British West Africa much less loyal to the metropole.

Education, Comportment and Colonialism

The colonial systems of education trained an educated elite which became increasingly important to the various colonial administrations in British and French West Africa. Eventually the most prominent members led movements of independence. To focus exclusively on the elite, however, would be to misjudge the full impact of colonial education. More than any other colonial policy, education reshaped the cultural identities of West African societies. At first glance this statement may seem grandiose, but a systematic examination of the colonial educational process underscores the prodigious impact of Western education on colonized populations.

In his book, *Colonizing Egypt,* Timothy Mitchell analyzes the impact of colonial education on indigenous society and culture in colonial North Africa. For Mitchell, the colonizers designed a system of education to create colonial order out of indigenous chaos—the creation of the "social order." In the mid-nineteenth century several schools, based upon Joseph Lancaster's model school in London, were introduced in Egypt.

> The school was a system of perfect discipline. Students were kept constantly moving from task to task, with every motion and every space disciplined and put to use. Each segment of time was regulated, so that at every moment a student was either receiving instruction, repeating it, supervising or checking. It was a technique in which the exact position and precise task of each individual at every moment was coordinated, to perform together as a machine. Authority and obedience were diffused, without diminution, throughout the school, implicating every individual in a system of order. The model school was a model of the perfect society.[22]

Educators in British and French West Africa organized their schools, primary and secondary, in ways similar to the Egyptian model. They made sure to regiment time and tasks. They made students adhere to dress and behavior codes—all in the attempt to control the body and, ultimately, the body politic. In his December 1930 statement on educational policy, Governor-General Jules Brevie stressed the centrality of education to the objectives of French colonialism:

> Up to now we have been concerned only with the training of the individual, the evolution of the native intellgentsia. More and more we shall have to turn our attention to large-scale education, to the training of the multitude in French West Africa. . . . Monsieur Carde, in his excellent circular of February 25th, 1930 . . . says: "We mean to bring about for the native a greater degree of progress in a few decades than he has achieved in one thousand years." Such progress can only be realised through education . . . Once the native's mind has become disciplined by the mastering of spoken French and the acquisition of skill in arithmetic—those gateways to new fields of knowledge—then we shall have to turn to practical issue and the betterment of the conditions of life throughout the villages. In order that the native may go to school, the school must be brought to the native.[23]

Clearly, Brevie thought education to be the prime mover in achieving French colonial objectives in West Africa. Through education, he wanted to transform "native" society. As Albert Charton, Inspector-General of Education of the French West African colonies put it: "In a word, then, the problem before us has still wider implications; it involves the whole question of guiding the future development of indigenous populations and of giving them a place in European civilization."[24]

Through education the colonizers attempted to literally and figuratively capture the bodies of the colonized by systematically subverting an old way of learning. Mitchell contrasts Muslim learning with renaissance learning, both of which consisted of the careful and cumulative mastery of increasingly difficult texts. In the world of Muslim learning, moreover, scholars built no conceptual barriers between text and world, no separation between the intellectualized activities of the mind and the sensible practices of the body, for "learning did not require overt acts of organization, but found its sequence in the logic of the practices themselves."[25] Colonial education, by contrast, was considered a set of organized instructions to be mastered in organized and regulated settings.

> These means of coordination were something particular and physical, offering what Michel Foucault has called a microphysical power; a power that worked by reordering material space in exact dimensions and acquiring a continuous bodily hold upon its subjects. Yet at the same time . . . this power was something meta-physical. It worked by creating an appearance of order, an appearance of structure as some sort of separate, non-material realm. The creation of this metaphysical realm was what made the education of the individual suddenly imperative—just as the microphysical methods were what made such education possible. Power now sought to work not only upon the exterior of the body but also 'from the inside out'—by shaping the individual mind.[26]

The colonizers did not shape individual minds through systematized instruction alone, though its importance cannot be minimized. They also shaped individual minds through a prescribed set of embodied practices.

What is it about embodied practices—dress, movement, eating, spirit possession—that enables them to profoundly affect the cultural dynamics of a group of people? British colonial officials grouped these practices under the rubric of "character development." "The three recognized lines usually followed in seeking to develop character are the inculcation of simple virtues by direct instruction, the formation of the right habits which deepen through practice into principle, and the influence of religious teaching with its expression in personal, school and family life."[27] In short, colonial authorities used education as the major means to the end of European cultural embodiment.

Recent studies in both history and anthropology suggest a strong linkage among colonial memory, embodiment, and the historical imagination. Following Bourdieu, Comaroff and Comaroff suggest that regimes attempt to create new people through the "deculturation" and "reculturation" of seemingly unimportant body habits and practices: posture, movement, dress, eating.[28] For Comaroff and Comaroff,

> Scrambling the code—that is, erasing the messages carried in banal physical practice—is a prerequisite for retaining the memory, either to deschool the deviant or to shape new subjects as the bearers of new worlds. Indeed, the individual salience of bodily reform in processes of social transformation is strong evidence that the human frame mediates between self and society. It is this mediating role, we suggest, that accounts for its privileged place in one widespread, yet poorly understood mode of historical practice: namely 'untheorized' collective action. By this we mean action that, while concerted, is never explicated, action whose logic seems vested more in corporal signs than in conceptual categories.[29]

This passage speaks directly to West African colonial cultures in which colonizers attempted to order the putative chaos of indigenous social relations. Indeed, the colonizers employed systems of education that regimented time, space, dress, instruction, and food to promote bodily reform, to borrow from the Comaroffs' language. They attempted to alter the body to enforce their will to civilize.

Comprised of new rules and regulations on domestic slavery, taxes, forced labor, chiefs, education, and bodily reform, West African colonial culture seems oppressive, if not overwhelming. Such a tidal wave of change must have crushed, or so the received argument goes, the peoples of West Africa. What did they think of the Europeans and their policies? Any number of Western commentators have offered their thoughts on the matter. Crowder writes:

> The European must have presented himself to Africans other than those from the coast, who by now knew him well, as an immensely complex and bewildering being. He possessed technological superiority and was fired with missionary zeal that compared only with that of the *mujihaddin*. It was also difficult to assess the extent and nature of his power. He came from overseas. The small pioneer party could be defeated, but those who had sent it?[30]

Historians like Steven Roberts write of the despondency that Africans, resigned to colonial culture, must have felt.

> [People] had their old life broken by the shock of European contact: the old order of tribal society, with its cohesion based on unquestioned rule of custom, has been forced into the background; and the native, deracialized by the shattering of everything which has previously guided him, drifts disillusioned and despairing, now knowing no hope, and now with the insane joy of the iconoclast aiding the outside forces in rending his life from top to bottom ... The future is not clear because the native, here a

French citizen and there a mere "subject," does not know where he can fit in. Seeing neither a place for himself nor hope for his children, he drifts in reckless despair or gives way to carefree insouciance.[31]

While the quoted remark is overstated and paternalistic it devolves from the well-known idea that when peoples are faced with rapid social change, when they are uprooted from the comforts of centuries-old traditions, they tend to lose themselves in the winds of change.[32]

Such commentary, of course, is a one-way street, for it does not take into consideration "actions vested more in corporeal signs than in conceptual categories."[33] It assumes, moreover, that the superiority of Europeans—and their technology—so devastated West Africans that the latter wallowed in despair. Nothing, as we shall see in the next chapter, could be farther from the truth.

Confronted with European military superiority, West Africans realized the impossibility of overthrowing colonial regimes. "Yet, no African people were willing to entrust their fate permanently to the European ruler. He seemed to represent some powerful, unthinking irrational force that argued little and interfered much in matters it did not understand or try to understand."[34]

There were any number of pragmatic strategies to cope with the European's rules and regulations. Some West African peoples managed to remain virtually isolated from continuous European contact. They paid their taxes, tolerated a distant authority, and secured a measure of cultural tranquillity in their isolation. Other peoples sought to cooperate with colonial administrations to gain a measure of political advantage. Still others pooled their resources to educate their children to better cope with the European presence.

And yet these pragmatic measures of avoidance and cooperation, realpolitik and resignation had little impact on the most onerous weapon of colonial cultures: the capturing, to borrow Timothy Mitchell's language, of West African bodies—through regulations, education, dress, food, movement and language. How did West Africans cope with bodily reform? Many colonial subjects partially adopted European ways. Some West Africans revolted against French and British authority. Others, as we shall see in the next chapter, reappropriated European bodily reforms (dress, movement, regulated time, food) in order to mock the European, to oppose his relentless efforts to sever the links of West Africans to their ancestors.

CHAPTER SIX

Embodied Oppositions

• • •

There is a great deal of good historical writing on how West African peoples rebelled against the French and British. The bulk of this literature—in French and English—consists of minute descriptions of military campaigns and the complicated analysis of diplomacies to end armed rebellions. The picture that emerges from this literature is a complex one characterized by much contestation and debate. Officials in the various colonial regimes heatedly debated the wisdom of military intervention and governance. West Africans themselves had a wide range of beliefs about the colonial administrations that sought to regulate them. As should be expected, there was a wide range of opinions and actions about active collaboration, passive resistance and armed rebellion. Usually a group's decision on how to react to the French or the British had more to do with the dynamics of local politics than with the quality of Euro-African relations.[1]

Much less has been written on the more subtle forms of colonial oppositions. These were expressed invariably in rituals, in the plastic arts, and in little-discussed everyday behaviors that took advantage of widespread European ignorance of West African languages and customs. These unarmed oppositions are often called "cultural resistance," and I intend to argue that they are in some ways more historically significant than well-documented cases of military resistance.

In this chapter, I would like to collapse the rigid distinction sometimes made between military and cultural resistance by defining West African challenges to colonial authority as embodied oppositions, all of which can be placed on a continuum. Baule warriors who ambushed French military columns certainly engaged in a form of embodied opposition. But so did Igbo sculptors who carved satiric images of white men and Europeanized Africans (collaborators). And so did Yoruba dancers who, dressed in ersatz tuxedos and evening gowns, waltzed in a rain-forest clearing. And so did the colonial servant whose public gesticulations ridiculed his European employers, ignorant of these small, but derisive, acts of defiance. These, too, are embodied oppositions, which, like all oppositions, involve some degree of risk.

I plan to present a sampling of embodied oppositions in colonial West Africa to set the context for the rise of the Hauka Movement in Niger—an embodied opposition to colonialism par excellence.[2] The cases range from well-known armed oppositions (El Hadj 'Umar, Samory Toure, and the Baule rebellion) to more subtle cultural oppositions (Igbo Mbari houses, Yoruba Egungun dancers, Baule "colonial" sculpture).

El Hadj 'Umar and the Tukulor Opposition

El Hadj 'Umar, a learned Muslim who belonged to a family of religious leaders, became one of West Africa's most important political leaders in the nineteenth century. Having spent much of his youth away from his home in the Futa Toro (in contemporary Senegal), he returned to his homeland in 1840 having traveled to Mecca, Sokoto (Nigeria) and Macina (Mali)—the latter two being West African centers of Muslim learning and political power. As a wealthy religious leader, El Hadj 'Umar attracted numerous disciples, whom he used as trading agents. Rather than settling in his homeland, the Futa Toro, he took his coterie south to the Futa Jallon, where the local leader permitted 'Umar to establish an armed religious community.

Having been converted from a Quadiri to a Tijani Muslim, Umar soon came to disparage the Muslim practices of the largely Quadiri populations of both the Futa Jallon and the Futo Toro.[3] He condemned the leaders of West African Muslim states for not accepting Tijani religious principles, and was seen as something of a Muslim revolutionary in mid-nineteenth-century West Africa. Whether 'Umar cynically used his religious fervor in a bold play for power is a debatable point. Whatever his motivations, El Hadj 'Umar mobilized his army of fervent followers and created out of the decaying structures of pre-existing states the Tukulor Empire.[4]

The expansion of the Tukulor Empire in the 1850s brought El Haji 'Umar into the conflict with French commercial and eventually French military interests. Before the advent of French imperial policy, indigenous West African rulers protected the French traders. Suddenly, the same rulers were told to accept French authority. This order resulted in several limited wars, including one with the Tukulor in 1854 in which the French fared badly. Soon thereafter, Paris sent Louis Faidherbe to govern Senegal.

Faidherbe and 'Umar soon came into direct competition over Senegalese resources, for France and the Tukulor Empire were essentially imperial polities. The powerless subject states of Senegal, which were caught in a political vice, found the French less worrisome than the Tukulor. From their standpoint the French, who steadfastly opposed the expansionism of 'Umar, were seen as potential allies. Measuring this sentiment, the French presented themselves—rather cynically—as the defenders of local independence. Despite the perceived strength of the French and their everchanging constellation of Senegalese allies, 'Umar continued to expand his political and economic sphere.

Between 1857 and 1860 Faidherbe and 'Umar fought a series of battles for the control of Senegambia. These ended inconclusively, though 'Umar had failed to eject the French from Senegal. A Franco-Tukulor peace treaty, which settled nothing but enabled each polity to reinforce power in their respective spheres of influence, was signed in 1860. For his part, 'Umar moved his operations eastward, conquering the Segu Bambara and campaigning in the Macina. For their part, the French consolidated their Senegalese authority.[5]

Faidherbe prudently remained wary of the Tukulor even after El Hadj 'Umar's death in 1864, for the Empire represented the most powerful force in the Western Sudan. The resilient power of Tukulor and the Empire's perceived threat to the French political and economic interests set the stage for more pervasive French military intervention in the Western Sudan. A long series of French military campaigns against various segments of the Futa Toro groups and the Tukulor brought on an era of French military adventurism, the aims and actions of which often undermined civilian authority in Dakar and in Paris. Soldiers like Archinard, who took military command of the Army of French Sudan in 1888, intentionally ignored civilian orders to cultivate Franco-African economic relations through peaceful contacts. Instead, the French military steered its own course, presenting the French government with uncontemplated and unexpected military *faits accomplis.* Understandably, military adventurism caused much bitterness among subjugated West African populations but also among civilian officials who had been humiliated. From 1860 to 1910, "no-nonsense" military actions provoked many rebellions in the French sphere of influence and opened festering resentments among the West Africans.

It is clear that El Hadj 'Umar's armed opposition to expanding French occupation had political and economic motivations. Tukulor and France constituted two imperial powers in nineteenth-century West Africa. The French were savvy enough to manipulate local fears of potential Tukulor rule to their political and military advantage. Despite El Hadj 'Umar's failure to dispatch the French from Senegal, Tukulor continued to oppose French military expansion, and with good reason: the French, largely represented in the local imagination by the soldier, threatened the political independence and power of the Empire. But was that all? What else did the French represent to El Hadj 'Umar and his allies? As Christians they were certainly considered a slovenly people, infidels who ate pork and who did not pray to Allah. From the learned vantage of 'Umar and his clan of religious leaders, the French must have seemed culturally ignorant, reckless, untrustworthy, and yet doggedly resolute in their territorial ambitions— people capable of "capturing", to use once again Timothy Mitchell's language, West African bodies. 'Umar and his followers knew that if they did not oppose the non-believing Europeans, the French would transform West African ways of living irrevocably. That was a cultural challenge that required embodied opposition.[6]

Samory Toure and the Wasule Opposition

Like El Hadj 'Umar, Samory Toure was steeped in Muslim learning and created an expansionist West African Empire. Samory's base of operations, however, was in the hinterlands of Guinea and southern Mali on either side of the Upper Niger River. Historians trace the origins of Samory's Wasule

Empire to 1870-75. From the beginning, Samory demonstrated superior skills as a tactician, diplomat, and administrator. He trained an army of soldiers, called *sofas*, who were respected, if not feared throughout West Africa. Like El Hadj 'Umar, Samory's imperial designs brought him into conflict with the expansionist designs of the French.

In the early 1880s the French began to build a railway that would, among other things, secure their Senegalese base. It soon became apparent that Samory's *sofas* had other ideas. In 1881 they unsuccessfully attacked Kita. In 1883 they attacked a French column in the railway construction area. In 1885 Samory overran the French post at Nafadie. In defeat, the French half-heartedly mounted what turned out to be a successful expedition against him. Neither side, according to Crowder, wanted a full scale war at the time. In 1886 Samory and the French signed the Treaty of Bisandougou. Through the Treaty

> the zones of expansion of France and Samory were delimited and a vague
> protectorate was established by France over his states, though it was a nomi-
> nal protectorate that they were able to assume by force of arms . . . Samory
> himself flirted with the idea of submitting his empire to a British protectorate.
> He certainly denied that he had accepted a French protectorate.[7]

In essence, the Treaty brought a halt to Samory's westward expansion. He instead fixed his gaze eastward and began military operations against prosperous Sikasso whose King, fearing a ruthless return by Samory, accepted a protectorate with France.

Ever the diplomat who understood realpolitik, Samory attempted to forge an alliance with Ahmadou, El Hadj 'Umar's son and head of the Tukulor Empire. Samory wrote: "If you continue to make war on your own, the whites will have no trouble in defeating you. I have already undergone the experience in trying my strength against them. Let us therefore unite. You will hit the French from the North, I will harass them in the South, and we will certainly manage to get rid of them."[8]

Ahmadou refused to ally Tukulor with Samory, which marked the beginning of the end of the Tukulor Empire, for Samory's message was prophetic. Shortly thereafter the forces of Archinard conquered Tukulor. For his part Samory continued his eastward expansion. When war broke out between Wasule and France in 1891, Samory adopted guerilla tactics. Part of his army would engage the French, while another segment conquered new lands to the east. As the French advanced, his people moved eastward, burning their villages as they departed.

> The most striking facet of Samory's military genius was his adaptability to the changing situation. First and foremost he realized the prime importance of maintaining his source of supplies of arms, ammunition and horses. Secondly, he brought the art of strategic withdrawal to near-perfection. And thirdly, so brilliant was his organization of men that he could move his sizeable army with surprising rapidity. Finally, he had an excellent intelligence system so that he had good knowledge of French intentions.[9]

This combination of strength made Samory France's most formidable adversary in West Africa. Samory resisted the French for more than 15 years. In 1896 the British defeated Ashanti and declared a protectorate over Sierra Leone, which meant that Samory could no longer receive arms from those sources. By 1898 the French had defeated Tukulor and had conquered Sikasso to the North and sent a force against Samory from the Ivory Coast to the South. These circumstance trapped Samory and the French captured him in 1898. His prophecy had come true.

Faced with technologically superior forces, why did Muslim leaders like El Hadj 'Umar, his son Ahmadou and Samory oppose the French with such brave resolve? Crowder provides a compelling answer: "For the Muslim societies of West Africa the imposition of white rule meant submission to the infidel which was intolerable to any good Muslim and helps to explain the ferocity of resistance of many Muslim leaders in the Western Sudan to the French advance when the odds were so clearly weighted against them."[10]

Such evidence suggests that for El Hadj 'Umar and Samory the European presence triggered a cultural as well as political crisis. Samory was a brilliant man who opposed the French not only to maintain the political and economic independence of Wasule, but also to preserve a way of life. He knew quite well, it seems, the irrevocable cultural power of the French to reform, regulate and capture the West African body.

The Baule Revolt (1893-1910)

The embodied opposition of the Baule people, who live in what is today the south central region of the Ivory Coast, stands in contradistinction to the oppositions of El Haji 'Umar and Imam Samory Toure. The Tukulor and

Wasule Empires reflected the religious and political passions of their Muslim leaders. In a sense, the French were not fighting Tukulor or Wasule, but El Hadj 'Umar and Samory. Baule society, however, consisted of clusters of fragmented entities—villages or small groups of villages—that had long been economic and political rivals. Whereas the Tukulor and Wasule Empires presented a united front in opposition to the French, various factions of Baule continuously forged and broke alliances with the French and each other. Unlike Tukulor and Wasule, the Baule had no pre-eminent leader, only paramount chiefs who as paragons of wisdom had no jurisdiction over warriors. Younger chiefs made the military decisions among the Baule.

Considering West Africans hapless and indolent savages, most of the French approached the Baule in the same way they approached Tukulor and Wasule. Their ignorance cost them dearly. Indeed, the picture in the Ivory Coast between 1890 and 1910 is, like that in Senegal, a very complex one of contested colonialism.[11] There was much difference in opinion among the Baule about how to confront the French. Some collaborated with the French as useful economic and military allies; others opposed the French militarily, ambushing exploratory French patrols, or razing military outposts. Still others shifted their allegiances following a pragmatic and utilitarian path of negotiation. Likewise, the military-civilian cleavage that so complicated and troubled French maneuvering in the Sudan persisted in the Ivory Coast. Many of the French soldiers were veterans of the Sudan's no-nonsense military campaigns. Scholarly civilian authorities like Maurice Delafosse and Charles Monteil took avid ethnographic interest in the Baule, learning their language and culture. Enlightened civilian authority, however, was no guarantee of peaceful Franco-Baule relations; hard-nosed military administration, by the same token, was no guarantee of armed hostilities.

Timothy Weiskel, whose excellent history *French Colonial Rule and the Baule Peoples*, describes and analyzes the Baule armed resistance, pinpoints three periods of open Baule revolt: 1893-1895, 1898-1903 and 1908-1911. One could argue that each of these revolts devolved not so much from changes in Baule political relations as from personnel changes in the French administration. Through their ill-informed adventurism, military administrations, it could be argued, provoked Baule revolt. Weiskel suggests that the historical record undermines that hypothesis. Instead, Baule revolts seem to have resulted from the disruption of labor patterns.

> In each period, then, it was over the issue of labor that the initial collabora-
> tive relationships between the French and the Baule repeatedly collapsed,
> triggering the archetypal sequence of events including the appeal for troops,
> the preliminary military interventions, the spread of resistance activity, and
> the administration's awkward dilemma as to whether it should reinforce or
> restrain the military [12]

The Baule tolerated the French, according to Weiskel, if and only if colonial policies did not disrupt their productive processes. For Weiskel, the armed struggle between the Baule and the French

> was but part of a more fundamental encounter. The essential confrontation
> was that between a persistently viable traditional economy and a nascent
> colonial economy. The former was based on the household production of
> exports of high value-to-weight ratio; the latter depended upon large scale
> production of cheap agricultural commodities of low value-to-weight ratio
> ... Between the French administration and the Baule the crucial issue at
> stake concerned the control over the disposition of the rural labour bound up
> at the time in household units of production.[13]

Weiskel presents a compelling economic argument that "explains" the presence and persistence of the Baule resistance. But is that all? There is little mention of culture in Weiskel's text. What did the Baule think of the French? Weiskel presents a wealth of French colonial opinion about environmentally determined Baule indolence, but there is not one quote from a Baule spokesperson. Did the Baule fear the French? Did they think, like the Muslim peoples of the Sahel, that the French were slovenly infidels who would ruin a way of life? Weiskel suggests that the Baule thought that the white man was a nuisance who had disrupted their supply of slave labor.

We also know from Weiskel's account, however, that during the revolt the role of Baule diviners expanded considerably. For the Baule the diviners provided some hope of ultimate victory. "Little is known of these quasi-prophetic figures, although it is clear that they were capable of inspiring Baule resistance sentiment on a broader basis than that afforded by the narrow range of kinship ties."[14] The French feared these eminently cultural figures who predicted the future, crafted fetishes for the present, and spoke out against French occupation. Accordingly, the French executed several of the more prominent diviners. There is also the matter of the

Beugre cult and oracle, the influence of which spread among several ethnic groups in the southern Ivory Coast. The Beugre provided a compelling story of the future that inspired the Baule and others during the final days of the revolt.

> These aspects of the Beugre cult anticipate in a rudimentary form several features of syncretistic millennial movements which subsequently swept through these same areas in the period immediately following the final defeat of the resistance struggle . . . The French finally crushed the armed resistance of the Baule and other groups in the Ivory Coast, but this process itself generated the conditions in which the prophetic appeal was likely to spread.[15]

Clearly, the power and appeal of the Baule diviners and the Beugre cult speak—if only indirectly—to the cultural dimensions of the Baule opposition, cultural dimensions that expanded exponentially after final "pacification" in 1911.

Carving *Colons* in Baule

Embodied oppositions also took on less military forms in West Africa: silence, ruse, individual defiance as well as an incredibly diverse array of plastic art forms that "savaged" the European. At first many West Africans were impressed with the overwhelming power of the white man. Yet as Julius Lips remarked in his 1937 classic, *The Savage Hits Back,*

> The impression of the white man's superiority did not last long. The natives began to know him better, and ceased devising tales which would explain his superiority. They soon found out that the white man was only another species of the human race. When they became familiar with him, they treated him to their mockery exactly as they did any member of their own tribe, especially when they recognized his weaknesses.[16]

Much of Lips' account of embodied oppositions to European colonial occupations described West African images of Europe. These included models of the European ships, statues of European military men carrying rifles and firing canon, carvings of colonial officials officiating, missionaries preaching, white merchants exchanging, teachers teaching, physicians healing, judges judging and explorers exploring.

Great masters of the plastic arts, the Baule of West Africa began to carve "European" figures sometime after the collapse of their armed resistance in 1911. It is much too simple to say that the European carvings were a

A Baule *Colon* carving.

"symbolic resistance" to the harsh European presence. In general, carvings of Europeans emerged from traditional Baule practices.

In Baule there are many "other-world" spirits which, if not attended to, can bring harm to people. Every Baule is linked to an other-world being of the opposite sex. People become aware of their connections to the other-world through a life crisis or through dreams. A divination session may reveal that a person's sterility results from the jealousy of the social person's other-world lover. "In such a case divination may … also … reveal that it is necessary both to represent this other-world person by a statue carved in human form to which offerings of food or money can be made on a regular basis and to consecrate one night of the week to the *blolo* person by sleeping alone."[17]

At some point, the Baule began to dream about European-like spirit spouses, which, following the tradition, were carved and fed. "A Baule statue in European garb," writes Phillip Ravenhill, "is neither a replica of a European nor an expression of a wish for a European other-world lover, but rather the desire the Baule other-world lover exhibit signs of success or status that dominate the White-oriented or dominated world."[18]

Ravenhill does not, however, ponder the question of why the Baule felt the need to exhibit white signs of success. We know that resistance movements among the Baule were brutal and murderous. We also know that the arrival of the Europeans seemed to stimulate a resurgence of Baule statuary carving. "If art is a means of mediated mystery," Weiskel writes, "perhaps these carvings helped the Baule appropriate and attribute meaning to the new elements in their lives under colonialism."[19]

In his review of the book, *Statues Colons*, Christopher Steiner draws attention to a Senegalese art dealer's mimetic interpretation of the original power and presence of *statues colons*. The author, says Steiner, draws on an oral tradition passed from father to son to reproduce a Senegalese art merchant's historical interpretation of the life of colonial statues in Baule.

> According to Thiemo Diop, they were originally conceived to warn people of the presence of Europeans in the area. "They were placed at intersections in the road, beside bridges, at the entrances of villages in order to warn the entire population." Later, he explains, the carvings were created as "fetishes"; sacrifices were made to them to drive away the colonizers.[20]

The ruminations of Weiskel and Steiner come close to the notion that is developed in this book; namely that mimesis, in this case Baule copies of European forms, is one way to mediate not the undifferentiated mystery, but the mysterious and incomprehensible power of the white man. Such mimesis was perhaps one—but not the only—way for the Baule to redirect some of that incomprehensible power into their private spaces.[21]

Waltzing in the Forest

Like the Baule, the Yoruba mimic the white man through the plastic arts. Unlike the Baule, the mimicry is performed as part of an entertaining masquerade, part of the Egungun cult. The Egun, a group that communicates with the dead, are intermediaries between the ancestors and the living. As such, an Egungun festival is a powerfully serious religious ritual.[22]

As in Hauka ceremonies, however, the boundaries between the religious and the social, the comic and the serious are never distinct. Indeed, there is a special group of Egun, the Agbegijo, the function of whom is to

Beke ime ala, **The White Man in the Ground.** Photo by Herbert Cole.

entertain at Egungun festivals. They entertain through mimicry, for all of their masks are exaggerated caricatures that mimic other ethnic groups, people with odd body features, typified social personalities (policeman, prostitutes) and animals.[23] Uli Beier claims that a highlight of the Agbegijo dances is the *ouimbo* masks: ". . . Europeans with enormous hooked noses and smooth black hair made from Colobus Monkey skin. They shake hands, say 'how do you do' and perform a ridiculous ballroom dance."[24]

The Agbegijo mimicry exaggerates social, cultural and physical difference. A naive functionalist reading of these performances would suggest that the display of masks reinforces Yoruba sociocultural norms by exaggerating difference through entertaining mimicry. Such an argument, however, seems incomplete, for it ignores the question of power. The *ouimbo* masks have been a feature of colonialism. Following Taussig and Benjamin, one sometimes copies otherness to make partial sense of it, to master it.[25] To see *ouimbo* dancers doing a waltz in a rural Yoruba village is singularly funny, but it also situates that village within a network of power relations, which, in turn, situates the village existentially. As in the Hauka case, some of the most powerful images are those that provoke laughter.

Mimicking Majesty in Igbo

Mimicking majesty reaches its peak with the *mbari* houses of the Owerri Igbo of southeastern Nigeria. *Mbari* houses are structures built in the forest that house collections of mud sculptures depicting Igbo deities, animals, European objects of status wonder (bicycles, telephones, sewing machines, watches, binoculars), European soldiers, colonial police officers and so on. A.A. Whitehouse, a British colonial official, took the first photograph of a *mbari* house in 1904, but the tradition of *mbari*, according to Herbert Cole, probably dates to the mid-nineteenth century. The "golden age" of *mbari*, however, took place in the 1920s and 1930s, which was also the "golden age" of colonialism in West Africa.[26]

Mbari is steeped in the religious life of the Owerri Igbo. The Owerri built them, at considerable expense, to appease a deity who was feeling neglected. In so doing, the people ensured adequate rainfall and good yam harvests. For the Owerri Igbo, building *mbari* houses was one way to gain control of a capricious, ever-changing universe populated by fierce animals, angry gods, and incomprehensible white men.

Underscoring Lips' prescient scholarship, Cole suggests that Owerri images of the white man involved humorous caricature. One *mbari* figure, ". . . *beke ime ala,* 'the white man in the ground,' recalls the myth of the white man's origin; he simply emerged from a hole in the ground . . . In this, as in most of the varied renditions of white men, there is an element of caricature. The nose is long and thin, and almost invariably supports a pair of eyeglasses."[27] In other Owerri versions of the white man, he is pith-helmeted and Janus-faced, on horseback, in a litter, or looking out of second story windows. Many of these figures make reference

> to the reputation white men had, in the early days of contact, for omniscience and omnipotence, as well as to the deviousness of slave traders. They also suggest that white men are not quite human. *Beke* had always been held in awe and still is, in many quarters, because of his appearance, forcefulness, and wealth. It is possible that the virtually mandatory inclusion of his image also reflects a desire for the psychological control, even capture, of his awesome power. When it first appeared, the imagery may also have related to an analogous desire . . . to rid the Owerri world of a formidable enemy by modeling his "portrait," and thus expecting an angry god to kill him.[28]

Mbari is such a gripping and unsettling case of non-European appropriation of Western embodied behaviors that it has caught the attention of several prominent social theorists. James Clifford uses *mbari* to problematize Western representations of "primitive" art.[29] He cites Cole and Chike Aniakor to underscore the creativity and inventiveness of an Igbo aesthetics that stands in stark contrast to the rather staid way that museum modernists represent *their* "masterpiece" art.[30] In many respects Clifford's analysis suffers from the same kind of decontextualization he criticizes. He never asks to what ends the Owerri Igbo erect *mbari* houses. Instead, he uses material from Herbert Cole's exhibit—and not his aforementioned monograph—to make valid points about prevailing and persistent Eurocentric primitivist visions in the "world" of Art. His arguments both make and miss the point, for Clifford ignores what Cole finds important in *mbari*: the desire to capture and utilize—for their own ends—the powerful status of the white man. From Cole's more ethnographic perspective, art can enter into a locally conceived and practiced power dynamic.

In his *Mimesis and Alterity* Michael Taussig is also much taken with *mbari* figures. Unlike Clifford, Taussig is particularly concerned with the physiognomically disruptive effects that *mbari* can have on Westerners. The *mbari*

White men "broadcasting" from an *mbari* house. Photo by Herbert Cole.

figure that grabs Taussig's attention is the aforementioned *beke ima ala*, "the white man in the ground," the Igbo version of the myth of the white man's origin. Here, Taussig presents a singular reading of the mud sculpture whose existential ambiguities frighten him and give rise to feelings of profound guilt.

> He frightens me this white man. He unsettles. He makes me wonder without end. Was the world historical power of whiteness achieved, then, through its being a sacred as well as profane power? It makes me wonder about the constitution of whiteness as global colonial work and also as a minutely psychic one involving powers invisible to my senses but all too obvious, as reflected to me, now, by this strange artifact.[31]

Taussig goes on to wonder how previous anthropologies might have neutralized the image through "Africanization," through historically, socially and politically inspired theoretization, all of which is illusory diversion.

> For the white man to read this face means facing himself as Others read him, and the 'natives point of view' can never substitute for the fact that now the native is the white man himself, and that suddenly, woefully, it dawns that the natives' point of view is endless and myriad. The white man as viewer is here virtually forced to interrogate himself, to interrogate the Other in and partially constitutive of his many and conflicting selves.[32]

Taussig's apperception of *beke ima ala* is a brute confrontation of historical and epistemological significance, but it is also a confrontation that again misses the point that Cole so modestly and respectfully articulates. Taussig seizes on his physiognomic response to *beke,* on how the mud figure "captures" his body so far removed from it in time and space. It captures him because it makes him aware of his own whiteness, of the global project of whiteness. What remains unexpressed, though, is the other side of the physiognomic equation. What did whiteness mean to the communities of Owerri Igbo that constructed *mbari* houses? One possible interpretation is that *mbari* attracts power that can be "captured" and controlled through mimesis, for the gods, angered by likenesses that reminded them of whiteness' invasion, might eventually kill the white man. Whiteness, then, was more than a global colonial project; it was a source of power that could be tapped to improve the lives of the (post)colonized.[33]

Embodied oppositions to whiteness in West Africa took on many forms: armed rebellions, individual defiance, remarkable ruses, mocking masquerades, and mimicking plastic arts. The purpose of these defiant acts was not to make white men feel guilty about their colonial and postcolonial beliefs and practices, but to master whiteness through mimesis, a way, as we shall see in a description and analysis of Hauka in colonial and postcolonial Niger (Parts Three and Four), of tapping into circuits of colonial and postcolonial power. Seen in this light, the Hauka spirit possession is very much an embodied opposition to colonial rule; it was an exercise in mastery through mime.

PART THREE

Migrating with the Hauka

♦ ♦ ♦

Thunderous Gods

◆   ◆   ◆

The distant rumble of thunder, some Songhay say, warns people of an imminent storm. The winds switch direction and if there is daylight, one can see the black clouds gathering on the eastern horizon. The winds stiffen and clouds of red dust sweep over some of the villages of Songhay: Tillaberi, Ayoru, Wanzerbe. Dust blots out the Sahelian sun. The temperature plummets. Rain drops dapple the parched earth. As the rumbles get closer, the wind howls, blowing rain across the village in sheets. Compounds fill with water; dry river beds gush with raging water. Dirt pathways thicken with mud. Dongo, the rumbling deity of thunder, has ravaged the countryside.

When Dongo's voice passes to the distant west along an irregular path ("Dongo's path"), it is sometimes replaced by Hauka voices. From the nooks and crannies of Tillaberi and Wanzerbe, they, too, rumble as they run, jump, and swan-dive into the mud on their way to the *zima's* (priest's) compound.

After one particularly devastating rainstorm in July of 1987, several Hauka ran and splashed their way through the streets of Tillaberi. One deity, Commandamant Bashiru, in the body of Bibata, a short, thick woman, came running into Adamu Jenitongo's compound. Hoarse from his "rumbling" along Tillaberi's muddy paths, Bashiru could barely speak. It was his charge to speak, however, and so he did. "I am Commandamant Bashiru."

Adamu Jenitongo shook Bashiru's hand and said, "A ma ye. A ma ye," ("may it cool down, may it cool down," he says, to ask the spirit to settle into the body of its medium.)

As he stood at attention, Bashiru pumped his arm forcefully as if he were marching double-time. "He is angry today. My father, the chief of the sky, is angry, *zima*. Angry. Did you not hear him?"

"I heard him," said Adamu Jenitongo. "He was angry today."

Bashiru stopped his double-time march motion and wagged his finger at the rest of us. "He was angry today. Our father was angry. Be wary of him. Make him an offering. Dance for him. My father is very, very mean. You must beware. You must not bicker or debate. You must act now if you want rain, if you want food, if you want your young children to live."

Bashiru balanced himself on one foot and saluted for what must have been two minutes. Stiff-legged, he marched to us and shook our hands. "I must go back to Malia," the name the Hauka give to their home, the Red Sea. A shudder pulsed through Bashiru's body as he flew through the air and landed on his back, splattering the mud.

What a spectacle! In a muddy compound, Bashiru, a "colonial military officer," takes the body of a young woman, which assumes a stiff military bearing—legs stiffened, posture straight, shoulders squared—a body through which directives are pronounced.

Bibata slowly pulled herself up to her knees. She coughed several times and called for water.

One of Adamu Jenitongo's wives brought her water and a piece of cloth to wrap around her naked, mud-caked chest. Adamu Jenitongo helped Bibata to her feet and thanked her.

"I salute your sacrifice," he said.

Bibata nodded, but said nothing. Moving her neck from side to side, she slowly walked from the compound. Her Hauka had already arrived in Malia; in Tillaberi, Bibata slowly took her weary body home.

Hauka spirit possession, of course, was—and is—much more than spectacle. Inspired by the Hauka deities defiance, Hauka spirit possession appropriates European and Europeanized African embodied behaviors to directly and indirectly challenge the colonial order. So far we have seen how Europe attempted to "capture" West African bodies and how West

Hauka spirit possession in Tillaberi, Niger (1977).

Africans mounted embodied oppositions to colonial rule. In Part Three of *Embodying Colonial Memories*, we shift our focus to the Republic of Niger, birthplace of Hauka spirit possession. What kind of sociopolitical context gave birth to and nourished the Hauka? How and why did they become thunderous gods? In Chapter Seven, we will trace the major events in the colonization of Niger, focusing, when possible, on their embodied repercussions. How do these events correspond to the emergence of the Hauka in 1925? In Chapter Eight, we chronicle the earliest Hauka ceremonies, the persecution of Hauka mediums, the establishment of Hauka villages, and the expulsion of the Hauka from the colony of Niger. In Chapter Nine, we follow the expelled *hauk'ize*, along with other migrants to the Gold Coast from Songhay to consider the Golden Age of the Hauka, which is admirably depicted in Jean Rouch's controversial documentary, *Les maitres fous*.

CHAPTER SEVEN

Colonizing Niger

♦ ♦ ♦

In the Western Soudan, the French Army, as we have seen, was inspired by independent and adventurous officers who paid scant attention to civilians in Dakar or Paris. Given their isolation, they often initiated military campaigns against indigenous populations without government authorization, boldly presenting their *fait accompli* to civilians in Dakar and Paris. In this way, the French occupied much of the Western Soudan between 1890 and 1900.

The peoples of Niger were among the last West Africans to lose their sovereignty to the thunderous rumble of French canons and rifle fire. Some of the literature on the Nigerien conquest and on early colonial rule in Niger minimizes the serious social and economic ramifications of French militarization.

> The French military conquest of Niger was motivated by two political and strategic considerations, both of which stemmed from interests outside of Niger itself: the ambition to create an empire stretching from North Africa to the Red Sea, while checking expanding British power, and the specific strategy of controlling and stabilizing the Lake Chad basin by defeating the Mahdists, who, under Sultan Rabeh, controlled Bornu.[1]

Standard accounts of the French conquest like those of Edmond Sere de Riviere, Robert Charlick, and to some extent, Finn Fugelstad, point to the relative ease with which Niger—especially Western Niger—was conquered.

"The conquest of western Niger," writes Charlick, "posed few problems"—for whom, one might ask.[2] Earlier histories present events in a chronological sequence, relying largely upon readings of military and colonial reports of reprisals and early attempts at governance. These accounts spend much time analyzing the structures and policies of colonial governments—very much histories from "above." What happened to rural peoples in the wake of French military conquest and governance? What happened to their local economies, their family structures, their systems of beliefs? How did the colonizing of Niger capture the bodies of its peoples? What strategies, if any, did these peoples employ to oppose colonial oppression?

Colonial Culture and the Conquest of Niger

The greatest weakness of the early and some later accounts of the conquest of Niger and of its colonial period, is that they lack a cultural focus. Many of them explore the intricacies of administrative structure. Others focus on military stratagems. Still, others consider indigenous efforts to resist, directly and indirectly, economic and social dislocation and change. Although these studies provide much useful information about colonial conquest and administration, they usually don't consider colonialism as a cultural process.[3] In a recent book, Nicholas Thomas suggests that

> colonialism has always been, equally importantly and deeply, a cultural process; its discoveries and trespasses are imagined and energized through signs, metaphors, and narratives; even what would seem its purest moments of profit and violence have been mediated and enframed by structures of meaning. Colonial cultures are not simply ideologies that mask, mystify, or rationalize forms of oppression that are external to them; they are also expressive and constitutive of colonial relationships in themselves.[4]

Colonial cultures, however, cannot be reduced to some unified cultural system; like all societies, they were riven with disagreements, contestations and internal struggles. Given Thomas' refreshing perspective, what, we can ask, were the cultural ramifications of colonizing Niger?

Military Conquest

Charlick is correct in asserting that the conquest of western Niger posed "few problems" for the French army. The most infamous military event of the conquest was undoubtedly the Voulet-Chanoine mission in 1899. Charlick writes that in 1898 the French sent a military column to Zinder, in eastern Niger, to conquer the Sultan. The mission failed. Captain Cazamajou and twelve of his eighteen men died during the campaign. The French response was quick and ruthless. The colonial military authorities organized the Voulet-Chanoine mission which pillaged its way through western and southern Niger, eventually defeating the army of Zinder as well as that of the Kel Elway Tuareg. Eventually the Voulet-Chanoine column joined another French Army column to engage and defeat Rebeh of Bornu, which enabled the French to create in 1900 the Third Military Territory of Niger.[5]

Although the atrocities of the Voulet-Chanoine mission triggered some outrage in the French press, colonial officials approved of its systematic effectiveness.[6] In his report of 1906 Ponty wrote:

> The conquest of the Djerma is of recent date. It goes back about seven years and we should remember how rapid it was. After the passage of the Voulet-Chanoine mission, which had left bloody traces in the villages it passed through, notably Sansanne-Houssa, where 400 people had been massacred, . . . the terrorized villages let us establish ourselves when we decided upon occupation. Without a murmur, they helped us by providing the provisions and porters we needed.[7]

Oliver de Sardan calls these colonial practices, the "politics of terror." From the French military perspective, pacification "posed few problems." From the perspective of rural peoples, pacification meant burnt granaries, razed villages, summary executions, and devastating famines. "Thought of the Voulet-Chanoine column remained in all the memories. Fear reigned in the countryside."[8]

The widespread fear was not exaggerated for in the early days of the colonial regime summary executions and cruel reprisals were not uncommon. The military authorities wanted to make examples of those who opposed them. Oliver de Sardan notes several examples culled from the colonial archives.

1. The village of Goudel, near Niamey, was fined 20 head of cattle because a certain Alpha Gao had criticized the military government.

2. The chief of the village of Tessa, along the Niger River, was executed by Cornu, because his agent, a certain Aouta, who went their to procure provisions (millet), was wounded by arrows. Cornu shot the chief, "because it was necessary make an example to maintain the native submission."[9]

These extortions, which the military called "requisitions," not only impoverished the rural peoples of western Niger, but made them vulnerable to famine. "The ligne de Tchad [another name for the Voulet-Chanoine mission], largely responsible for the devastating famine between the years 1901-03 and thus the death of thousands, was nothing other than the concentrated expression of a systematic politics of . . . pillage."[10]

After seven years of village burnings, "requisitions" of food and porters, several groups in western Niger mounted a futile revolt against the French. The most notable battle occurred at Karma, a riverain village some 40 kilometers to the north of Niamey. The revolt was immediately crushed.[11] Writing in 1906, Loffler used the language of colonial culture to describe what had happened during the 1906 revolt.

> The *discipline* imposed on the native, *discipline* that unique circumstances determined, was, in my view, of the meanest sort. Our occupation, in effect, affirmed itself by a regime of terror to which the natives submitted . . . Our response to the attitude of an constrained and fearful population was over-confidence [my emphasis][12]

And yet, such overconfidence seems reasonable given the ease with which the French Colonial Army crushed the revolts of Kobtitende and Karma in 1906.

Many Songhay/Zarma chiefs, like Zermakoy Aouta of Dosso, decided to collaborate with the French early during the period of pacification. Following the depressing failure of these revolts, the Songhay/Zarma disengaged completely from armed opposition, their chiefs recognizing the futility of military resistance to the French. From 1906 onward, Songhay/Zarma populations engaged in generally unarmed opposition to French authority.

We are told from any number of sources about the social disintegration that French "pacification" precipitated, but what cultural impact did pacification have? Historians note that "pacification" terrorized the local population that feared massacres, village burnings, and famine. We also know that the *raison d'etre* for such heinous practices was to, in the words of Loffler, a military official, "impose discipline," which meant to regulate activity, to "capture" a colonized body.

And so at the end of the era of pacification (circa 1915), what cultural attributes did *anasaarey* (Europeans) have in the eyes of the pacified? It can be reasonably assumed that Europeans were considered soldiers (*sodje*). Soldiers took what they wanted: food and porters. Soldiers imposed discipline through terror: they fined or executed those who disobeyed them. Soldiers were tough, merciless men. They lacked courtesy and respect. And they were feared. Such may well have been the foundation of colonial culture in (western) Niger.

Colonial Culture, Taxes, and Forced Labor

The administration of occupied Niger differed in degree rather than in kind from that of other territories in French West Africa. As in the other colonial territories, the colonial administration of Niger imposed taxes and forced labor to discipline and govern the territory, practices which changed the sociocultural dynamics of the peoples of Niger.

During the early military years of colonization, taxes took the form of obligatory "requisitions" of food and other needs of the administration. These practices continued after 1922 when the military administration no longer governed Niger. The various local administrations required much food for their personnel—both French and Nigerien—as well as for their animals. Every year,

> soon after the harvest, local authorities stocked up for the coming year— mostly calculated stocks since there was always an excess—the necessary millet to provide not only for its needs, but also for the Administration's native agents . . . who also benefitted from the advantages of the requisition which was not small.[13]

During the civilian administration of the Niger, however, local administrators paid for the provisions they required, but at a price far below the market rate.[14] Thus these forced requisitions further impoverished rural peoples in western Niger. The needs of local colonial authorities, of course, varied throughout Niger. In the west, the site of the colonial administrative center, the authorities required many more provisions than in the Hausa-speaking areas to the east.[15]

Following the failed 1906 revolt, the French installed what Charlick calls "puppet regimes" in western Niger.

> With the effective imposition of puppet regimes, the plight of Nigeriens worsened. Although they had little real autonomy, leaders like Gado Namalaya, chief of Fillingue, could act in a more heavy-handed way than had been possi-

ble prior to the colonial conquest as long as they were loyal to the French.
With French support they could levy abusive taxes for personal gain virtually without fear of popular uprisings.[16]

Indeed, "little by little the notion of taxes grew larger and more refined.
The tax would no longer simply supply the replenishment of posts, but
nourish the resources of the territorial budget."[17] Imposed officially in 1906
the head tax tripled between 1906 and 1916. By 1911, moreover, taxes could
no longer be paid in cowery shells, the pre-colonial currency. Rural populations now had to pay their taxes in francs.[18]

Taxes provoked the partial monetarization of rural economies in Niger.
People needed to grow surpluses of staple crops like millet, sorghum, and
rice, or grow cash crops like peanuts or cotton—to raise the necessary
funds to pay their head taxes. Such monetarization, for Olivier de Sardan,
was not purely and simply a brute introduction to capitalism, but yet
another colonial extortion, part of a politics of punition and terror; a
substantial additional burden to a depressed and terrorized population.[19]

Through *agents indigene* like the aforementioned Gado Namalaya of
Filingue, local administrations also conscripted able bodied men into
forced-labor gangs. As discussed in Chapter Five, the abolition of slavery,
the foundation of the precolonial order among the peoples of Niger, was
more than an enlightened European response to the moral repugnance of
slavery; it enabled local administrations in Niger (and elsewhere) to recruit
unpaid labor to build the colonial infrastructure. Some of these freed slaves
found their way into "villages de liberte." Others simply provided their
local administration ten free days of labor a year. Indeed, many of the post
offices and roads in Niger were built through the employment of forced
labor.[20]

There were two other forms of forced labor, according to Oliver de
Sardan: forced recruitment, in which the colonial administration paid the
laborers a salary permitting the authorities to work them for longer periods of time (two or three months)[21]; and the military draft, in which rural
peoples in Niger were taken into the army to fight in World War I and II.
Indeed, Ousmane Fodji, who was to become high priest of the Hauka in the
Gold Coast, was drafted to fight in World War I (see Chapter Nine).

A special French legal code sealed the powerless fate of peoples in Niger.
Called the *indigenat*, this code, which was decreed on 21 November 1904,

considered Nigeriens to be subjects, rather than citizens, which meant that they were to be governed by decrees rather than laws. The code also meant that local administrators, for any reason, could arrest and try any of their subjects and sentence them to 15 days in prison. The code also stipulated 26 offenses which included ". . . nonpayment of taxes, disrespectful attitude towards administrators, disrespectful speeches, remarks, even songs intended to undermine respect for the French, a non-collaborative attitude and failure to carry out (or to carry out properly) an administrator's order."[22] In relation to the

> Commandant, ie. the local chief administrative officer, law-maker (in the sense that he could interpret local customary law as he wished), judge, police chief, military commander, prison superintendent, tax-collector, chief medical officer and much more, the average African was powerless. He was left with three alternatives: to obey, to migrate somewhere else if possible, or to revolt. Indeed, as can be seen from the provisions regarding requisitions, a mere tacit acquiescence to French rule would not do. The French required nothing short of active collaboration. The administrators on the spot in Niger wielding, if anything, even more power than their colleagues in other parts of French West Africa, because of the difficulties of communication within their territory, made it practically impossible for superior authorities to keep a watchful eye on the local administration and to see that directives and orders were carried out at the local level.[23]

The Nigerien confrontation with French colonialism was brutal and terrifying. Peoples lost their political autonomy and their economic independence during the short period of 7 years (1899-1906). The French imposed taxes. The French "freed" the slaves not for noble humanitarian reasons, but to facilitate the recruitment of forced labor while weakening the power of traditional chiefs. They replaced independent chiefs with their own agents who exploited their new found authority as eager-to-please tax collectors and forced-labor recruiters. Their eagerness made them among the most reviled people in rural areas.

In the language of colonialism's culture, the administrations of the Niger territory were entities that demanded absolute and unwavering respect and discipline. Put another way, the colonial authorities of Niger sought to regulate the behaviors, to literally "capture" the bodies of their "subjects" through regimens, through legal decree, and through colonial practice. Lack of "acceptable" discipline and respect—lack of regulation—resulted in arrests, trials, fines, imprisonment, and sometimes summary execution. The French occupation of Niger condemned most rural people to poverty and powerlessness. Considering the risks, it is altogether remarkable that rural peoples defied—albeit indirectly—French colonial rule in Niger.

Indirect Oppositions

This defiance, usually practiced by individuals or small groups, took on many forms: trickery, fraud, insult, silence in response to orders. Although these forms of indirect opposition posed no threat to the colonial administrations of Niger, they rendered the colonial enterprise less efficient and provided a small measure of satisfaction to those under its yoke.[24]

Rural peoples hid their assets to avoid giving them to the French authorities. Consider the frustrations of several colonial officials responsible for local censuses.

> Everywhere there reigns the same taste of fraud, the same bad esprit. I couldn't express without interminable goings-on all the trickery employed by the population to hide their herds and dispatch their goods.[25]

> During the census no precise information was supplied by the natives. They invariably answered they owned nothing at all. Questioned about the origins of numerous animals tracks, they answered that they came from the animals of neighboring villages coming to drink at their wells; naturally in the village so named we obtained identical answers.[26]

Colonial officials often considered these behaviors examples of "native passivity," but Idrissa Kimba, and especially Olivier de Sardan, consider them acts of resistance to colonialism.[27]

Another individual act of this opposition was sorcery. Acts of sorcery to sabotage a harvest, a public works project, or to sicken or render mad a colonial official also defied the colonial order in no uncertain terms.[28] Called "mean chief medicine," these sorcerous acts are used in Songhay when chiefs exceed their authority.[29]

Although scholars like George Spittler, Kimba, and Olivier de Sardan write on the application of trickery and fraud during the colonial era, these practices of defiance and opposition existed during precolonial times and continue in the present (see Chapter Ten).

Not all these acts of what I call embodied opposition were strictly individual. Consider what Olivier de Sardan calls the "breakup of villages." Prior to the French occupation, it was not an uncommon practice for villagers in such isolated regions as Simiri in western Niger to spend the entire rainy season at bush camps near their fields. This practice, providing its participants a measure of unregulated freedom, continued during the colonial period (and continue today) in rural Niger. Yet the villagers often paid a substantial price for such defiance. The French routinely burned small "abandoned" villages. They also searched for and destroyed rural granaries, storage facilities that "hid" local provisions. Despite the exceedingly high price of rural flight, people in isolated regions continued the practice.[30]

Migration

During the French occupation of Niger, thousands of young men migrated to the Gold Coast. In so doing they migrated from a staid rural French regime of regulation to a dynamically urban British sphere of influence: two different systems of production and politics. The Nigerien *sujets* were not alone. In the first decade or so of French rule, as already mentioned, tens of thousands of single young men migrated from the Sahel to the Guinea Coast.

There are a wide variety of explanations for this mass movement to the south. Some of the French administrators considered migration, which was usually seasonal in nature, to be a social consequence of the abolition of slavery. Freed of their servile responsibilities, they reasoned, the (former) slaves left their masters in droves. In an administrative report of 1911 it was estimated that one-third of all the slaves in the Sahel had migrated to the Guinea Coast.[31]

Other scholars like Jean Rouch saw persistent migration as the continuation of a process that began in the mid-nineteenth century when Songhay/Zarma warriors migrated to the Gold Coast in search of adventure, booty, and power. During the colonial period, economic adventurers replaced the mercenaries. Despite the shift from military exploits to economic adventurism, rural peoples in Niger continued to regard the migrants as heros.[32]

Indeed, the historical romance of migrating Songhay/Zerma mercenaries is critiqued by a later generation of scholars.

> The young Zerma/Songhay began to go as seasonal laborers to the Gold Coast, mainly to the Kumasi region, following in the footsteps, as it were [but

> pushing farther to the south than], of their nineteenth-century warrior ances-
> tors, who had conquered the Mamprusi-Dagomba region . . . It is probable
> therefore that there occurred among the 'adventurous' Zerma/Songhay a
> form of culture transfer in favor of migrant labor. In particular, the long and
> at times perilous journey to the Gold Coast became part of a 'modernized'
> initiation ritual.[33]

Adventure no doubt played some role in the "initiation" of migrants
during the colonial period. But was that all? Consider the comments of
Nicholas Leca, a French colonial official, in his 1939 annual report.
"Emigration is the natural consequence of heavy burdens of our occupation."[34] According to Schmitt, another colonial administrator in Niger,

> the mass migrations of young people capable of working has alarmed the
> canton chiefs who complain of the serious difficulty of supply laborers . . .
> requested by the T.P. [Public Works Departments] and the requisitions for the
> work of the cercle. It is not doubtful that the recruitment, the laborers and the
> diverse supplies for the T.P. are, in part, the reason for these periodic displace-
> ments.[35]

Considering the evidence of the brutal exploitation of the French *militaires*
and *civils,* migration must be considered in a more nuanced fashion.

In a recent study, Thomas Painter argues that the urge to migrate to the
Gold Coast sprang not from the spirit of adventure but from the need to
escape French economic exploitation. For Painter, migration was an escape
from the pernicious politics of French colonialism in Niger.[36] Olivier de
Sardan sees migration, among other things, as an escape but also a refusal
to accept the colonial exploitation:

> It is true that escape was not the only motive of the migrations. Psychological
> causes (liberation from family constraints, prestige of the voyage and the
> initiatic character of the expedition) or economic causes (earning money on
> the Coast to send that which would pay for taxes, millet, or bride prices) are
> often advanced.[37]

Olivier de Sardan's position corresponds to that of several French colonial officials in Niger. And yet the colonial administration did little to stem
the flow of migrant labor from Niger to the Gold Coast. Officials in Niger,
he argues, probably found it useful to let the men go to Accra and Kumasi.
The earnings they sent home ultimately paid local taxes and provided for
the "requisitions" needed by local administrations. From the standpoint of
the French administration, migration was "indispensable."[38]

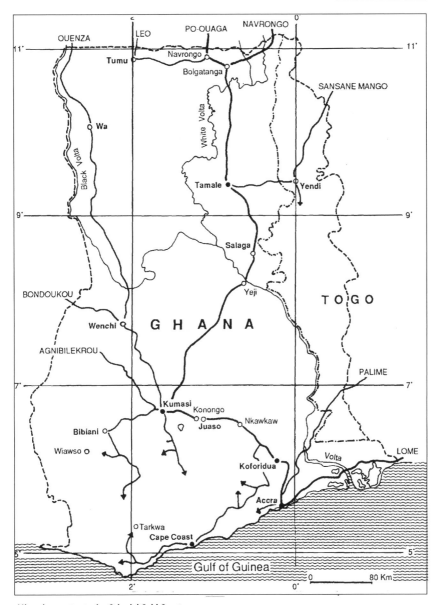

Migration routes to the Colonial Gold Coast.

Colonial Culture and Social Change in Niger

There is an ongoing debate about the impact of colonial culture in Niger and other colonies in French West Africa. No scholar denies the uniformly brutal character of colonialism in Niger. Several scholars contend that although the French used different methods to brutalize their colonial *sujets* in Niger, brute reality was nothing new to these rural populations. Brutality preceded and followed the colonial period in Niger.[39] For writers like Olivier de Sardan, colonialism precipitated new relations of production which prompted widespread and social change.[40]

The degree of change, however, varied from region to region. Some writers contend that colonial culture had its greatest impact in western Niger among the Songhay/Zarma, from whose ranks the French drew the majority of their local and regional agents.[41] Although the impact of money in rural economies was varied, everyone, after 1911, had to pay taxes in francs, which meant that rural people devised various strategies to pay their taxes. In the west, the young men who migrated to the Gold Coast often sent their money home to be used to pay taxes. In Hausa-speaking regions in the east, young men grew cash crops to earn, in part, their tax money.[42] Whether these kinds of economic changes amounted to, in Olivier de Sardan's language, "a rupture" which brought on new relations of production, is debatable.[43] What is important to note is that like Islamization, colonialism constituted a major event in the history of the peoples of Niger, an event with profound sociocultural implications.

Colonization thus exploded the pre-existing domestic economy, introduced foreign exchange, prompted widespread and large-scale migrations, required the cash cropping of cotton and peanuts, reoriented family relations, and undermined the authority of local and regional chiefs. These events, of course, cannot be analyzed independently for they are interdependent. Obligatory requisition of food and animals and the imposition of taxes required a shift in economic practices.

Migration also profoundly affected family relations. Whereas prior to colonization younger males led socially and culturally constrained lives, during the colonial period, their economic and social importance grew exponentially, as they became earners of money. In areas where people grew labor-intensive cash crops to pay their taxes, farmers had to divert labor from staple crops like millet and sorghum, which reduced reserve supplies of foodstuffs. Cash cropping, in effect, made rural peoples more vulnerable to famine.[44]

Taxation and forced-labor recruitment had devastating internal political effects. The French wanted to reinforce the authority of their agents: the collaborationist local and regional chiefs. But these policies, which precipitated mass migration, had the opposite effect. They undermined patriarchy and transformed the chief into a reviled figure. Social life had been transformed.[45]

Colonialism's culture, however fragmented and contested it may have been, added one indisputably new element to the cultural matrix in Niger: the white man or in Songhay, the *anasaara*, who had slipped into local consciousness. Like economic and social changes, the local conceptions of Europeans varied significantly from region to region. But one could say that the white man had several general attributes. If he wasn't a military man, he had a military bearing. He possessed a limitless supply of food and enjoyed eating meat (mostly taken from rural peasants). He hired servants and porters. He could not be trusted. He did not work with his hands. He was resolute and punished those who did not demonstrate proper discipline and respect. For all intents and purposes, the *anasaara* was what the Songhay called a "hard man."

Hard Men and Cultural Defiance

In Niger most French officials tried hard to be hard men, and, as we have seen, many of them succeeded. They squelched their *sujets* with oppressive requisitions, forced-labor details, excessive head taxes, and brutal punishments. The resilient *sujets* persevered. Some were insubordinate; others tricked the colonial authorities. Many more retired to isolated stretches of the bush or migrated, most often seasonally, to the Gold Coast.

Given their seemingly easy victory, many French officials in Niger became overconfident of their supreme power. They were soon taken aback by the armed revolts in 1906 and in 1916. The more seasoned the colonial official, the more wary his attitude toward West African political and military capacities. The French had long experience with formidable Muslim resistance, having fought long and hard against the likes of El Hadj 'Umar and Samory, both of whom used Tijani Islam as a means of maintaining the particularly African identity of their regimes. In this schema, Africans were believers, and Europeans were infidels whose presence destroyed the cohesion of the community of believers (*umma*). A divided community, it followed, explained a wide variety of catastrophes: loss of sovereignty, drought, famine, epidemic. But there is more, for as Timothy Mitchell has shown, the confrontation of Europe and the Muslim world was more than merely political; it was profoundly cultural, opposing distinct epistemologies, ways of organizing space, time, and systems of embodiment.

In 1908, Venel, the military commander of Niger, focused only on the political ramifications of Islam. "Politically, the Muslim religion will undoubtedly constitute a powerful connection shared by all our subjects (to fuel) . . . a general rebellion."[46] With ever-generous hindsight, then, it came as no surprise that Islam inspired the minor revolts that occurred in Niger in 1906 and again in 1916.

Many French officials realized that they could not—and should not—attempt to stamp out an increasingly important religion. Wisely, they tolerated Islamic practices, all the while maintaining surveillance of major clerics who potentially posed threats to their regimes. Administrators also attempted, rather successfully, to co-opt Muslim clerics who hailed from aristocratic families—yet another ploy to calm potentially volatile Muslim communities. This *realpolitik* resulted in Islam's exponential growth in Niger.

> The Zarmas who were once fetishists have all converted to Islam, just what we could hope to happen. This religion has certainly highlighted their bad instincts, but the evil that it carries in itself goes beyond the good we can expect from it. The country is worked by Islam; the errant clerics, disguised dioulas, all the silk-tongued merchants find help and refuge either in Birni or Say. All one needs is a serious external influence to provoke a maraboutic movement.[47]

French colonial policies provided the ingredients to feed such religiously-inspired movements throughout West Africa. Although the colonizers living in the region considered Muslims infidels who sapped the western Sahel of its resources, the French government nonetheless took a pragmatic, political approach toward Islam. They tolerated Islamic practices and indirectly promoted migration—two factors that favored the development of Maraboutic Movements—the centers of which lay outside of Niger.

A case in point is the Mourides of Senegal, a Sufi order founded after Ahmadu Bamba, a Muslim cleric, experienced a revelation in 1891. In Mouradism, one achieved piety and devotion to Allah through hard work, which in Senegal meant the cultivation of peanuts. Bamba soon gathered many followers who, in turn, controlled large tracts of land. The French administration exiled Bamba to Gabon in 1895 and to Mauritania in 1902.

When Bamba returned to Senegal in 1912 ". . . he had some 70,000 followers. The French administration finally set up close ties with the Mouride *marabouts* on the basis of shared interest in peanut commerce . . ."[48]

Economic and sociopolitical circumstances limited Mouridism to Senegal. The case of Cheikh Hammala's movement, however, was altogether different. Hammalism, an outgrowth of Tijanism, the sufi order of El Hadj 'Umar and Samory Toure, was first and foremost a religious phenomenon that, because of the sociopolitical factors of the colonial situation, became a widely diffused "anti-colonial" political movement. By 1914 the French had come to terms with transforming it from a revolutionary threat to the colonial order into

> a kind of established church with quasi-official status. "Reformed" Tijanism—the Hammaliyya—was at first preeminently a religious, nonconformist, dissident movement, but insofar as it was directed against an officially recognized, semi-officially supported "church," it was bound, willingly or not, to assume a political significance.[49]

Hammalism emerges from what Pierre Alexandre calls the "mystery" of Chiek Hammala's teachings. Hammala was born in Senegal in 1883 or 1884. Although he received a fine Islamic education, he never became a great scholar. His fame and influence spread through his written messages, sent to minor Tijani clerics, that criticized the faults of orthodox Tijanism. Cheik Hammala also provoked the ire of orthodox Tijani officials by praying with an unorthodox eleven-bead rosary. In time, a large number of adherents extolled the Cheik's humility and piousness. Such renown fired the hostility of orthodox Tijanis who aligned themselves with the French and demonstrated none of the Cheik's humble piety.

Although Cheik Hammala was ostensibly a reclusive apolitical figure, the French considered him a revolutionary who had the capacity to incite peasant resistance. In most respects, however, Hammala was ". . . a reactionary since his avowed aim was a return to the purity of olden times. However, his influence was objectively subversive . . ."[50] In Senegal, tensions between the Tijanis and the Hammalists grew during the 1920s and 1930s. The teachings of the Cheik attracted two kinds of adherents: intellectuals like Tierno Bokar, Hamani Diori, and Ahmadou Hampate Ba; and warriors like Yakouba Sylla.[51]

In 1940 a band of Hammalist warriors reputedly attacked an encampment, killing more than 400 people. The French reacted swiftly and decisively. They executed 33 Hammalists, including three of the Cheiks's sons, and threw 600 others into prison. In 1941, they exiled Cheik Hammala to Algeria, where local Muslim authorities found his presence intolerable. Attempting to maintain the religious peace in Algeria, the French sent Hammala to the Cevennes in the south of the France in 1942. He died there in January of 1943. Cheik Hammala's exile and death, however, did not prevent the spread of his influence, especially among the "warrior" branch of the Hammalists. In 1941 Hammalists attacked a café in Bobo-Dioulasso and killed six Europeans.[52]

After World War II, the revolts spread to other parts of West Africa. One such disturbance, noted by Vincent Monteil, took place in eastern Mali in 1947. According to Monteil, Moussa Aminou, the leader of the revolt,

> who claimed he was a *sharif* and called himself Cheikh Moussa ben Mohammed Lamine was a Songhay marabout. Born around 1906, he had made a trip to Ghana around 1919 and another to Morocco in 1947. He first settled down in Dori in Upper Volta, until 1940. From there, he went to Nioro in order to initiate himself to Cheikh Hamalla and the 11 grain rite of the Tijani. Then he established himself in Wani, near Bourem upriver from Gao on the Niger. On March 26 1949 he declared a holy war, mounted his white horse and whipped up the faithful, who beat up the administrator. The troops reestablished order and killed eight of the murderers. Wounded, the marabout died the next day, 27 March due to lack cf treatment.[53]

In the end, " . . . the most important of the traits which set Hammalah apart from other contemporary leaders of messianic-prophetic protest movements is the fact that he did not borrow anything from European sources—from colonial and missionary innovations."[54] Indeed, Hammalism was a movement to return to the piety of the past, an ideology that triggered, in turn, a popular reaction to the colonial situation. As West Africa approached independence, however, Hammalism faded away.

Was Hammalism the solution to the cultural disintegration brought on by colonial culture? One could say that French colonial culture in Niger—and West Africa as a whole—snuffed out early forms of organized dissent, leaving Islam as the repository of African identity. For most of the peoples of Niger, however, Islam represented a powerful, but foreign, influence. It provided a formidable framework from which to maintain a sense of African community, but it was only a partial answer to the cultural and political devastation of French colonial rule in Niger. Islam was the religion of the Arabs, but not of the ancestors. Many peoples in Niger believed—and still believe—that the ancestors controlled many of the natural and social forces: sky, soil, wind, clouds, water, and power. Sometime in the past the ancestors ceded that control to spirits who, if appeased through offerings, would protect the peoples of Niger. Much like the Islamic reasoning associated with protecting the harmony of *umma*, spirit possession priests claimed that failure to pay homage to spirits would bring on drought, famine, epidemic and loss of sovereignty. As we shall see in the next chapter, colonizing Niger produced another religious phenomenon, the Hauka spirits, who, unlike the Hammalists, attempted to master the master by appropriating his embodied behaviors.

CHAPTER EIGHT

The Birth of the Hauka Movement

♦   ♦   ♦

They came from Malia, the Red Sea, these Hauka, these "sons and daughters" of Bilali. Muhammed's black African confidant, Bilali was a man, who, as the mystical alter-ego of Dongo (the deity of thunder), possessed the power to burn villages and kill villagers without remorse. The Hauka, the descendants of Dongo-Bilali, captured some of their father's power.

They came to Niger in July of 1925, a scant three years after Niger had formally been transformed from a military territory to a French colony. They came on the wings of the Harmattan, the wings of the desert wind.

When they landed in Niger, they found a country occupied by whites, who, like Dongo, had burned villages and killed villagers without remorse. They found a land in which the whites had "requisitioned" food and animals, imposed taxes, forced young men to work, squelched armed revolts and punished any form of insubordination with steep fines and imprisonment. For many people in Niger, the whites must have seemed to possess incomprehensible power.

And so they came from the east, from Malia and took the bodies of their first mediums in the village of Tondigandia in the Kurfey of south central Niger. Nicole Echard describes the earliest gusts of what she calls the "Babule Movement" (which later became known as the Hauka Movement):

The Babule begins during the 1925 harvest following the return to the village of a woman called Shibbo who had lived in a neighboring region. There, she had been "attacked" by the "Europeanne," a female spirit of the brand new Babule family, and she returned along with a few mediums of these new spirits as well as with musicians-griots who knew their melodies and their demands. In one month the movement was organized under the guidance of Shibbo-the-Europeanne. About 100 people, considered as soldiers, formed a collectivity under the authority of general staff that copied the French military hierarchy. The Europeanne ordered the manufacture of rifles: the blacksmiths were capable only of reproducing the form and only the bayonet was usable. During the day, men and women, who had abandoned the harvest after Shibbo's return, went to the bush to train for guerilla war. Guard duty was organized, and lookouts were assigned positions in the village. Every evening there was a spirit possession dance during which the Babule came to hunt witches.[1]

Hauka spirit possession in Tillaberu, Niger (1977).

Echard goes on to describe how the Babule "soldiers" travelled through the Kurfey to proselytize their movement.[2]

In the first reports about the Hauka "agitation," French officials also wrote about wind gusts from the east:

> It is good to point out a kind of crazy wind that originated in the east that blew over the Kourfey and Tondigandia cantons last July. In most of the villages young people in the guise of "bori" (spirit possession genies, in Haoussa) had formed groups that parodied our military institutions. They played majors, captains, lieutenants all the way down to the bottom of the hierarchical ladder. Everyone amused themselves by drilling with well fashioned minuscule wood rifles. A woman, the sister of Dangalamdia of Chikal, had been the instigator of the movement, explicitly directed against us! Elsewhere, certain natives spread the gossip that one had to cut the throats of all chickens to please Allah and that mosques had to be taken into the bush, and that sexual promiscuity had to exist. The origin of this movement and these rumors is unknown. After the commander of the circle learned of these facts, several punishments were announced and several palabres sufficed to bring complete calm to the situation.[3]

The official underestimated the potential power of the Hauka, however; they spread, as Echard notes, from Dogondutche to the north and the region of Filingue.

> Following 1926, [there is] serious trouble in Kourfey. The movement comes from (Dogon)Doutchi. A woman from Chikal, Chibo, and her father, Ganji created a sect that copies our administration and wants to supplant our authority. Young men and women gather, found villages, name governors, commandants, doctors, drill with wooden rifles, arrest local guards . . . Chibo goes into trance, preaches insubordination, invites non-payment of taxes and work refusals. The movement amplified in 1927 . . . Census: no one [cooperates]. The energetic guards and the calvary of Mayaki (the Kourfey canton chief) corrected the Sudies [a subgroup of Songhay/Zarma]. Several of the ring leaders were exiled for 10 years in the Ivory Coast.[4]

Even before *they* came from Malia to Dogondoutche, officials reported much agitation in Kourfey. In 1926, the canton's populace refused to pay their taxes. "The spirit of individualism and insubordination skillfully brought to bear by the ring leaders in Kourfey has made its imprint. We are witnessing the development of an opposition born in Chikal and Louma in the rival clans to those of Mayaki. This agitation is aggravated by the 'gadji' (. . . the zarma word meaning genii, or the father of Chibo, the first hawka medium?)"[5] In 1927 adepts of the sect declared that we ". . . could turn bullets to water, that there was no longer a chief in the Kourfey, and that at last, the moment had come for Gandji and Chibo to take their place. . ."[6]

In 1927 the political conflict escalated. Although Jean Rouch's informant, Alhadji Mohammadou, situates the birth of the Hauka in Chikal rather than Tondigandia, he provides some remarkable details of the early moments of the movement:

> It all started during a dance of girls and boys. During the dance a Suji woman, Zibo, who was married to Timbuktu *sharif* began to "win" a spirit. They asked who he was. He said: 'I am Gomno Malia,' (that means the Governor of the Red Sea). The people said that they didn't know this holley (spirit). But the others came upon the boys. They said their names, but we didn't know them. They said: 'We are the Hawka, the strangers (meaning the guests) of Dongo.' This happened at Chikal, very near to Filingue. Several days later, all the boys and girls of Filingue had "won" the Hawka. Filingue's chief sent a message to Niamey in order to tell the commander of the region, Major Croccichia, that the woman, Zibo's Hawka had ruined the country. Croccichia said that they should all be rounded up and brought to Niamey. The chief rounded up 60 boys and girls. They were brought to Croccichia's. Croccichia locked them up for three days and three nights without food. He brought them out, and they danced until they "won" their Hawka. It was Zibo who began by having Gomno Malia, and Croccichia called his guards. He summoned Zibo and slapped her. He said to her: 'Where is the Hawka?' He continued (to slap her) until Zibo said: 'There are no Hawka!' It all happened this way until they all said: 'There are no Hawka.' Then Croccichia sent them all back to Filingue. People in Filingue expelled Zibo who went to Dori. The Hawka did not come back to the other villages. Soon they had spread throughout the country.[7]

That same year, other villages in Kourfey refused to pay taxes to the French administration. In Tessoua, to the east of Maradi in Hausa country, Islamic militants attacked the administrative center in Tessoaua, killing one European and three guards. French officials linked this Muslim "agitation" to the Hauka—an unlikely alliance considering the mutual hostility of Hauka adepts and Muslim militants.

When the brutalized Hauka mediums returned to Filingue from Niamey, the chief, Gado Namalaya, expelled them. They trekked to other villages in the Filingue district and to other cantons and founded new Hauka cults. The movement spread widely. By Februrary of 1927 the colonial administration noted that there were Hauka adepts in all the villages of the Filingue district. They considered the Hauka rivals "of the established order represented in the chieftaincy, the backbone of the administrative system created by the

French."[8] In March of 1927, Gado Namalaya, the old chief of Filingue, died. The French supported the candidacy of Chekou Seyni, one of Gado's sons. Chekou, however, was not unopposed. Manifesting themselves as a political force, the Hauka supported a rival candidate. This action was an intolerable affront to French authority. To make matters worse from the French perspective, the Hauka seemingly founded their own villages in the bush and putatively created their own society, which was overtly anti-French. The French found in the Hauka " . . . the presence of an open dissidence, a society, the members of which openly defied the social, political and religious order. It is here that we discover the most original aspect of the Hauka movement: their total refusal of the system put into place by the French."[9]

Following this bold political confrontation, the French authorities, as already noted, expelled Zibo and three others to the Ivory Coast for ten years. There is virtually no published or archival material on Zibo and her father, Gandji. We know little of the personal circumstances that prompted their principal roles in the birth of the Hauka movement.[10]

Discourses of Resistance and Identity

The emergence of Hauka spirit possession in July of 1925 jolted the French authorities in Niger. Administrators and collaborating chiefs like Mayaki and Gado Namalaya quickly took measures to make outlaws of these new adepts who carried spirits that, in effect, made outlaws of the colonial occupiers. Put another way, the Hauka became outlaws who made outlaws of those who outlawed them.

What are we to make of the emergence of these spirit outlaws whose mediums so threatened French authority that they were exiled to other French colonies? French authorities clearly understood the Hauka movement in purely political terms. The administrators write of parody, of challenge to French authority, of imitation of the French military hierarchy. The French responded to the "Hauka agitation" in the same manner they dealt with other acts of insubordination in Niger—with severe punishment. They arrested and fined Hauka mediums. They exiled the principal instigators.

The French administrators, of course, had little knowledge of indigenous religious practices. For them, spirit possession (*bori*, in Hausa and *holle hori* in Songhay) was no more than a theatrical stage of political resistance. Parodying the French military, it seems, meant blatant and unpardonable insubordination. They knew little of the complexities of Hausa or Songhay spirit possession, little of the way new spirits are incorporated into the respective spirit pantheons. They knew less still of the symbolic and cultural importance of spirit possession in Hausa and Songhay/Zarma culture.

Given their pyrotechnic histrionics, the Hauka have understandably attracted the descriptive and analytical attentions of several scholars. The first description of Hauka possession, a graphic one at that, appears in the last frames of Jean Rouch's first ethnographic film, *Au pays des mages noirs* (1946). Later, Rouch wrote about the Hauka in his magisterial *La religion et la magie Songhay*. Rouch, however, doesn't attempt to explain the Hauka phenomenon. The same can be said for Rouch's provocative film, *Les maitres fous*, which is long on images and short on explanations.[11] Fugelstad, an historian, both describes and analyzes the emergence of the Hauka. In his early attempts at explanation, he considers the Hauka—much like the first-hand French observers—as an overtly political manifestation.[12] In a more nuanced and sustained work on the colonial history of Niger, Fugelstad attempts to account for the Hauka as a complex cultural event. He suggests that the Hauka represented a way to comprehend colonial domination from an indigenous perspective and to tap into an ever-evident, ever-impressive powerline of European "force" and use it to local advantage.[13] Such recircuiting, Pamela Schmoll has argued, " . . . represents a very 'Hausa' strategy for coping with situations of domination and oppression. . . ."[14]

Fugelstad's notion of the Hauka as the attempt to tap into European power is intriguing but underdeveloped in his book. At no point does he fully consider the Hauka movement as a discourse of resistance and identity. For his part, Olivier de Sardan is careful to consider the Hauka movement as both a religious and a political phenomenon brought on by what he calls "la rupture coloniale."[15]

For Olivier de Sardan, among others, *la rupture coloniale* created a social context ripe for the florescence of multi-ethnic movements. Prior to French occupation, rural populations preoccupied themselves with household matters, lineage concerns, local religious rites, village politics, and to a lesser extent, matters of ethnicity. These sociocultural preoccupations did not disappear following the French occupation, but the occupation did reduce their social significance. As we have seen, local village chiefs became puppets; taxes, migration and cash cropping altered the social matrix of the household; and the *indigenat* transformed independent peoples into *sujets* subject to the mercurial whims of local administrators.

In this sociopolitical context, argues Olivier de Sardan, two sociocultural movements grew: Islam (as articulated by Hammalism) and the Hauka. Although Olivier de Sardan astutely notes the mutual antagonism between Islam and the Hauka, he argues for a more abstract commonality. Much like Islam and its pan-ethnic community of believers, the Hauka unified ethnic groups. The Hauka ". . . created a membership that transcended family, village, ethnic group, and language all the while excluding the colonizer . . . "[16] He suggests that only a "native" could become a Muslim or a spirit-possession dancer. [17] In practice, Olivier de Sardan is quite correct. It would be unthinkable, though not impossible, for a Frenchman of the colonial era to convert to Islam. As for spirit possession, it is clear that not everyone can join the circle of possession dancers. The Songhay say, for example, "boro kan mana gaanu si windi," which translates roughly as "the uninitiated cannot join the circle of possession dancers." Still, mediums of possession troupes, be they among the Hausa or Songhay/Zarma, are of various ethnic backgrounds. They are "called" to their spirits through a series of initiatory rites that begin when a future medium is marked with spirit sickness.

Refining his argument, Olivier de Sardan goes on to suggest other points in common between development of (Islamic) Hammalism and the Hauka, both of which

> are born in the margins of religious systems in the process of mutating, under the disapproving stare of the existing clergy, both of them stem from a veritable religious logic, the inheritors of a long symbolic history, became the carriers of visions and political conflicts that transcend them [ie the other religions, my comments], both of them had an essentially rural, popular, and spontaneous coloration.[18]

In both cases, Olivier de Sardan argues quite convincingly that the Hauka and Hammalists exploded religious traditions in the countryside. Put in more contemporary language, the Hauka and Hammalist movements embodied a politics of identity and resistance which, because of its trans-ethnic character, attracted legions of faithful followers: people in rural Hausa and Songhay and, as we shall see in the next chapter, migrants to the Gold Coast.

Olivier de Sardan's argument, as far as it goes, is apposite. From my vantage, however, the differences between the Hammalists and the Hauka are far more interesting to explore. In Niger at least, Hammalism was the product of an exotic religious tradition. The Hauka evolved from locally developed religious practices. More important, however, is the different way that Hammalists and Haukas articulated their viewpoints on French occupation.

As noted in the previous chapter, the Hammalists preached about the dangers of the occupying infidel. In this respect, Hammalism reassembled the politics of such great resistance warriors as El Hadj 'Umar and Samory Toure. For Hammalists the return to simple religious piety would pave the way for a millenarian revolution: the force to expel the infidel occupiers and return power to the community of believers.

Hauka expression differed markedly from that of the Muslim Hammalists. From the beginning, the Hauka spirits mimed the colonizers, their institutions, and their entourage of collaborators. As such, the Hauka created in Niger a highly complex and subtle mimetic discourse. Indeed, the Hauka constituted an embodied opposition to the French occupation. Therein, I would argue, lies its popularity, its resilience and, ultimately, its political power.

Mimesis, Embodiment, and the Birth of the Hauka

The mimetic faculty, to recall what we discussed in Chapter Three by way of Michael Taussig, enables a person to grasp that which is strange, other. In other words, one mimes or copies something or someone—in our case the colonial hierarchy in French-occupied Niger—to comprehend and master it. Adopting the insights of Taussig and Benjamin, we can say that the power of the mimetic faculty devolves from its fundamental sensuality: copying the French Governor entails contact, which is electroshocking to both intended and unintended audiences. Using this theoretical framework, the appearance of Governor Malia and his entourage of generals, majors, and Senegalese *tirailleurs* like Bamabara Mossi would have been *jolting* to the French administration, their collaborators and to the established religious order. The colonial record is unequivocal in this regard: the emergence of the Hauka shocked the established order. Accordingly, the administrators punished the Hauka quickly, decisively, and brutally, to make them an "example" of what happens to those who are disrespectful and insubordinate outlaws.

Most of the previous writing on the Hauka, including my own, has neglected the sensuousness of its mimetic nature. Olivier de Sardan's brief analysis of Hauka possession neglects this sensuality.[19] Fugelstad considers the Hauka a way of mastering domination, of redirecting European power to African networks, but fails to take the analysis one step further—into the power of the mimetic faculty, into the power and resilience of embodied oppositions.[20] Benjamin teaches us that miming creates an electrical storm of sensations that enable people to understand and master that which is strangely powerful. Following this logic, we can argue that peoples in Niger copied the French Major, for example, to comprehend and master him— literally through their bodies.[21]

Muslims never sought to copy the infidels through Hammalism; they prayed and acted to expel them, thinking the white man an inferior, unre-deemably compromised being. For the Hammalists, infidels belonged to the category, *cefeeri*, or non-believers, for whom death meant a long and painful fall into the fires of hell. They prayed to avoid the fiery fate of non-believers. Pious Muslims didn't want to copy these infidels, but many may have feared that European occupation would condemn them to the infidel's fate.

By contrast, the Hauka sensually grasped the power of the French: their guns, the ability of their armies to conquer, their seemingly endless supplies of men, weapons and food, their stern resoluteness, their ability to inflict pain and to regulate. The French became the epitome of ever-desired hard-ness. How to interrupt those circuits of power and tap some for the people? The answer may well have been through symbolic appropriation, through the rearranged circuitry of mimesis. In place of steel rifles, Hauka drilled with wooden ones. In the place of the Major's bullwhip—a real body regu-lator—they cracked whips fashioned from automobile fan belts. In place of immaculate uniforms, they wore inverted gourds or pith helmets if they could find them. Hauka walked and talked like soldiers. They held meet-ings like soldiers at the end of which they made declarations—to refuse to pay taxes in the early years, for example. Although the guns, whips, and uniforms might not have been exact copies of the "originals," the (military) protocol, to paraphrase Jean Rouch's text in *Les maitres fous*, remained the same.

The origin of the Hauka in 1925, however, marked only the beginning of a politically and culturally significant phenomenon. The Hauka shared much with other embodied oppositions in British and French West Africa. Like Baule "colons," Igbo *mbari* houses, and Yoruba *ouimbo* masquerades, Hauka appropriated European facial gestures, postures, gaits, speech and body movements. Unlike the Baule, Igbo, and Yoruba examples, however, Hauka also directly mimed the European bureaucracy that regulated the bodies of their mediums. Unlike other West African examples of embodied oppositions, moreover, Hauka was also a pluri-ethnic, transnational phenomenon. The Hauka flew to Niger on the wings of the wind of the east, the Harmattan, which originated along the African shores of the Red Sea. Never a soft breeze, the wind carried the Hauka farther south and west to the Gold Coast, the Mecca of Hauka, *their* ultimate destination.

CHAPTER NINE

Transgressing to the Gold Coast

· · ·

Migration from Niger to the Gold Coast has a long history, and so by the time the Hauka first visited Niger, the trails to the Gold Coast were well worn. Migrants followed long-established slave routes. Early migrants like Alpha Hano and Gaziri, the nineteenth-century leaders of a band of Zarma mercenaries, traveled on horseback to Dagbon in the north central region of the Gold Coast. From there they went north to Gurunsi lands which they plundered for more than 40 years.[1] The great majority of migrants, as discussed earlier, travelled from Niger to the Gold Coast during the colonial period. In the early years, most of them walked from Niamey to Kumasi or Accra. As time passed many more traveled at least part of the way on trucks and trains. No matter the route or the means of transportation, the Gold Coast was the Mecca for literally hundreds of thousands of migrants seeking some escape from the economic and social privations of French colonial rule in Niger and Mali.

The migrants from the north may have travelled light, but they never left home empty-handed. They brought with them their longstanding pride, their inestimable energy, and their religious practices. These men from the north built mosques in Kumasi and Accra; one of them, Mounkaiba, erected a Hauka spirit compound in a forest in the south of the Gold Coast. High priest of the Gold Coast Hauka in the 1940s and 1950s, Mounkaiba succeeded Ousmane Fodie, the Hauka's first high priest in Ghana.

The Hauka in the Gold Coast. Photo by Jean Rouch, *Les maitres fous.* Courtesy, The Center for Visual Communication.

According to Jean Rouch, the Hauka came to the Gold Coast around 1929 and first appeared during dances staged in Asuom. The Hauka spread quickly to Kumasi and Accra. Rouch suggests that it was Ousmane Fodie's priestly zeal that propelled the Hauka far and wide in the Gold Coast. As we have seen in the previous chapter, however, the power of Hauka mimetic practices were likely to have struck resonant chords in the migrant enclaves of the Gold Coast.[2]

Like Zibo of Chikal, the life of Ousmane Fodie, for which there are but the scantiest details, seems fascinating and unusual. Ousmane Fodie was born in Dosso, Niger, and served—he was most certainly drafted—in the British Army during World War I, meaning that Ousmane Fodie had been subjected to British as well as French colonial culture. We don't know when or where he was conscripted (probably in Nigeria), or where or when he served. We don't know if he was one of the Hauka "ringleaders" whom the French exiled beyond the borders of Niger. We do know from Rouch's texts that one year after his arrival in the Gold Coast, Ousmane Fodie had become the high priest of the Hauka.[3]

From 1930 to 1935 the Hauka performed their rites in the southern Gold Coast without incident. In 1935, however, Rouch's informant, Tyiri Gao, the spirit-possession priest of Kumasi, spoke of a violent dispute between a Hauka medium—most probably spirit possessed—and a young Hausa woman. As a result the colonial authorities outlawed further Hauka ceremonies. Forty days after this decree had been issued, a span of time which corresponds to the Muslim period of mourning, Ousmane Fodie called a "meeting" of all the Hauka mediums in the Gold Coast, a meeting which amounted to a full-fledged spirit-possession dance. In Tyiri Gao's words:

> The celebration began about seven o'clock in the morning, but at noon the police arrested everyone. That evening, a guitar player played in the prison. The Hauka possessed their dancers. They broke down the prison door and escaped. Then, that same night, two fires broke out. In Koforidua the church burned, half the village of Kibi burned, and eight Hauka dancers were killed; the governor of the Gold Coast became alarmed—Is it because we arrested the Hauka that in only one night there have been so many accidents? Who are these Hauka? The governor ordered Ousmane Fode and Amani to explain what the Hauka were. The governor authorized them to have a place in Nsawam, Accra, and Akwatia. In this way the Hauka remained in the Gold Coast.[4]

Rouch was unable to determine if Tyiri Gao's story corresponded to real events, but said that the "Golden Age of the Hauka" in the Gold Coast began in 1935 and lasted to 1943, the year that Ousmane Fodie died.

Tyiri Gao's account underscores the considerable evolution of the Hauka. His tale bears some resemblance to El Hadj Mohammadou's story of the origin of the Hauka in Filingue in 1927. In both accounts, Hauka spirit-possession activities provoked local and regional colonial officials. In both cases, the Hauka were officially outlawed, thrown into jail, and publicly humiliated. There are other points in common. In Niger, the French authorities harshly punished the people associated with the Hauka. The ringleaders were expelled. Other mediums fled to the hinterland or to such other colonial territories as the Ivory Coast, Upper Volta and the Gold Coast. In the Gold Coast, the Hauka high priest, much like Zibo a decade earlier, arranged a ceremony to challenge the colonial authorities. Although the British authorities arrested the Hauka mediums, their spirits soon came into their bodies, and, like the arrested Hauka in Niamey, they broke out of jail.

There the resemblance between the two accounts ends. For, in Niger, the putative jailbreak prompted harsh reprisals from Major Croccichia. In the Gold Coast, by contrast, the Hauka allegedly escaped and fires erupted. Like their mercurial "father" Dongo, the Gold Coast Hauka took their revenge by burning villages. Whereas, in Niger, the French would have in all likelihood responded to such defiance by fining villagers and imprisoning the *malfaiteurs* (precisely their tactic in dealing with the "agitations" of the Hauka in 1925 and 1927), in the Gold Coast, the Governor wondered if the colonial officials' imprisonment of the Hauka had caused "all these accidents." In the face of such brute power, which was, unbeknownst to him, an expression of the mythic power of Dongo, he asked "Who are the Hauka?"[5]

Tyiri Gao's story also suggests that the Hauka's indomitable force compelled the Governor of the Gold Coast to invite Ouseman Fodie to his palace. He wanted to educate himself about this violent and potentially dangerous force. After their "roundtable" discussion, the Governor revoked the order banning the Hauka and allowed them to perform their rites at three designated sites.

Confronted by the putative challenge of British colonial authority, the Hauka reacted with the fury of Dongo, a fury that could not be ignored. In this way the British Governor presented the Hauka with a colonial stamp of approval; accordingly, the Hauka celebrated a sweet victory which led to their Golden Age in a faraway land.

Evidence from Rouch suggests that after 1935, the Hauka could stage ceremonies without official interference. Lack of interference did not mean acceptance, however. The autochthonous populations of the southern Gold Coast found Hauka ceremonies bestial, a similar reaction to that of the established religious orders in Niger.[6] The popularity of the Hauka nonetheless increased among the migrant communities in the southern Gold Coast.

Since most of the Nigeriens in the Gold Coast migrated seasonally, there was a great deal of two-way traffic along the old slave routes.[7] Hauka mediums undoubtedly took part in these migratory comings and goings. Following the events of 1927 there is no mention of Hauka "agitations" in Niger. But in 1937, two years into the "Golden Age" of the Gold Coast Hauka, Brachet took note of more "agitations" in Tondigandia, the site of the first Hauka manifestations. This time a man named Hima Wakou sparked the unrest after his return from a long trip to the Gold Coast. As before,

> There were new late night meetings, refusals to obey the chief, dog, sheep and chicken sacrifices—a fetishist agitation that troubled the inhabitants. Hima became the leader of a certain number of young men who had returned from the Gold Coast. In April of 1937, P. Pinyard had convoked them, but they refused to budge. The head of the subdivision went to Kobi and found there open opposition to his orders among the young men coming from the Gold Coast. He punished Diga, the village chief, Dougaza and Natoni, the clan chiefs, Tassaky, a former infantry man, Alimine and Koarakoy and Timbo, also young men who had come back from the Gold Coast with disciplinary prison sentences. Two days later, Sinka, the sorcerer, Sala, Siddo, Alou and 15 people from Kobi left for Niamey to complain. Sinka was given a disciplinary prison sentence and the affair ended there.[8]

But "the affair" didn't end there. Hima Wadou seemed to have gotten away. Perhaps he returned to the Gold Coast? We also know that a similar series of events occurred in Tondigandia in 1941. Migrants continued to leave Niger for the Gold Coast, where they joined Zabrama communities in which Hauka priests staged periodic Hauka ceremonies.

Les Maitres Fous

By the time Jean Rouch and Roger Rosfelder first traveled to Accra and Kumasi in 1951-52 the Hauka were well established in the Gold Coast. Following Ousmane Fodie's death in 1943, it appears that the Hauka cults remained active in several of the major cities of the southern Gold Coast.[9] Mounkaiba, a migrant cocoa farmer, had replaced Ousmane Fodie as the Hauka high priest.[10] In 1954 Rouch returned to the Gold Coast and screened some of his films. He made contact with the Hauka in Accra and they invited him to film their yearly festival at Mounkaiba's compound. This trip resulted in Rouch's incomparable, *Les maitres fous*, Europe's first underdetermined take on the Hauka. Because of its unequivocable directness, *Les maitres fous* is considered one of documentary cinema's most controversial films.[11]

Much has been written about *Les maitres fous*, but most of this scholarship—including my own—has neglected the mimetic power of Hauka images. For most writers and for Jean Rouch himself, *Les maitres fous* is an indictment of colonial culture in West Africa, a classic and powerfully evocative examination of cultural resistance.[12] George DeVos suggests that the power of the film devolves from its brutal honesty.[13] Rena Bensmaia writes that *Les maitres fous* captures the essence of British colonialism in the Gold Coast: the British exploitation of Africa.[14] My own initial readings of the film focused on Rouch's attempt to document exotic alterity. His camera creates a surreal scene of spirit-possessed men who sacrifice and eat dogs and who, without bodily harm, thrust their hands into pots of boiling dog stew. Rouch's purpose, I have suggested, is Artaudian shock: he wants his images to jolt his audience—Europeans, mostly—into awareness, change.[15] The primary supposition in this writing is that *Les maitres fous* is a film about the articulation of colonial tensions, about how the powerless are able to resist, albeit only theatrically, the racism and terror of those who dominate them.

Those readings of the film—and the Hauka phenomenon—focus more on the politics embedded in the moment than on the memories embodied in the Hauka themselves. Such readings also assume that Hauka spirit possession represents something, perhaps a body of articulations, that constitutes a counterhegemonic colonial discourse. It would be foolish to contest such apposite insights.

And yet readings that consider the Hauka phenomenon as one of many examples of colonial resistance and counter-discourse (which I don't deny) describe and analyze only one of two dimensions that the Hauka shape. The second dimension, of course, is that of sheer, brutal power—the ever-present, ever-feared and ever-respected force of Dongo—which is tapped though mimesis. As noted in Chapter Three, Michael Taussig's *Mimesis and Alterity* zones in on one side—our side—of the Hauka power equation. The Hauka, he argues, copy us with brute honesty, and such refraction troubles Taussig and others who have squirmed in their seats during screenings of *Les maitres fous*. And yet the Hauka are separated from us by time, space and screen. What is it, then, about the images of the film that trouble us so? What is it about the film that so revolts us? Surely, it is something more than the excess

***Les maitres fous* engaging in sacrifice.** Photo by Jean Rouch, *Les maitres fous.* Courtesy, The Center for Visual Communication.

of a particularly gruesome symbolic inversion. Taussig suggests that the force of such distant power devolves from the mimetic excess—an overloaded circuit, without a breaker—of mechanical reproduction, the surfeit of mimetic power found in the cinema.

> The film with its ability to explore the optical unconscious, to come close and enlarge, to frame and to montage, creates . . . a suffusion of mimetic magic. Here film borrows from the magical practice of mimesis in its very filming of it. The primitivism within modernism is allowed to flower. In this colonial world where the camera meets those possessed by gods, we can truly point to the Western rebirth of the mimetic faculty by means of modernity's mimetic machinery.[16]

On the participant side of the screen, we can also point to the reinforcement of the mimetic faculty in West Africa through the framework of spirit possession—a longstanding attempt by Songhay and others tap into circuits of natural and political power.

Jean Rouch once said that the Hauka disappeared after Ghanaian independence. "There are no Hauka deities," he once said, "named Kwame Nkrumah."[17] Perhaps they disappeared in Ghana, but not in Niger. Even in 1994, Hauka continue to mimic Europeans and Europeanized Africans in the villages and cities of western Niger. Rouch's statement is one that partially isolates the Hauka from their history and the cultural context of their appearance in West Africa. If the Hauka "represent" anti-colonial discourse, how and why do they continue to attract adepts in the post-colony? How have they survived the "rupture" of independence? Why have they flourished in contemporary western Niger?

Clearly the Hauka, just like contemporary regimes of African post-colonies, compel us to explore the textures, contours, sounds, and embed-ded memories of new analytical terrain.[18] As Mbembe points out, quite correctly, the old binary oppositions of resistance/passivity, subject-ion/autonomy are not useful. As we can see in the case of the Hauka, these categories can actually "cloud," to use Mbembe's language, our compre-hension of (post)colonial relations in Africa—and elsewhere.

Taussig understands quite well the power of cinema to frame and mold images of the Hauka. Possessed gods possess a camera held by an admit-tedly entranced filmmaker, all of which produces a magically reproduced surfeit of mimetic force: power oozes from the mouths of the gods, making European audiences squirm and sweat in their seats. But the images of *Les maitres fous* also unsettle African film audiences, especially those filled with intellectuals, for whom the brutal scenes of spirit-possessed black men chomping on a freshly slaughtered dog reinforce racist, primitivist stereotypes of the Dark Continent.[19]

And what about popular audiences in West Africa? Ghanaians of all reli-gious persuasions denounced the "bestial" nature of the Hauka, even though most of them had never seen *Les maitres fous.* In the Zabrama community of the Gold Coast, Muslim clerics denounced the Hauka in the same manner as Muslim clerics denounced them a generation earlier in Niger: they were the devil (*Iblis*) who had taken the bodies of black-skinned infidels. Despite these condemnations—or, perhaps, because of them—Hauka flew back to Niger "on the wings of the western wind." They landed in Niamey, Dogondoutche, Dosso, Ouallam, Tillaberi, Ayoru, Tera, Dargol, and Wanzerbe, where, even after independence, they took new mediums and attracted new audiences.

Once they returned to Niger, how did the Hauka portray themselves? On numerous occasions over the years I saw gods mimicking Europeans. Comedians and masters of exaggeration, the gods of force sometimes held burning bushes in their hands and ate poisonous plants, sacrificed dogs and knocked down mud-brick walls with their heads, all the while maintaining a rigid military bearing: stiff legs, squared shoulders, erect postures, precisely mechanized drill movements, including salutes, about-faces, attention, and formal salutation (hand shaking). As rigid disciplinarians, Hauka ordered their people—the Nigerien audience—to follow orders and obey decrees. The Hauka threatened them with reprisals if they did not—threats that most certainly evoked for some the force of the no-nonsense French military administration in Niger. Although Hauka mimicry often made audiences laugh, they also used their extraordinary power to frighten people. "Do what we say," one Hauka told me in 1987, or else!" "Or else," Adamu Jenitongo once told me, meant "burned villages, burned granaries, burned fields, burned minds (boiling head, in Songhay)—the fiery fury of Dongo and his offspring, the Hauka. In a very real sense, the Hauka make the case that they are beings who have tapped into European power, a power they openly express through word and deed. That makes them frightful. Like the European, they demand rigid discipline, unflinching respect, and unwavering loyalty—or else!

The birth, growth and ongoing presence of the Hauka is not, then, exclusively a representation of counterhegemonic colonial discourse; nor is it simply a capsulized reflection of "la rupture coloniale." It is also the electroshocking appropriation of European power—through the mimetic faculty.

The true test of Hauka power, however, comes not in 1925, not in 1927, not during their "Golden Age" in the Gold Coast, not on some dusty dune in western Niger during the early years of Niger's postcolony. Rather, it comes when the *Les maitres fous* take leave of their dusty village dunes and fly to Niger's capital, Niamey. During the second government of the Republic of Niger, a military regime, they sweep into the presidential palace, which was then controlled by the late General Seyni Kountche, himself a Hauka medium. In time, *Les maitres fous* become *le maitre fous*, who, as we shall see in Part Four, ingeniously mimed the Hauka mimicry of the French military to empower his regime. The force of the Hauka might prod the people forward along his path of power and glory.

Transforming State Power

The Hauka Movement in the Postcolony of Niger

Crossing Ceremonial Boundaries

• • •

Boundary crossings are sometimes dangerous; they always involve premeditated risk. Sometimes boundaries mark a space of challenge. As one approaches a line, one considers the risks and decides to cross or not to cross the boundary. One thinks of Gaddafi's "line of death," which the US Navy crossed without one sailor dying. The U.S. Admirals knew that Gaddafi could hardly challenge the might of the American Navy.

Boundaries of all sorts crisscross the spirit world in western Niger. Some are permanent, invisibly separating the spirit and social worlds. Others are fleeting as when spirit priests trace a magic circle (*kelle*) into which the uninitiated are not allowed. What happens when such a boundary is crossed?

Take the following story, which I paraphrase, told to me by the late Sorko Mounmouni Koda of Mehanna. Sorko Mounmouni tells a tale of Dongo, the "father" of the Hauka, the Songhay spirit who burns villages, punishes people who disobey him, and executes those who insult him.

During one rainy season lightening struck and killed several farmers in their fields, near Niamey, capital of Niger. From the vantage of some Nigeriens, these sorts of deaths are attributable to Dongo's displeasure; they also prompt spirit-possession priests to organize a Dongo *hori*, a ceremony at which people ask Dongo how to avoid more suffering and death. Accordingly, a Niamey spirit-possession priest organized such a ceremony.

Before long Dongo shuddered into the body of a frail old woman dressed in homespun indigo cloth—Dongo's cloth. Dongo roared at the crowd, wagging his forefinger at people as he pranced around the priest's compound. With the same forefinger, Dongo drew a line in the sand, again wagging his finger. The priest interpreted the gesture.

"Anyone who crosses Dongo's line will die," he said.

The din of the audience subsided as a tall barrel-chested man dressed in fatigues and a red beret marched up to Dongo's line. "You are all devils," he was reported as saying. "This is the product of charlatans." He pointed to Dongo, now dressed in his flowing black robe. "You are not Dongo," he thundered, "you are nothing but an old woman."

People in the audience moved away from the soldier, who by his dress was probably a border patrolman. He spoke again: "I will show you that these devil dances are nothing but a ruse. I will cross this boundary."

At that, the soldier crossed the boundary and collapsed on the sand. Someone hailed a taxi. People carried the soldier to the taxi so he might be rushed off to the hospital. No one knew for sure what happened to him, but someone said that he died before he reached the hospital.

As in the case of Tyiri Gao's story of the Hauka jailbreak and the eruption of fires in the Gold Coast, there is no way to determine the veracity of the tale. But surely this question of veracity here is beside the point. These kinds of stories are part and parcel of the Dongo mystique, which is primarily a mystique about fiery, unexplained power that frightens people. The story also reveals sociopolitical cleavages among spirit-possession players (deities, mediums and others), the military (the military, police, educated civil servants), and Muslims (some of whom are members of the educated elite, some of whom are peasants (*teleke*). In short Dongo's power overwhelms that of the Islamically inspired, partially educated, French-speaking soldier. Taken as a metanymn, Dongo's power overpowers the forces that govern Niger, supplanting that of invincible Allah. Dongo commands respect and generates fear. Lest we forget, the French colonial military commanded just such respect and terror and used it to govern the Colony of Niger with a firm hand. The Hauka, as we have seen, used the mimetic faculty to tap into this perceived power. Although the specific identities of some of the characters in this play may have changed in the postcolony of Niger, the dynamics of power relations have remained virtually the same.

CHAPTER TEN

Independence and the Postcolony of Niger

◆　　◆　　◆

The postcolony is a chaotic, fragmented entity, the pluralities of which defy business-as-usual scholarly analysis. And yet there is some regularity in the postcolony's chaos. Just as the seemingly infinite mutable patterns in cloud movements or gushing streams have "structures," so in the complex chaos of the postcolony there is what Mbembe calls an "internal coherence."[1] Indeed, postcolonies are characterized by a system of signs—a discourse—in which the state creates significantly empty symbols—veritable simulacra. The postcolony,

> is not, however, just an economy of signs in which power is mirrored or *imagined* self-reflectedly. The postcolony is characterized by a distinctive art of improvisation, by a tendency to excess and disproportion as well as by distinctive ways in which identities are multiplied, transformed, and put into circulation. It is likewise made up of a series of corporate institutions, and apparatuses which, once they are deployed, constitute a distinctive regime of violence.[2]

Mbembe also argues that postcolonies in Africa at least consist of what he calls, "the commandament," the French term used to mark a colonial regime that wields absolute power and that tolerates nothing less than total discipline and obeisance.[3]

And yet, Mbembe does not suggest that the postcolony is brutally and simply a regime of terror. For him, postcolonial relations cannot be reduced to analyses of domination, resistance, and collaboration; they are

Hamani Diori, First President of the Republic of Niger. Courtesy, Office National de le'Edition et de Press.

much more complex and subtle. In postcolonies, he suggests, there emerges a certain conviviality that familiarizes and domesticates power relations and leads not to resistance, but to the "zombification" of the *commandament* and their subjects. Considering Reagan's regime in the United States, for example, one can add that mutual zombification is not unique to the African postcolony. The conviviality and complicity of power relations in Reagan's America lead to a certain kind of impotence. Reagan happily took naps as the nation felicitously went to sleep.

Just as quotidian rituals, advertising rites, and political myth-making led to a remarkable period of "political success" in Reagan's America, so in the postcolony routine rituals reinforced ". . . the commandament's own institutionalization (its *recherche hegemonique*) in its capacity as a fetish to which the subject is bound . . . "[4] At the same time, the subject in the postcolony displays ". . . a talent for play and a sense of fun which makes him *homo ludens par excellence,*"[5] Such capacity and necessity for play, of course, split the postcolonial subject's identity into so many fragments—peasant, laborer, member of the party, member of an ethnic group, Muslim, Christian, citizen.

In this chapter, the Republic of Niger is considered as a chaotic and fragmented postcolony that exhibits most, if not all, of the attributes that Mbembe articulates. The space of the postcolony, as we shall see in Chapter Eleven, is one that nourished the Hauka, who, after all, have been *spiritus ludentes par excellence.*

Movements Toward Independence

Prior to World War II, the French regime in Niger was in Mbembe's language, the *commandament,* a colonial government that used terror, real or perceived, to maintain iron-fisted rule. Following World War II, several factors lead to growing sociopolitical change in colonial Niger. First, there emerged in the late 1940s a small elite which gained a degree of legitimacy at the expense of "traditional" chiefs whom the French had used to collect taxes, supply labor, and enforce discipline. In opposition to these chiefs, the new educated elite stressed economic development, which, they hoped, would steer Niger onto the path of independence. Second, there appeared a small working class in major towns. These workers had aims and interests similar to those of the new elite. Third, the French reconstituted their colonial empire under the Fourth Republic, which meant that Africans, no longer the completely powerless *sujets* of the *indigenat*, could run for office and represent their peoples in the French Parliament.

Change in the metropolitan political climate brought on an era of West African electoral politics. In 1946, a group of educated Nigeriens formed the Parti Progressiste Nigerien (PPN) which was affiliated with the Francophone West African, Rassemblement Democratique Africaine (RDA). As Robert Charlick suggests, the great majority of the PPN leaders were not from chiefly families. As commoners, they promoted a vigorous program of socioeconomic development that would supplant traditional authority following independence.[6] Indeed, the PPN chose Hamani Diori, a commoner, as their candidate for the French Parliament. He was elected in 1946.

In a colony governed by colonial and chiefly authority, the PPN had a very narrow electoral base. Since he initially viewed the PNN as a radical force, Colonial Governor Toby worked assiduously to splinter its growing power. And why not? PPN members routinely "agitated" in the country-side to weaken the hold of collaborationist chiefs, the lynch pins in the French machine of colonial governance.

These were the radical years of Diori and his PPN cohorts. Toby's politics of fragmentation worked well—at first. In 1948 Toby lent his support to a rival, more conservative party, the Union Nigerienne des Independants et Sympathisants (UNIS). PPN, which had been allied to the French Communist Party, fared badly in that year's elections. PPN quickly realized that they needed French support to win future elections. Ever the political pragmatists, PPN severed its ties with the communists and allied themselves with a right-center party. In the cities, their stronghold, PPN continued its "agitation" politics, their attempt to undermine chiefly authority. In the rural areas, however, they bribed local leaders to bring in the vote and fanned the fires of ethnic divisiveness. This partial ideological transformation made the PPN more palatable to the French and laid the foundation for the first regime of the Republic of Niger.

Not all the leaders of the PPN agreed with the pragmatic politics of Hamani Diori. Djibo Bakari, Diori's cousin, founded the Union Democratique Nigerienne (UDN) in 1954, an overtly radical party which appealed to oppressed peasants in the countryside and downtrodden workers in cities. Being a trans-ethnic party, Djibo built a substantial electoral base. He organized a Youth League and a Free Women's Association, the aims of which were to create new sociopolitical structures in rural areas. These radical organisms posed major threats to existing rural authority. When the new Socialist Government of France replaced Governor Toby with a socialist colonial governor in 1955, Djibo pragmatically switched the UDN's affiliation from the French Communist to the French Socialist party. In 1956 the radical UDN formed an improbable coalition with the Bloc Nigerien d'Action (BNA), a rurally based, conservative party of traditional interests. The French supported this coalition, according to Charlick, because they thought it represented the best opportunity for economic reform. In May 1957 the UDN-BNA took control of the national government.[7]

Given the imminence of independence, Djibo Bakari, the leader of the coalition, seemed to be on his way to becoming the Republic of Niger's first president. Then came General de Gaulle's Fifth Republic and the great choice: to remain or depart from the French Community. To remain meant self-rule with little international autonomy. To depart meant ". . . immediate independence from France against President Charles de Gaulle's explicit wishes, and . . . the . . . risk . . . of . . . a total break with France."[8]

Two weeks before the referendum, Djibo announced his decision to seek immediate independence. He renamed his party, *Sawaba*, which in Hausa means "freedom." France's response was immediate. De Gaulle dispatched a forceful new governor, Don Juan Colombani, who quickly took measures to crush the *Sawaba* Party. Colombani used his office to persuade Nigeriens to remain in the French community. When the vote was tallied on September 28, 1958, eighty percent of the voters elected to cast their fate with France. Colombani indicated that he would support the parties that had resisted *Sawaba*. Djibo's government resigned on October 19, 1958.

The Governor disbanded the old National Assembly and called new elections, in which the PPN-dominated Union Pour la Communaute Franco-African (UCFA) won the majority of the National Assembly seats. In the election Djibo as well as Hamani Diori lost their bids for the National Assembly. On December 18, 1958 France declared Niger a republic in the

French Community. Emerging miraculously unscathed from his electoral defeat, Hamani Diori was named President. Historian and author Boubou Hama became President of the National Assembly.

> In the space of the next twenty months the PPN, aided extensively by its French advisors and the French police, established the outlines of a repressive one-party regime in Niger. One by one, opposition organizations were banned, and rights to oppose the regime were limited. Early in 1959 all political meetings were outlawed, and Sawaba supporters were physically beaten in several demonstrations. Sawaba deputies to the National Assembly were refused permission to speak, and in May 1959 they were simply barred from the chamber and replaced with PPN deputies following an annulment of the December 1958 election returns from Zinder and Tessoua.[9]

Indeed, Niger had become, for all intents and purposes, a postcolony. The new Government designed its administrative practices to create ". . . a world of meanings all of its own, a mastercode . . . "[10] In so doing the Diori regime started a government newspaper, *Les Temps du Niger*, broadcast messages from a government radio station, and outlawed opposition labor unions while promoting its own. In this way, the Diori regime attempted ". . . to institutionalize its world of meanings as a 'socio-historical world,' and to make that world fully real, turning it into a part of people's common sense not only by instilling in the minds of its *cibles* [or 'target population'], but also in the imaginary of an epoque."[11] Such consolidation of power propelled Niger toward formal independence on August 3, 1960.

Diori in His Postcolony

Like many of the first presidents of the former French colonies of West Africa, Hamani Diori had a profound French connection. He was born in Soudoure, which is near Niamey. As an adolescent, the French selected him along with his compatriot, Boubou Hama, to attend the prestigious William Ponty School in Dakar. Trained as a primary school teacher and a translator, Nigeriens elected Diori to the French Parliament in 1946, which meant that he spent increasing amounts of time in Paris. Early on, Diori seemed quite the political pragmatist, shifting his "radical" party from the left to the right center in 1954 to impress Governor Jean Toby. After Djibo Bakari proclaimed his Sawaba Party in 1958, the French Governor, Colombari, gave his support to those, including Diori, who had "resisted" the "radical separatists." Even with French support, Diori lost his reelection bid in 1958. No matter. The victorious UCFA snatched him from the jaws of defeat and named him President of the Republic of Niger. Taking cues from ever-present French advisors, the unelected president built an oppressive single-party government. Diori most certainly owed his presidential appointment, like much else in his life, to French support. In the "presidential system" he constructed, Diori vested himself with absolute and complete power, relying, once again, upon the aid and advice of the French army and police, both of which were garrisoned in Niamey. From atop his edifice of power, Diori tolerated no opposition, no insubordination. As Charlick argues, " . . . Diori's priorities were clear: to create a powerful state to manage these threats (from political opponents) and to consolidate his own position and the power of his inner group . . . "[12]

Diori's reliance on the French continued throughout his regime. Several military officers attempted to oust him in 1963. His greatest threat, though, came from the Sawaba, which in 1964 mounted a feeble attack against his Government. In 1965, a Sawaba agent attempted to assassinate him. As Charlick notes, Diori used these events to tighten his control. He created a Presidential Guard and a secret police force, the latter headed by a trusted French intelligence official, Jean Colombani.[13]

Following these abortive attempts at sabotage, Diori gained a firm and commanding hold on power. An era of relative prosperity and tranquillity ensued. Diori earned the reputation as a lavish party-giver who hosted expensive receptions at the Presidential Palace for official events like Republic Day (August 3) or Independence Day (December 18). In 1970, Diori held a reception for Peace Corps Volunteers. The lavishness of the reception overwhelmed—and pleased—many of us who attended. Several sheep had been slaughtered and roasted. Large supplies of traditional Nigerien dishes—all spicy and aromatic—had been wonderfully prepared. There was much to drink. And to make us even giddier, the President and his wife, Aissa, personally hosted the event, which was held on the patio of the Presidential Palace, sitting on a bluff majestically overlooking the Niger River. The President spoke of how proud he was to meet young Americans willing to live in the bush and learn Nigerien languages.

While Diori consolidated his power and successfully charmed Peace Corps volunteers, his wife, Aissa, used her eminent position to build a fortune. A beautiful Fulan woman for whom the greatest wealth resided in cattle, she increased exponentially the size of her herd, which was tended on a large farm along the Niger River, west and south of Niamey. Like other members of Diori's inner circle, she also invested brilliantly in real estate. The owner of scores of villas in Niamey's fashionable Plateau neighborhood, she rented her dwellings to diplomats and French Cooperants (technical and "development" experts, professors, financial and security advisors) for high prices.

During this period of consolidation, Diori coveted close ties to the French. He relied increasingly on the advice of his personal security advisor Jean Colombani. Even on Sundays, Colombani would sometimes attend Diori's weekly English conversations with Peace Corps Volunteers.

His power secure, Diori embarked on plan to extend his power to rural areas. In the countryside, as Diori well realized, people often felt little or no allegiance to the postcolony. Diori called this program "Animation," which

> was primarily designed to produce a breakthrough in agricultural production and export revenues. It was hoped that this breakthrough could be accomplished by establishing channels for 'mass' participation controlled by the state. Participation in newly structured cooperatives, it was believed, was to be the key to increasing the productivity of small farmers. By establishing cooperatives based on such natural sociological units as the village community, Diori's advisers hoped to attract the willing and enthusiastic participation of rural producers.[14]

To implement this scheme to increase the production of cash crops, Diori established a new government agency which recruited village representatives as links to the national government—a way of recircuiting power in the countryside.

The scheme, which in some ways reassembled the early PPN program of rural "agitation," failed miserably, probably for the same reasons that early PPN "agitation" had little impact. Confronted with schemes of the urban modernizers, rural peoples remained suspicious. The apt Songhay proverb,

> gondi bero gusu, a go no, a si no, naane si,
> (If one doesn't know if the big snake is in its hole, he or she lacks confidence
> [to step over it]),

suggests that if one lacks confidence he or she hesitates to embrace the unknown. Rural peasants often told me in 1969 and 1970 that they didn't trust the government and its "unknown" programs.

One could argue that Diori designed his animation program as a symbol devoid of meaning, a simulacrum, in Jean Baudriard's sense. The same could be said for Diori's party, the PPN, which Diori and others built to win elections. Following Diori's presidential appointment, the Party played, at best, a tenuous national role. Through benevolent neglect Diori allowed the PPN to decay. Run down *maisons du parti*, which could still be found in most of Niger's towns in the late 1960s and early 1970s, testified to the PPN's obsolescence. For most rural peasants, the PPN stood, purely and simply, for extortion. Each time I took a bush taxi between Tillaberi and Niamey in 1970 and 1971, police stopped our vehicle and asked to see papers. If peasants had no papers, the police forced them to join the Party—for 300 francs CFA. Party membership card in hand, the police happily permitted them to proceed on their journey.

Following 1968, the Diori regime had no program other than its own self-maintenance. The extravagant state rituals at the lavishly appointed Presidential Palace stood as symbols of the Nigerien postcolony, symbols of rampant corruption, of the elite's insouciance in the face of such increasingly difficult problems as a lackluster economy, persistent drought, and incipient famine. Like his colonial predecessors, Diori had a singular response to administrative failure: raise taxes. According to Charlick, the Government of Niger took up to 40% of the rural peasant's income.

> As the drought intensified in 1973 and rural incomes declined dramatically, efforts to collect taxes became more persistent and brutal. When village headmen failed to produce the stipulated tax receipts, they were beaten and occasionally jailed, and when villagers could not pay their taxes, the police and agents of the traditional chiefs confiscated their tangible property, including seed, farm tools, and even cooking utensils.[15]

As the suffering in Niger reached epic proportions, so did the Diori Government's theft of international food relief shipments. In response to a student strike, Diori dispatched the army to break it and sentenced the ring leaders to ten years in prison.

Diori's support rapidly dissipated and the Nigerien Army overthrew him on April 15, 1974. Diori thought that his fall from grace devolved directly from the withdrawal of French support. That is incontestable. He also thought that the French opposed him because of the growing Islamization of Niger. In an interview published in *Jeune Afrique* in 1984,

Aissa Diori, Niger's Premier First Lady. Courtesy, Office National de l'Edition et de Press.

Diori said that "In February of 1974, it was decided that Saudi Arabia, Libya and Morocco would augment their aid to Niger, which would promote the spread of Islam and the teaching of Arabic. That was very badly taken by Paris."[16] Given the riches of Niger's uranium reserves, he suggested, France was worried that Niger might escape from the French sphere of influence. Diori went on to say that the French organized the *coup d'état.* During the period of his greatest power, the French had agreed to intervene militarily if there were a threat to Diori's regime. Even though the French military in Niger could have easily crushed the Nigerien Army, they elected to do nothing. "In particular, Michel Jobert, who was then at the Elysee," Diori suggested, "refused to intervene with French troops."[17]

In short order, the military arrested Diori and other high-ranking notables. During the palace raid, they killed Diori's wife Aissa, who openly resisted the attack. Diori's location in the postcolony shifted from the Presidential Palace to a military prison. In the end, it seems that he still knew little about the dire difficulties of the peasant's life in his postcolony.

CHAPTER ELEVEN

Peasant and Hauka in Niger's Postcolony

• • •

In Diori's postcolony, political malpractices precipitated the kind of zombification of which Mbembe and others have written. In his time Diori lived comfortably, lavishing upon himself and his family the spoils of power: increasing amounts of money stolen from public funds. They invested this hot money in Niamey real estate, spent it on the purchase and upkeep of mansions in Normandy, and deposited it in Swiss bank accounts. Self-aggrandizement and enrichment can create, following Mbembe's argument, a very peaceful kind of insouciance. Why worry about drought, hunger, death and disease in the countryside? Why, indeed, when one enjoys a sweet life? It is such insouciant zombification that may well have prevented Diori from grasping the peasant's point of view or from comprehending the "colonial" ironies of the postcolony's political and administrative practices. These practices included, lest we forget, (1) a steep tax burden; (2) forced requisitions of grain, seed, and tools; (3) the use of chiefs and the military to collect taxes; and (4) stiff prison penalties for insubordination or open political dissent. As one weary peasant told me in Tera, Niger in 1969, "Nothing has changed." Indeed, in Diori's postcolony, considering the legacy of French colonialism in Niger, the players had changed, but the script remained very much the same.

If zombification is to work politically, however, it must be mutual. While the elite of the Diori regime basked in a zombified insouciance, many peasants yawned, shrugged their shoulders and blamed their plight on "fate," itself a very powerful form of zombification.

Peasants in Niger's Postcolony

From 1960 to 1974, Hamani Diori lived in the sumptuous air-conditioned comforts of Niger's Presidential Palace. A chef trained at the Cordon Bleu School in Paris prepared his meals.[1] For peace and quiet, he could stroll in the well-manicured palace gardens or repair to his wife's riverbank farm. Frequently he escaped the dust and heat of Niger to travel to Europe, Asia or other African capitals.

From 1960 to the present, Soumana Youcouba, a rural farmer, has lived in a mud-brick compound situated on a dune near Tillaberi's secondary school. He has had no running water, no electricity, no air-conditioning, no garden. His wife has never owned a riverbank farm. He periodically leaves Niger for Ouagadougou to collect his military pension. Soumana, who is Diori's age-mate, is a World War II veteran, who spent time in Europe as well as the Gold Coast.

At the end of World War II, Soumana resigned from the military and returned to the countryside to farm millet, sorghum and cow peas. He is still a strong man who can easily farm two or more fields. And yet, even the most arduous labors of the best farmers can sometimes yield nothing in the drought-plagued ecology of western Niger.

During many of our conversations, Soumana would sift sand through his hands. "This," he would say time after time, "is what I grow my millet in."[2]

From 1968 to 1974 rainfall dropped precipitously in the Sahel.[3] Each successive year brought lower millet yields. In 1973 and 1974 a great famine gripped Niger. Hundreds of thousands of people died; millions of people hungered for food. For Soumana Youcouba those years were tough ones. What was it like to live through a failed crop? Soumana claimed that 1973 and 1974 were difficult, but not as hard as the famine of 1984.[4]

The cool-dry season ended in mid-February 1984. The sun moved higher and higher in the sky, and the hot-dry season unfolded with temperatures reaching their peak in mid-April. In March, before it became too hot to work, Soumana cleared his fields. Foraging cows, sheep, and goats had devoured the millet stalks, leaving in their wake inedible stumps, which

Soumana uprooted on two successive mornings. His field now ready for planting, Soumana remained at home during the peak of the hot season (April-May). "No one goes to the fields during the hot season."[5] With good reason—shimmering heat burns one's skin. Hot season temperatures often exceed forty degrees centigrade (102 degrees Fahrenheit), and in Tillaberi, one of the hottest villages in Niger, they often climb to well above forty-five degrees centigrade.[6]

Something strange occurred in April of 1984; it rained, and rained hard. Called "mango rains" because they fall when mangoes are ripe for picking, these early downpours are blessings. They remove disease-carrying dust from the air, wiping out, for example, meningitis, which strikes western Niger in March and April. Convinced of a good season of rain, some Tillaberi farmers sowed their fields. Thinking the early rain a fluke, Soumana remained at home to wait for later rains, which came, in fact, in early May— also early for Tillaberi farmers. This time Soumana planted his field. Perhaps 1984 would be an extraordinary year. Two weeks after the May sowing, Soumana's millet germinated and emerged from the sandy soil.

Confident Tillaberi farmers spoke about record harvests. But overconfidence gave way to worry. The young millet plants needed additional rain to survive the intense May heat. The sky, however, remained cloudless, and hot, dry desert breezes swept across Tillaberi east to west, ensuring rainless days. Their millet plants dying in the dry heat, Tillaberi farmers watched the sky for rain, which, in 1984, did not come.

In 1984 Soumana's field yielded no millet. Most people in Tillaberi went hungry; some starved to death.

Soumana thought to the past, the bygone years when people respected age-old traditions.

> When I was younger in Nemega, we always had good harvests. That's because we followed our ancestors' path. Every year, we sacrificed a black bull to the genie of Nemega Mountain. Every year we staged a rain dance to appease the spirits. We respected our ancestors. We respected the spirits. And now, look at our fields. People today have no respect. They prefer to save the expense of sacrifice. But what does this stinginess bring? Look at our fields. Look![7]

The people to whom Soumana referred are, of course, the young, many of whom have never seen such rituals, and the educated elite, many of whom officially mock such beliefs and practices. For people like Soumana such mockery leads to disasters like the "demise" of the border patrolman who dared to cross Dongo's line of death, or the demise of millet crops which no longer grow along Dongo's path—the path of rain.

Soumana Yacouba's position in Niger's postcolony is one of increasing alienation. His increasing age alienates him. His ethnicity, Songhay, alienates him from the other ethnic groups in Niger (Zarma, Fulan, Tuareg, Arabs, Hausa, and Kanuri). These forms of alienation were no strangers to the members of the elite during the Diori regime. Early on, Diori's party, the PPN used longstanding ethnic enmities as a political tool—with much success.[8] Diori understood well the strong ties that bound traditional elites (chiefs and aristocrats) to local populations of peasants. But Diori, it seems, never fully understood the political importance of a widening trans-ethnic gulf separating modern elites and peasants. Issaka Boulhassane's visit to Mehanna, Niger, in 1977 is a case in point.

During one of his vacations in 1977 Issaka Boulhassane, a Songhay noble from the Mehanna region who had studied nursing in France, visited Mehanna and stayed with me for one week. I welcomed the company of this worldly gentleman who spoke four languages and who had versed himself in local lore. Then in his late forties, Issaka exuded robust health.

Issaka's arrival attracted swarms of relatives and other clients of his family. He gave gifts to his nieces and nephews, his aunts and uncles, his "brothers" and "sisters." And then came the clients who had been in service to his father: smiths, bards, musicians, all of whom received small gifts. And then came the destitute, for whom Issaka had reserved a few coins. He looked at me and smiled.

"I never leave Mehanna with money. You know what they say?"

"What?"

"If a noble is penniless, he will give you the shirt off his back."

For lunch and dinner the compound was filled with cronies who ate fine food: millet paste covered in oily peanut and tomato sauces. They washed down these delicacies with unfiltered river water. Despite my reserves of boiled and filtered water, Issaka, a state nurse in Niger with more than 20 years of experience, opted to drink the untreated river water. The disregard of his own professional preachings soon resulted in nausea and dysentery. I offered him clean water once again.

"I'll drink the same water as my brothers," Issaka said.

I soon understood the reason for Issaka's insistence on drinking untreated river water. One afternoon just before the two o'clock Muslim prayer, a local noble, one of Issaka's cousins, came into the compound.

"Is the *anasaara* there?"

"The *anasaara*?" I asked, perplexed. "I'm right here. I'm the *anasaara*."

"No, no. Not you," said the noble, a bit flustered. "I'm looking for Issaka."

Times had indeed changed. This man, Issaka, the son of a renowned chief, had been called an *anasaara*.

I asked Issaka about that incident when he returned from prayer. He told me that when people learn the European's language or live in the European's land, they, for many people, become Europeans. "It works the same way as the Songhay saying, *Boro kom, goro maiga windo ra, inga no maiga no.* (The person who lives in the nobles compound becomes a noble)."[9]

From the vantage of his Mehanna relatives, then, Issaka's exotic knowledge and experience made him other: strange, bizarre, and, in some matters, someone they could not trust. Events like his visit made Issaka painfully aware of his ambiguous social position in Mehanna. Suddenly and painfully, peasants added the attribute of exotic knowledge to the semantic field of *anasaara* traits. One Mehanna elder frankly admitted to me: "Once one of ours learns French, he is lost to us forever."

When Hamani Diori went off to the William Ponty School, he left his village forever. From the Nigerien peasant's point of view, Issaka Boulhassane had become a white man with black skin, and shared this putative trait with other members of the educated elite.

The cracks of this social cleavage first appeared during the latter part of the colonial period. They widened into a chasm during Diori's regime. Was Diori blithely unaware of the growing mutual suspicion and enmity between those who had and had not "read"? Perhaps he was well aware of the new social cleavage, but didn't care about it. How else can one explain an increase in the rural tax burden during the famine years? How else can one explain why he ordered the army to collect taxes and to requisition goods as people starved to death? Despite these gruesome excesses of power, however, there were no popular rebellions or uprisings during the last years of the Diori regime. One wonders why not? The answer may be that in the postcolony, zombification knows neither class nor regional boundaries.[10]

The Hauka in Niger's Postcolony

Did zombified independence in West Africa render the Hauka culturally, socially and politically superfluous? Jean Rouch reportedly thought so. As noted in Chapter Nine, Rouch argued that the Hauka movement had become irrelevant in independent Ghana; no Hauka called Kwame Nkrumah had appeared there. That, as I suggested earlier, is a reading that considers the Hauka purely and simply a reaction to colonial culture. Did Hauka spirit possession disappear completely in Ghana? Not necessarily. Following independence, many Songhay and Zarma men remained in Ghana, where they lived in the Zabrama neighborhoods of Accra, Kumasi, and Assuom. As foreigners in independent Ghana, they were likely to be as dispossessed as they had been during British rule. Evidence suggests, more-over, that Ghanaians did not much care for the Zabrama.[11] Indeed, resentment of Zabrama and other strangers grew until President Busia expelled all foreigners from Ghana in 1969. If the Hauka movement, as I have argued, is a way that dispossessed Nigeriens tap into circuits of power, why wouldn't Zabrama stage ceremonies in independent Ghana?

Regardless of the nebulous fate of the Hauka movement in Ghana, it is clear that Hauka spirit possession never abated in colonial and postcolonial Niger. Hauka spirits stomped in front of Jean Rouch's camera near Firgoun, Niger in 1946 as well as in Simiri, Niger in the early 1950s.[12] During the Diori years, Hausa, Songhay and Tuareg peoples staged spirit possession ceremonies on a regular basis. In Songhay ceremonies, Hauka stormed into the bodies of mediums. Whenever the Tooru, the nobles of the Songhay pantheon, appeared, the Hauka came to guard them. A generation earlier, African soldiers protected their (post)colonial commandants in a similar way.[13]

Hauka Spirit Possession in Tera (1969)

The Hauka came to Tera, Niger during the colonial period. Although some of them may have traveled to the Gold Coast, many chose to remain behind in the houses (*hu banda*) along the shady shores of Tera *bongu* (pond). In

December 1969 one of them came to Tera to invade the body of his medium. Lulled by the melodious cry of the one-stringed guitar and electrified by the thump of the gourd drums, Lokotoro, the French Doctor, stormed into the body of a slight, short man wearing a white laboratory coat. Lokotoro threw himself on the ground. He threw sand all over his body and shoved handfuls of it into his mouth. He stood up and scanned the audience. He stomped and spit sand at the audience. Fixing his gaze on the audience, he lunged menacingly toward them. Three men restrained him before he could strike anybody. He came closer to the edge of the audience, closer to where the American secondary school teacher stood. Lokotoro's eyes bulged. A blood vessel throbbed in his forehead. He groaned. Saliva frothed from his mouth as he broke loose from his restrainers and came toward the teacher.

"Is the man crazy?" the teacher asked someone in Songhay. "Oh no," responded another spectator. "He is not a man; he is one of the Hauka. You must go up and greet him. He will not harm you."

The teacher refused, but people told him that if he didn't greet the Hauka, the spirit would wreak havoc on the village.

And so the teacher approached this Lokotoro. He thrust his open hand toward the teacher's hand. "Sha vas?" he asked in pidgin French.

"Fine," the teacher answered, still quite afraid.

Lokotoro then insulted the teacher's mother's anatomy, much to the delight of the crowd.

The teacher protested, which provoked even more laughter.

Lokotoro insulted the teacher's father's anatomy.

The teacher protested once again; laughter erupted. Filled with a mixture of laughter and fright, delight and fear, the teacher was led away from the scene.

There have been any number of readings, including my own, of this and similar Hauka episodes. Some of the readings have focused on the dramatic impact of Hauka histrionics.[14] Others have considered Hauka antics from the vantage of Foucaultian discourse and counter-discourses.[15] Still others have seen the symbolism of the Hauka in terms of colonial ruptures. So far I've argued, following Mbembe, that these kind of binary categories cloud the issue of life in the African postcolony. They also fail to explain

A Hauka initiation ceremony in Tillaberi, Niger (1981).

adequately the ongoing presence, indeed the growth, of the Hauka in the Nigerien postcolony.

This ceremony consisted of much more than "horrific comedy"; it was the site of colonial memory grafted onto a space of postcolonial despair. On this multiplex stage, spirit-possession players also used the mimetic faculty to attempt to tap into restorative power.

Consider the plight of people living in Tera in 1969, nine years after Niger's independence.[16] Tera has been in many ways a forgotten town in the Republic of Niger, for it is situated west of the Niger River, a kind of nowhere zone. In 1969 no bridges connected the east and west banks of the river in Niger. To cross the river one could take a ferry in Niamey or Farie or a dugout just about anywhere along the Niger. If one of the ferries suffered a mechanical failure—not an uncommon occurrence—mail and other deliveries, including medical supplies for Tera's dispensary, could be delayed for weeks. People in Tera often told me that they felt invisible. Some people liked invisibility. That way the state left them alone. For others invisibility meant danger. Without the state, how could they cope with drought, disease and unscrupulous local officials?

Tera disappeared in a thick cloud of desert dust in 1969-70. But invisibility was but one of Tera's synergistically connected problems. The dusts of invisibility made the town's perennial water shortages even more difficult to bear. One large well supplied the drinking water for western Niger's largest town. People who could not pay the modest well fee gathered scummy water from a large, shallow pond. People who drank unfiltered and unboiled Tera water suffered from a variety of gastrointestinal disorders: guinea worm, dysentery (amoebic and bacillary), gastroenteritis, infectious hepatitis, and so on. Those who suffered so could expect little, if anything, from the understocked and inadequately staffed state medical facility.

Invisibility and thirst constituted normal ingredients in the recipe of Tera's social misery. In 1969, however, nature added drought to the list. Low rainfall in the summer of 1969 translated to a millet shortage. Peasants that year harvested only enough food to feed their families for part of the year. To compensate, they would have to buy millet on the open market or from the state agency. Corrupt officials in the state agency sold much of their millet to ruthless speculators soon after the harvest. The speculators held onto their millet until supplies ran down and then sold it at inflated prices. State officials and rich merchants lined their pockets at the considerable expense of the peasants.

Farmers often complained bitterly to me about the inequities of the corrupt system. Powerless and invisible, they did what they could for their hungry and sick families as thirst, hunger, and epidemics like meningitis swept over Tera. One old man said to me in 1970: "It is good that we have Diori, but he is no different than the French people. We are no better off today than before." What to do in a powerless, zombified state? Some of Tera's peasants fervently prayed to Allah for rain, health, food, and water. Others asked the Hauka deities to intercede on their behalf, to tap into the power of yore to bring rain, food and laughter into their lives.

Lokotoro swooped down to Tera from the spirit world. He listened to people's pain and offered tonics for their painful powerlessness. Embodied in the spirit's borrowed flesh were powerful memories of long dissipated ancestral power. The ancestors understood the mysteries of nature and culture; they stabilized life in western Niger. And so the people shook Lokotoro's hand and listened to his advice, taking from him small measures of the power he had brought from another world, another time.

Hauka Spirit Possession in Mehanna (1976)

The Hauka also visited Mehanna during the colonial and postcolonial periods in Niger. One December night in 1976, the Hauka came to Mehanna. Pinpoints of light flickered in the blue-black sky of midnight. Meteors streaked through the night like tracer bullets—a cosmic fire-fight. Perhaps this celestial light show compelled the Hauka to take their mediums' bodies that night. From a distance, the anthropologist occupying the body of a European could see two Hauka brandishing fiery branches above their heads. One of them threw his burning bush to the ground and lit a torch which he held to his bare chest.

The anthropologists's companion, Idrissa Dembo, urged him to quicken his pace. "You must see Zeneral Malia (the General of the Red Sea) and Lokotoro." Zeneral Malia was not in uniform, but Lokotoro wore a pith helmet and carried a syringe. As soon as Lokotoro spotted the anthropologist, he greeted him.

"Sha vas? (How's it going)," Lokotoro demanded.

"Ça vas? (How's it going)," the anthropologist asked.

"Sha vas?"

"Ça vas?"

"Me ne Doctor. (I am called doctor.)"

"Ni Doctor? (You're a Doctor?)"

Laughter interrupted the exchange. Playing by the rules of the spirit-possession game, the anthropologist ritually mocked Lokotoro. The audience found the game-playing hilarious.

"Alahamdu lilaahi. Enchante. (Praise be to God. Enchanted.)"

"Sha vas?" Lokotoro repeated.

"Ça vas?"

"To, Anasaara hinka no. Tu as conay? (Okay. There are two Europeans here. Do you know it?)"[17]

More laughter. Lokotoro was ridiculing Europeans, and the anthropologist was appropriately mocking his mocking. They were both being obdurate, playing out the exaggerated roles of two "Europeans."

In this exchange, a black man stood before the white anthropologist, frothing at the mouth, holding a syringe. The black man said, however, that he was a white European. The white anthropologist played along with the charade, stating that the black man was, indeed, a white European. Then the anthropologist code-switched into French to signify recognition of the black man's European status and said that he was enchanted to meet the black-white man. They participated in a veritably absurd comedy, an African version of what Artaud once called the Theater of Cruelty.[18]

Lokotoro left the anthropologist to examine a young girl who had been ill.

"Lokotoro, I've taken my daughter to the *Alfaggey* (Muslim healers), and the hospital people. The *Alfaggey* gave her potions and amulets. The hospital people pricked her with needles and gave her pills. In the name of God, Lokotoro, my daughter is still sick."

Lokotoro examined her, blew on her left arm, and injected her with his syringe, which contained a milky fluid.

"She'll get better now, good woman."

Lokotoro returned to the anthropologist. He said: "To l'argent (Okay. I want money).

The anthropologist gave him a hundred-franc piece. Lokotoro put the coin in his shirt pocket.

"*Anasaara*," Lokotoro said, "sha vas?"

"Ça vas."

"Mershi (Thank you)."

In this sequence Lokotoro addressed the anthropologist as "*anasaara*," which signified that they were no longer in the same social category. "*Anasaara*, ça vas?" is a linguistic device that many Songhay use to distance themselves from Europeans. The Hauka and the anthropologist were suddenly in different social categories; the Hauka had objectified the anthropologist as the generic rich white man and asked him for a contribution— a comic slap in his white face.

The bizarre histrionics of the hulking, frothing black figure of Lokotoro mimicking a white physician and equating himself with the only "other" white person in the audience was also a means of defining Songhay people *vis à vis* Europeans. On a more interpersonal level, the theatrical interaction created and maintained distance between encroaching European civilization—the anthropologist in this instance—and the boundary of Songhay identity.

After completing his grand rounds, Lokotoro joined his fellow Hauka, Zeneral Malia and Commandament (Major) Bashiru for a roundtable conference about witches in Mehanna. Their conclusions:

"Mehanna people are lazy," Zeneral Malia declared.

"Most Mehanna people are witches," Lokotoro proclaimed.

"Mehanna babies should have wet nurses," Commandament Bashiru suggested.(One becomes a witch by ingesting a witch's breast milk.) "Mehanna must express more reverence for Dongo," Commandament Bashiru continued, "If not, witch sickness will kill many people."

The three Hauka motioned to the musicians, a violinist and a drummer, to play. And they did, faster, faster, and faster until the three dancing Hauka did backflips onto the sand. After five minutes of vigorous massage, Sorko Djibo, a spirit praise-singer, revived the exhausted mediums.

Like the initial readings of the Hauka spirit possession in Tera, this one tells only part of the story. The focus of the reading above is on blackness, whiteness, identity gymnastics, and on how play can suspend disbelief. The reading also suggests that Hauka spirit possession is still about cultural resistance. Although the white man no longer governs the Republic of Niger, his sociocultural power lingers. The Hauka, like Dongo, draw a line that the white man, even anthropologists occupying the bodies of white men, should think twice about crossing.

But the reading doesn't inform us about the alienation and powerlessness of people in Mehanna in 1976. Like Tera, Mehanna is a village off the beaten track in Niger's western-most district. Unlike Tera, Mehanna has neither a post office nor an administrative center. By the same token, Mehanna is more visible than Tera, for it hugs the west bank of the Niger River. This geography makes Mehanna something of a commercial center, where food is relatively abundant in good harvest years.

Mehanna's geography, however, didn't improve the plight of its inhabitants in 1976. Despite the availability of food, many Mehanna people suffered from sicknesses that year: malaria and bilharzia (the scourges of the Niger River), hepatitis, guinea worm, and the other gastrointestinal diseases one gets from living in unsanitary conditions. In 1976-77 Mehanna people suffered through a meningitis epidemic. Even the most prosperous of Mehanna's merchants lost sons and daughters to the disease.

The juxtaposition of relative abundance and widespread suffering prompted Mehanna people to think of witchcraft, for their village was—and still is—reputed to have the highest percentage of witches per capita in all of Songhay. In Songhay witches are jealous creatures. They pounce on the weak; they prey on the prosperous. At the slightest sign of human vulnerability they steal souls and eat them, bringing rapid and painful death to their victims. Showing no mercy, their power inspires fear and respect. Powerless and resigned—zombified—people in Mehanna spoke of hunger, disease, death and witchcraft—all the more reason for some of them to organize Hauka ceremonies that year.

Commandament Bashiru brandished a burning bush over his head, a sign, the people told the anthropologist, that threatened the witches in Mehanna. Those who control fire—the French colonialists, Dongo, and the Hauka, Dongo's "children,"—are more powerful than witches. To touch a Hauka, to shake his hand, is to come in contact with power; it is, to borrow Taussig's language, contact with mimetic excess. Such proximity to power and magic is tempting; it compels mothers to seek cures for their hapless children and energy for the daily ordeals that they must face. The ceremony is "deep" play and serious theater, all in the endless effort to access grids of power through contact with mimetic excess. Perhaps contact with the Hauka is one way to confront zombification in the Nigerien postcolony.

Hauka "Clubs" in Tillaberi (1987)

In the late 1960s the presence and power of Adamu Jenitongo, Tillaberi's principal possession priest, created a certain unity among the village's spirit-possession players. Adamu Jenitongo staged most ceremonies in his compound, into which descended spirits from all the spirit families in the Songhay pantheon. Adamu Jenitongo's was the central arena of Tillaberi spirit possession activities. By 1976 several rival spirit-possession priests

A medium dancing at a Hauka "club" social (Tillaberi 1987).

disrupted much of the previous unity. Several compounds became the locus for spirit-possession rituals. Dissension poisoned the social and ritual atmosphere in Tillaberi, transforming a cohesive spirit possession troupe into mutually hostile fragments.[19]

Such fragmentation created space for new social arrangements and invented traditions. The most significant of these is the Hauka "club" of Tillaberi. The club consists of young men and women whose common Hauka mediumship forms the foundation of their association. In earlier times these mediums would have spent much time with spirit-possession elders like Adamu Jenitongo. By the late 1980s they spent much of their time with one another. They partied together, held informal meetings in their compounds, and audaciously staged more openly exclusive meetings during community spirit possession ceremonies. It was the Hauka club of Tillaberi that coordinated the Hauka Roundtable described in the Prologue of this book. The club "discovered" Commandamant Mugu's (the wicked major) altar in the bush southeast of Tillaberi. There, they staged ceremonies, replete with music, dancing, and sacrifice. As Issifi Aboulaye, the "chairman" of the club told me: "If the Commandamant wants blood, we give it to him. If the Commandamant wants perfume, we give it to him. Whatever the Commandamant wants, we give."

The Tillaberi Hauka club made a series of contemporary adaptations to suit its young and modern aficionados. Although the Tillaberi Hauka mediums participated in other spirit possession ceremonies, which are usually held on Thursdays and Sundays (days of the spirits), they scheduled their own ceremonies and sacrifices on Saturdays. Saturday, of course, is the only "official" day off that does not coincide with a traditional spirit day (Sunday). Logically, it is an unequivocally perfect day for a Hauka festival. It is at once free of both Islamic or traditional spirit association and linked to contemporary government practices. Saturday is a good time to attempt to recircuit government power for local uses. "We get the functionaries to come if we have a Saturday festival," Issifi Adboulaye told me.

The foregoing doesn't explain why Aboulaye Issifi and his friends would organize a troupe within a spirit-possession troupe in Tillaberi. Why create a separate organizational structure for the Hauka? Part of the reason may be generational. Young mediums and would-be spirit possession priests sometimes chafe under authority of conservative elders. Like Aboulaye Issifi, they want to assert their independence.[20] Part of the reason may be economic. By establishing a distinct Hauka troupe, young mediums would not have to share fees with older, more established spirit priests and mediums. Part of the reason may also stem from a realistic appraisal of ritual effectiveness. Since 1970, the standard of living in Tillaberi has declined. Although Tillaberi now has a paved road, electricity, three secondary schools, the administrative offices of the Niamey province, and new small-bore wells that provide clean water, the cost of living there has risen sharply. Incomes for most people, however, have declined. Many more goods are available today, but most people don't have the money to pay for them. Annual rainfall has tapered off, meaning that less food is produced in the region, which means that cost of feeding a family has risen exponentially. Many peasants in Tillaberi have complained to me about how well the civil servants, whom they refer to as *anasaarey* (Europeans) live. For them the government, called *hiinekoy*, the possessors of force, has a monopoly on power. One way to get a share of that power may be to mimic it through Hauka rituals which are free and clear from non-Hauka medium supervision. In some respects, this move is one that a community can use to break the bonds of postcolonial zombification.

Zombification, Postcolonial Niger, and the Hauka

Zombification characterized the tone of sociopolitical relations during the first regime in Niger's postcolony. Most members of Hamani Diori's government lived a life of sumptuous insouciance. Most of them chose to ignore the suffering in the countryside. Peasants lived a life of austere insouciance. Most of them chose to ignore their ability to change their lives. In this zombified space of devil-may-care, there emerged what Mbembe calls the postcolonial subject.

> If there is, then a 'postcolonial subject,' he or she is publicly visible . . . in the common daily rituals that ratify the *commandement*'s own institutionalization (its *recherche hegemonique*) in its capacity as a fetish to which the subject is bound; and, on the other, the subject's deployment of a talent for play and a sense of fun which makes him *homo ludens par excellence*.[21]

Mbembe goes on to say that such ludic practices enable postcolonial subjects to splinter their identities, changing constantly their personae, all of which render superfluous the analysis of postcolonial relations in terms of resistance and domination, discourses and counter-discourses.

Hauka spirit possession in Niger's postcolony is certainly a ludic performance that enables postcolonial subjects to fragment their identities into so many mimicked personae of power: judges, lawyers, doctors, truck drivers, generals, majors, presidents. These ritual performances are ludic par excellence, but they also frighten people. In so doing they are cruel in the Artaudian sense; they wake people from their zombified reveries and jolt them into temporary awareness.[22] As Abdoulaye Issifi told me in 1987, "we need the Hauka more than ever. They do good work for us."

And so in the space of Niger's postcolony, the significance of Hauka spirit possession expanded. Why would spirits that mimic colonial personages and colonial behaviors become more and more important in postcolonial rural villages? One reason may be purely economic. Hauka ceremonies attract large audiences which fill the possession troupe's coffers, enabling mediums to cope with the economic constrictions of the postcolony. Another reason may be that peasants feel an increasing alienation in the postcolony. Through contact with mimetic excess, Hauka ceremonies may tap into the resources of postcolonial "owners of power" (*hiinekoy*). Perhaps Hauka ceremonies lend themselves to the carefree conviviality of which Mbembe writes, a periodic conviviality that both confronts zombification and shields people from the seemingly incessant surveillance of oppression.

In the early years of Niger's postcolony, the Hauka had their roundtables on rural dunes, saluting one another, offering advice to their audiences, and serving as symbolic conduits of "European" power. No matter how powerfully the Hauka performed on the dune, the people in the Presidential Palace ignored them—until Lt. Colonel Seyni Kountche took power in 1974. A Hauka medium himself, Kountche attempted to use Hauka aesthetics to de-zombify the Republic of Niger. Many of the Hauka, as we shall see in Chapter Twelve, left their rural dunes in 1974 and triumphantly entered the Presidential Palace. Planned de-zombification, however, failed to transform Niger into a modern industrial state; rather, it brought on a reign of truculent oppression which re-zombified socio-political relations.

CHAPTER TWELVE

The Hauka and the Government of General Seyni Kountche

◆ ◆ ◆

In the zombified space of the Diori years, as we've noted in the last chapter, there were no popular uprisings in response to massive corruption or to Diori's excessive taxation of rural peasants in years of drought and famine. As one official in the Nigerien Ministry of Foreign Affairs cynically told me: "Nigeriens are a tolerant people; they expect their leaders to be corrupt and excessive."

There are limits, of course, to toleration. During the last years of the Diori era, the Nigerien military obeyed presidential decrees to collect taxes and requisition rural goods. By April of 1974, however, Diori had passed the limit of the military's tolerance. Led by Lt. Colonel Seyni Kountche, the Nigerien Army toppled Diori from power, killing his wife, Aissa and imprisoning his cronies.

From the very beginning, the Kountche regime stressed its military bearing, its no-nonsense style of austere government, and its insistence on honesty—as opposed to the corruption of the *ancien régime.* Putting the rhetoric of austerity into practice, Kountche, who was quickly named chief of state as well as head of the Supreme Military Council (hereafter CMS, the acronym for *Conseil Militaire Suprème*), refused to move into the Presidential Palace. Instead, he remained in the more modest quarters of the Army Chief of Staff, part of his attempt to create a new regime—a new system of bureaucratic practices, a new world of meanings. In this chapter,

Lieutenant Colonel Seyni Kountche assumes power. Courtesy Office National de l'Edition et de Press.

we shall re-read the history of Niger's second regime, looking at official texts and attempting to uncover unofficial subtexts, all of which demonstrate how Kountche—intentionally or not—manipulated Hauka aesthetics to consolidate power, design his program for progress, and promote a general state of fear in the population.[1] This fear enabled him to govern Niger with little serious opposition; it also paralyzed the population, ensuring, in part, the failure of his regime.

Fatigued Leaders

The morning after Kountche's *coup d'état* a photographer shot a group portrait of the entire military government. Except for Colonel Henri Dupuis, the senior ranking officer, the soldiers presented themselves in fatigues, boots and berets—field dress.

In the early days of the Kountche regime, the military prepared itself both for symbolic and logistical battle.

The first task of the new government, which Kountche governed through the CMS, was purely logistical. The coup took place at the height of the 1974 famine, and the military wanted to feed starving populations. Sending food convoys into the previously ignored hinterlands would promote good will among the peasants and provide a powerful symbolic counterpoint to the *ancien régime*. And so, shortly after the coup, life-saving convoys began to deliver food to hungry peasants.

But there was more to establishing a symbolic counterpoint to the *ancien régime*. Ever the shrewd politician, Kountche took measures to create a new symbolic order. The scope and character of the new symbolic order was brought into relief in the inaugural edition of *Le Sahel*, published on April 29, 1974, two weeks after Kountche's coup. On the first page, a brief message announced: "*Les Temps du Niger* [the title of Diori's newspaper] has lived its life. *Le Sahel* has come to take its place." The message goes on to say: "*Le Sahel* wants to better aid what its predecessor didn't know how to do—the transformation of mentalities and attitudes; it wants to energize our economic (vitality) and the evolution of our people."[2]

In the same issue, Sahidou Aliou, editor-in-chief of the newspaper, wrote an editorial that commented on a Kountche speech delivered to the wholesale merchants of Niamey. In addition to the specifics of the speech, Sahidou Aliou wrote about its tenor, suggesting that it was not the least bit tender, but direct, blunt.[3] Indeed, Kountche was addressing many of the people responsible for the famine that afflicted Niger at the time of the coup. Tenderness would not have served his political interests. To the Hauka, it should be added, tenderness is an undesirable trait; it demonstrates weakness.

Accordingly, Kountche projected himself as tough and resolute. Among his first public statements was: "It is a matter of putting our house in order."[4]

In introductory remarks to his *Jeune Afrique* interview with Kountche, Jos-Blaise Alima wrote: "With his severe expression, his frail body and his under-average height, Lt. Colonel Seyni Kountche would pass by easily unnoticed. His physique, in any case, contributes to making him an invisible man. However, when he speaks, one takes notice because of the great disproportion between the fragility of his silhouette and the strength of his voice."[5] Alima's description, it should be noted, also evokes a non-descript Hauka medium suddenly transformed by the force of his spirit.

Through word, image, and action, Kountche's gang constructed an image of resolute toughness—an image "sans tendresse." These are certainly "military" images, but in postcolonial Niger they also evoke Hauka subtexts. And so, during the first weeks of the new regime, the military ministers travelled through rural areas to learn from the peasants the problems of life in rural Niger. They also took pains to explain the nascent program of the new government.

One month after taking power the CMS expelled the French military from Niger. On a concrete political level, Kountche dispatched the French to eliminate a potential threat to his incipient power. The French garrison in Niamey was better equipped and better trained than the Nigerien Army. The CMS knew well that "... a secret agreement foresaw a rapid French intervention if Mr. Diori Hamani would be in difficulty. Before being taken by surprise, they [the military] still feared an *a posteriori* intervention."[6] Before the expulsion several difficulties arose between France and Niger. The most troubling problem concerned Major Langlois Estaintot, head of the French garrison in Niamey, who had allegedly attempted to provoke a counter-coup. Kountche expelled Major Estaintot from Niger on April 28, 1974, which escalated Franco-Nigerien tensions. However, the May 9, 1974 mission to Paris of Major Sani Souna Siddo, vice-president of the CMS, soothed Franco-Nigerien relations.

Given the complexity of constructing new symbolic orders in the post-colony, one must look beyond narrow questions of security to comprehend the importance of the expulsion of the French military from Niger in 1974. We should not forget that years after his fall from power Hamani Diori claimed that he was abandoned by the French military,[7] which, in retrospect, is tantamount to saying that the Kountche regime had little to fear from French military adventurism. Besides, Kountche surely realized the

Captain Moussa Sala, Military Minister. Courtesy, Office National de l'Edition et de Press.

symbolic victory he would earn by expelling the French military. First, the expulsion severed an important link between Niger and France, which clearly distinguished the practices of the old and new regimes. Kountche constructed the old regime as tired, uninspired, weak, timid, and corrupt; the new regime was, by contrast, energetic, inspired, strong, bold, and honest. Second, the expulsion demonstrated powerfully the courage, daring, and undaunted power of the CMS. They faced down the French army, the ultimate symbol of power in Nigerien colonial consciousness, and, like the Hauka, did not blink. Indeed, the CMS had faced down the very institution that had razed and pillaged villages, that had requisitioned goods and provoked famine, that had established forced labor gangs and pernicious head taxes. Kountche, in short, had defeated the *commanda-ment*, which in Mbembe's language,

> embraces the images and structures of power and coercion, the instruments and agents of their enactment, and a degree of rapport between those who give orders and those who are supposed to obey them without, of course, discussing them. Hence, the notion of 'commandament' is used here to refer to the authoritarian modality par excellence[8]

Diori never really established a real *commandament*. Although he remained in power for 14 years, his dependence upon the French bolstered an image of a handcuffed leader. To oppose Diori would be to oppose the French Army and Government. In expelling the French, Kountche used tough images to establish his own *commandement*, a powerful, fearless, Hauka-like authority completely free of French military influence.

His independent *commandament* established, Kountche set out to reap the rewards of his symbolic move. He surrounded himself with a new scientific brain-trust and decided to rely primarily on Nigerien resources, labor and initiative to combat the drought and famine of 1974. Kountche quickly decided to cut tons of fat from externally funded and financed development projects. He continued to send scores of grain-filled trucks to the famine zones. As stated in *Jeune Afrique,* "the results recorded in two months of battle against the drought are a sign of dynamism."[9]

In August of 1974, Kountche wanted to transfer this dynamism, this military "can-do" attitude, to what he openly and intentionally termed "*le commandament*," which for him consisted of Niger's *prefets, sous-prefets,* mayors, and district administrators. Four months following the coup d'etat, Kountche laid down the law to his administrators. "In front of those whom you administer," he told these civil servants, "you must constitute with the military, if not a single body, a single mind."[10] Kountche went on to stress the absolute necessity for loyalty, integrity, justice, and civic duty. He also outlined a work program for his *commandament*. Clearly, Kountche had redesigned the lines of authority, creating a *commandament* in which the ultimate local and national authorities wore military uniforms. The CMS had established its rule; the people respected, if not feared, their force, a force that had expelled the French military from Nigerien soil.[11]

So far I have presented a primary reading of the first four months of Seyni Kountche's regime. Kountche and the CMS took power and rapidly consolidated it. They presented themselves as tough and unsentimental, dynamic and bold, fearless and decisive.These, one could argue, are straightforward military attributes that undergird a more general military ethos. In the Nigerien context, however, military attributes are pregnant with cultural significance. Kountche's "*homme de force*" military projections, as I have already suggested, also constructed a subtext, for these military attributes also constitute the ethos of the Hauka.

During the colonial period and the Diori regime, the Hauka entered the bodies of their mediums. Confronting the distant but ever-terrifying *hiinekoy* ('owners of power'), they mimed the French military in an attempt, as I have argued, to master its force, or better yet, to use its inexplicable power to get rid of the oppressors. In so doing the Hauka appropriated the French military ethos and its attributes, vying to use them to redirect power. The Hauka alternatively saluted and sneered at their spectators. They alternatively impressed and frightened their audiences with unrestrained boldness, brute force, energetic dynamism, and fearless decisiveness. On the dune the Hauka solved local problems and seemingly pumped energy and power into their audiences. In the Presidential Palace, Kountche brilliantly reappropriated a military ethos that was, as I have argued, refracted through a framework of Hauka aesthetics. Like the Hauka, the fatigued leaders, military ministers all, swaggered about the Nigerien countryside. They strutted, sneered, and made sure to have their tough-guy photographs appear in every issue of the *Le Sahel*. Even if most Nigeriens could not read the rhetoric of the new regime on the pages of *Le Sahel*, they certainly could appreciate the photos of the fatigued leaders participating in official ceremonies, formal audiences, and other public encounters. Through brute force of will, the military ministers relieved the dire conditions of the 1974 famine. Like the Hauka, they faced down their opponents—the French—and didn't retreat. In one formal act, they accomplished what no other Nigerien group had been able to do: expel the French military from Niger. The CMS had entered an ambiguous, but

Commandant Sani Souna Siddo. Courtesy, Office National de l'Edition et de Press.

powerful space. Drawing strength from his military successes and from longstanding Hauka symbolism, Kountche declared the first real Nigerien independence from France. To his great credit, Kountche led his people onto a path of putative pride, prudence and power. Where would this path lead? Could Kountche have known that the path of power is frought with duplicity, that the underside of Hauka's path is what the Songhay call *zamba*: betrayal.

Sani Souna Sido's Sedition

Hauka spirit possession ceremonies present an arena of much contestation and debate, all of which reflect the diffusion of power in the Hauka *commandement*. In *Les maitres fous* how one can never forget the fury of the General of the Red Sea who ceaselessly complains: "It's always the same. No one will listen to me. It's always the same." In *Les maitres fous* and other Hauka ceremonies, the deities openly argue, debate and compete with one another. Just as harmony is fleeting among the ever-competitive Hauka, so it was among the military ministers of Seyni Kountche's CMS. Although the fatigued leaders projected an image of harmony to the press and the public, there appeared to have been much inner dissention. The internal strife sometimes became so great that evidence of it slipped through the hermetically sealed doors of government deliberation.

Like Istambula, the chief of the Hauka, Kountche, tolerated no open defiance to his authority. In March of 1975 he condemned Major Gabriel Cyril to a military prison on the shores of Lake Chad, almost 2000 kilometers from the capital of Niamey. Although *Le Sahel* accused Major Cyril of corruption, *Jeune Afrique*'s Siradiou Diallo wrote that Cyril had been imprisoned "for having challenged the chief of state during a Council of Ministers meeting."[12] Similarly, Kountche condemned Squadron Chief Boulanga Manga to the military prison of Agadez for refusing to leave his ministerial post to take up the duties of a *prefet*.

Kountche's man-of-force rigidity and severity no doubt precipitated any number of conflicts among his military colleagues. The relationship between Kountche and Sani Souna Siddo, the vice-president of the CMS, sparked much competition. Reporters for *Jeune Afrique* frequently called Sani the brains behind the coup d'etat and the *eminence gris* of the new regime. Unlike Kountche, Sani maintained many close relationships with personalities of Niger's political past. He was the Brutus-like confident of Aissa Diori who visited the Dioris the evening of the coup. Reporters for *Jeune Afrique* wondered how long two such competitors could share power. Not long at all.

On August 2, 1975, Sani Souna Sido, Maitrouré Gadjo, and Djibo Bakary, Diori's old nemesis from the left, were arrested for plotting the overthrow of the CMS. Djibo and Sani both coveted the Nigerien Presidency—for different reasons. Ever the radical, Djibo wanted to transform Niger into a socialist state. Six months after Diori's fall, Kountche invited Djibo to return to Niger after 15 years of exile in Guinea. He did so in October of 1974. Soon after his return, Djibo began to criticize the conservative nature of the CMS. Sani and Maitroure Gadjo, the former director of SEPANI, the national peanut corporation, allegedly convinced Djibo to join them in their plot to oust Kountche. The CMS uncovered the plot well before its leaders had time to put their plan into action.

Sani Souna Sido seemingly received the harshest prison sentence; he died of what *Jeune Afrique* described as "natural causes" in 1977. Sani's treatment established a standard. From 1975 onward Kountche reserved his most merciless punishment for military traitors, for he expected nothing less than total obedience from his brothers-in-arms, some of whom were, like their leader, Hauka spirit mediums. In a front page editorial published on August 6, 1975, *Le Sahel* accused Sani of selfish ambition. "Knowing that the principles of the CMS compromised his real persona, and desiring to move on to supreme honors, ardently wishing to safeguard interests that he saw threatened, Sani Souna Siddo was thus ready to ally himself with the devil to satisfy his ambitions and safeguard what seemed to him essential. . . ."[13] The editorial went on to link the ambitions of Sani and Djibo Bakari: "Although evidence of a coup attempt exists, evidence for a broader plot linking Sido to Djibo is so tenuous that Kountche probably fabricated it or exaggerated it simply to consolidate his position."[14]

Kountche used the plot to distance further the policies and practices of the CMS from those of the *ancien régime*. Sani Souna Siddo's demise increased Kountche's power considerably, for Sani's departure eliminated the person who was at least initially Kountche's most substantial and serious competitor. Kountche's quick discovery and rapid response to the uninitiated plot also bolstered the image the President wanted to project to the public: a man of steel nerves who, to use words from a Songhay magic incantation, would "not step back, not step back" when confronted with danger. Like the hunters of yore (*gowize*), Kountche possessed the courage to face down and master his adversary. Like the Hauka, his fearless face and bold behavior mesmerized the public. This man projected an unsettling force designed to, in Kountche's own words, "frighten Nigeriens."[15]

Military Madness

After quashing Sani Souna Siddo's uninitiated plot to overthrow his regime, Seyni Kountche revved-up the engine of his Hauka-inspired symbolism machine. To solve its problems, he told the people of Niger on September 4, 1975 that Niger must be tough, resilient and self-reliant—a statement that mimicked the ethos of the French military as well as the Hauka. To promote his brand of self-reliance, President Kountche continued to travel about the countryside. In Maradi he told an assembled group of administrators: "It is not by remaining in the intimacy of your salons that you can know the problems of our populations."[16] Photos in the same issue depict Kountche as a rigidly dedicated and thoroughly tough leader who would solve the country's serious problems. These photos, like those of the military ministers reproduced in this book, reinforced the managed impression of dynamism.

The elements, it should be mentioned, helped Kountche to mold his image. The heavens produced good rains in the summer of 1975, enabling most farmers to harvest enough grain to feed their families, and this after Kountche and his CMS had prayed for rain in July of 1975.[17] In announcing *Operation Sahel Vert* in the summer of 1975, Kountche asked Niger's youth to participate in the battle against desertification by planting desert-stopping trees in the Nigerien countryside. In the eyes of foreign observers, Kountche became a man who kept his promises, a man who had a plan of action to develop Niger. Many Nigeriens saw a tough, dynamic man who brought rain and food: the kind of image that gives a leader an unspoken, but ever-present supernatural edge.

In February of 1976, Kountche reorganized his government. Nearly two years after taking power, the President decided to admit civilians into the corridors of power. Military ministers, however, retained the most powerful portfolios—defense, finance, telecommunications, health, foreign affairs, and development. Kountche assigned to technocrats and administrators such lesser portfolios as planning, mines, commerce, youth and sports, justice, public works, rural development, and presidential communications.

Kountche's decision was no doubt a practical one. Running a state takes expertise in diverse domains which means that non-military specialists had to be recruited for important technical posts. On the symbolic plain, the decision demonstrated a brute confidence. One could say that Kountche had stabilized the core of his military government to such a degree that he could entrust ministerial portfolios to civilians. Such confidence comes with the maturation and solidification of power.

In March of 1976, Kountche decisively exercised that power, annulling all class advancements and closing the prestigious Ecole Normal d'Administration (ENA), the principal training ground for the civil service's elite. The CMS closed ENA following a student's disrespectful act and the student body's decision to protest that student's expulsion. In response to this student defiance, the CMS issued the following statement on March 8, 1976:

> Following an undisciplined act by a student toward a Nigerien professor, and in the hope to maintain discipline in this establishment and to assure consequent good administration, the (ENA) disciplinary council, after deliberation, decided to expel him. With the announcement of this decision, the friends of the student, the majority of whom are state functionaries, decided to boycott their classes. . . .With regard to all that has occurred, the CMS decided to annul all class advancements at ENA and temporarily close this school.[18]

In the same issue of *Le Sahel*, the editor comments on the closure of the school, suggesting that the CMS could not tolerate insolence or lack of discipline, especially in those students who would one day be state administrators. Although the CMS would tolerate civilians in their government, this action underscored their absolute intolerance of civilian or military indiscipline.

Such unflinching rigidity must have alarmed many Nigeriens, including an important contingent in the military, for on March 15, a group of Hausa and Tuareg military officers, commanded by Batallion Chief Bayere Moussa, National Police Captain Sidi Mokhammed, and Ahmed Mouddoum, a trade unionist, mounted a bloody revolt against Kountche.

Kountche quickly repulsed the revolt. The CMS rapidly arrested and imprisoned the ringleaders. *Le Sahel* attempted to minimize the seriousness of this attempted *coup*. Reporters stressed how quickly and decisively forces loyal to President Kountche reacted to this military challenge. In fact, in its "spin" on the coup *Le Sahel* characterized the plotters as ambitiously corrupt, unstable drug abusers—terms similar to those used to describe Sani Souna Siddo.

Sidi Mokhammed was part of the National Police Force. After having been imprisoned for graft, the Nigerien Army family rejected Sidi Mokhammed. This man who claimed last Monday to have taken the destiny of Niger in his hands with Major Bayere Moussa, who presented himself as the Army's intellectual as well as the brains of the historic events of 15 April 1974, was a drug abuser.[19]

Le Sahel goes on to assassinate the character and capacities of Bayere Moussa, claiming that he incompetently managed the affairs of the Rural Economy Ministry. When the CMS arrested Bayere Moussa, he was found wearing ". . . 3 kilos of amulets and gris-gris."[20]

In its more critical reportage of the attack, *Jeune Afrique* wrote openly of the coup's seriousness. At first, observers believed that the attack claimed twelve lives. Later accounts put the toll closer to fifty.[21] *Jeune Afrique* also scoffed at the idea that the coup was simply the expression of individual ambition.[22]

In a subsequent issue of *Jeune Afrique*, Siradou Diallo reported extensively on the attempted putsch. He suggested that the *coup* attempt had profoundly shocked Kountche. Was the attempted *coup* merely a matter internal to Niger, or was there foreign support of the failed assault? Diallo reported that the mutinous soldiers were given arms that they did not know how to use. These were allegedly supplied by Gadafi's Libya, which for some time had been attempting to stir up ethnic animosities in neighboring Niger.[23]

The 1976 coup attempt, in fact, brought into the open seething ethnic conflicts and rivalries that have troubled Niger since independence. Although they did not constitute a majority of Niger's population, Zarma-Songhay from the west held power in both the Diori and the Kountche regimes. The Hausas, the majority population in Niger, had always been excluded from the circle of power. The two governments of Niger, moreover, openly discriminated against nomadic Tuareg groups that had often refused to recognize state sovereignty. Was it coincidental that Bayere Moussa, a Hausa, and Sidi Mokhammed and Ahmed Mouddour, both Tuaregs, represented these excluded populations?

One week after the attempted coup, Kountche staged a press conference during which he stated: "Any Nigerien who will unleash ethnic problems through the use of arms will be severely punished."[24] Kountche went on to describe in some detail how the coup was organized, revealing its princi-

Captain Bayere Moussa. Courtesy, Office National de l'Edition et de Press.

pal instigators. Rather than confronting the ethnic divisiveness that the attempted coup expressed, Kountche called for national unity, a sentiment expressed in *Le Sahel*'s headline of March 22, 1976, "One Army, One Nation."

One month after the coup, the CMS executed seven of its principal leaders, including Bayere Moussa, Sidi Mokhammed, and Ahmed Mouddour. Shaken by this military madness, Kountche also began to pay more attention to the needs of the troops. As Charlick writes:

This coup attempt was significant for three reasons. Since most of the civilian and military participants were from the Hausa and Tuareg ethnic groups, it introduced the specter of open ethnic conflict. Kountche warned of tribalism and narrowed the basis of his regime almost entirely to followers drawn from the Zarma group. It also marked the beginning of strained relations with Libya, since Kountche charged that Libyan agents had been involved. In addition, Kountche was reminded of his debt to a broader group, the army, since it was only through the continued loyalty of many key military units that the coup had been thwarted. From this point on, Kountche was careful to attend to the needs of the military, although he continued to limit its role in policy-making.[25]

Up to this point, my reading of the second plot against the Kountche Government shares much with typical analyses of the volatile politics in postcolonial Africa: coups and counter-coups, ethnic politics, and international adventurism. There is one document, however, a declaration handwritten by Bayere Moussa, that compels one to wonder about unstated motivations. Had the coup succeeded, the note would have been broadcast on Radio Niger. In its edition of March 17, 1976, *Le Sahel* printed Bayere Moussa's handwritten message.

> *Countrymen, Brothers and Sisters of Niger,*
> In the name of the Nigerien officers and soldiers aware of the incessant evil perpetuated by a regime of men who are unstable, cowardly, who are enslaved by a dictator inspired by Satan, I, who speak to you, Major Bayere Moussa, announce to you that from this moment, liberty is recovered at the end of this incompetent and tyrannical regime. I would like to assure you that this noble action comes from the "base," that is to say inspired and wanted by conscientious soldiers and countrymen.[26]

One interpretation of this declaration would be that Bayere Moussa wanted to get even. Kountche had already removed him from his ministerial post for "incompetence." The President had also imprisoned other military ministers for "corruption," incompetence, blind ambition and outright sedition. Following the attempted coup, Kountche belittled its organizers as irremediably corrupt, insatiably ambitious, and mentally unstable drug abusers. The newspaper reported that Bayere Moussa wore three kilos of "protective" amulets to suggest his "irrational" belief in spirits and magic.

In his declaration, however, Bayere Moussa stresses his patriotism and his opposition to the tyrannical rule of a man, Seyni Kountche, "inspired by Satan." The last statement needs to be unpacked in light of our previous analysis. How are we to interpret "inspired by Satan" in light of the curious proximity of Kountche's aesthetics and those of the Hauka?

No politician anywhere wants to be labeled an evil person. In Niger, public politics is inextricably connected to Islam. Nigeriens expect their leaders to demonstrate some degree of Muslim piety. They do not expect them, moreover, to openly endorse such pre-Islamic beliefs and practices as sorcery and spirit possession.[27] Kountche's call for unity, for example, articulates the Muslim ideal of *umma*, the harmonious community of believers, all humbled in their equal devotion to Allah. *Umma* is the antithesis of tribal divisiveness. When Muslims in Niger publicly state that a person is evil or inspired by Satan, they are suggesting one of two possibilities. The first is that the person is disruptive, a person who is bent on destroying a community's *umma*.

The second interpretation is more pernicious. In the Nigerien political context, as I've already argued, one can never forget the proximity of politics, power, and spirits. In his statement Bayere Moussa, we should remember, argues that Kountche's gang suffers from mental instability, cowardice, and enslavement to the rigid leader who is inspired, if not enslaved, by Satan. Was Bayere Moussa indirectly suggesting that Kountche was enslaved by the Hauka, by the Songhay-Zarma spirit world?

In 1925 the Muslim Hammalists referred to the emergent Hauka as "diable," or devils. Indeed, Muslims throughout Niger often refer to spirits as "diable." People often say "That one has a diable," or "His diable has made him quite sick." Invariably, pious Muslims in Niger link the "diable" with evil; they further suggest that the medium who carries the "diable" is mentally unstable. Could Bayare Moussa's declaration be an indirect critique of Kountche's Hauka-inspired aesthetics, an indirect plea to free the nation from the tyrannical grip of a Hauka spirit medium posing as a military president? It would be foolish to declare such an incomplete interpretation completely valid. But it would also be foolish to ignore the intent of the unstated message of Bayere Moussa's declaration. In time the personal rule of Seyni Kountche became more and more narrow and oppressive. In time, the spell of the mysterious Amadou Oumorou (known as Bonkano) captured more and more of President Kountche's attention. Was it coincidental that Bonkano claimed to come from a family of famous spirit possession priests? Perhaps Bayere Moussa paid the ultimate price for his prescient message?

Prosperity and the Development Society

In the late 1970s Kountche further consolidated his power. If the profile of a military minister became too prominent, Kountche would reassign him to a distant prefecture or to an even more distant foreign embassy. From 1976 to 1981 ". . . Kountche ruled by balancing the interests of the military and, to a lesser extent, those of the civilian bureaucracy with his own interest in maintaining centralized, tight, highly personal control."[28] This monopoly on participation in the Government led to labor and student protests, which led to sporadic co-optation of protest leaders and to widespread repression. Meanwhile Kountche resurrected the *samariya* movement, which, in Charlick's words, "was a serious effort to mobilize rural energies and create popular support for the regime."[29] Based upon the traditional Hausa model for village youth groups, *samariya* clubs planted fields, engaged in public works like building mosques and other structures and organized social events. But ". . . the new Samirya movement differed markedly from the traditional form in that it was directed by adults and was given its marching orders by external authorities rather than village youth leaders."[30]

Meanwhile, Niger's uranium mining efforts brought a flood of capital into the country. Market conditions in the late 1970s as elsewhere propelled the price of uranium skyward. Financial prosperity combined with relatively good grain harvests made Niger's light burn brightly in economic metropoles. Kountche used the new prosperity to finance several ambitious building projects that changed the Niamey skyline. In short order the CMS oversaw the construction of L'Hotel Gawey and the Palais de Congress as well as a new national football stadium and basketball arena. Kountche also made plans to build the Cendaaji dam, which would enable Niger to supply its own electric power.

In this period of prosperity, Kountche introduced his Société de Development (Development Society) in 1978-79. With the Development Society Kountche proposed to seriously change Niger's economic and political systems. "Kountche's motivations at the time were two-fold: to broaden his base of political support and to produce a breakthrough in the rural economy so that government revenues and the national income would not be so heavily dependent on uranium."[31] After three years of planning the structure of the Development Society emerged in 1982. It consisted of a series of nested development councils organized at the village, district, and regional levels. Charlick contends that the Development Society's ideology of grass-roots participation in national development and policy was a fiction. The Development Society's

> planners evoked the need to construct a new society on the basis of tradi-
> tional principles of social solidarity and *concertation*, or pulling together. It
> is now quite obvious that what they had in mind was much closer to the true
> principles of Nigerien politics, which stress, not democracy or mass mobi-
> lization, but hierarchy and elite management through personal rule and
> patronage.[32]

In other words, Kountche designed the Development Society as a way of reinforcing his power throughout Nigerien society.

Despite the rhetoric about the participation in and the democracy of the Development Society—themes much appreciated by Reagan's White House—the Kountche regime became more and more repressive between 1982 and Kountche's death in 1987. As always, Kountche demanded absolute loyalty from his cronies, none of whom were secure in their posts. In 1982 Kountche rearranged his government, firing, demoting and promoting 132 senior civil servants. This move enabled him to change five of his seven *prefets* as well as the mayors of Niger's major cities: Zinder, Niamey, Agadez and Maradi. "In 1981 only three members of the original CMS were still on the national political scene, and by January 1983 two of those had been dropped from national decision-making roles."[33] The most shocking dismissal, however, involved Moumouni Djermakoy Adamou, who had been the first Foreign Minister of the Kountche regime. At the time of his dismissal, Djermakoy had been the president of the National Development Council. Charlick speculates that Djermakoy's dismissal resulted from his distaste for the increasing political and supernatural influence of the ever-present Amadou Oumarou, more generally known by his nickname Bonkano.

The Zealous "Zima"

In Songhay there are two major deities. There is *Iri koy*, which translates liter-ally to "our chief." *Iri koy* is the High God of the Songhay cosmos, and the equivalent of Allah. The other almost unknown deity is called *zamba koy* which translates literally to "the chief of betrayal." *Zamba koy* governs the

Captain Mounmouni Djermakoy Adamou. Courtesy, Office National de l'Edition et de Press.

world of sorcery, a world of amoral power relations in which only the most powerful are able to deflect the treacherous intentions of rivals.[34] It is said that the path of the Songhay sorcerer and *zima* (a spirit possession-priest) is one of *zamba*, a path on which the most able practitioners are relentless seekers of power.[35] Bonkano knew this path well and his betrayal of Seyni Kountche speaks to the treachery of those who would follow *zamba koy*.

Bonkano and Kountche met in 1969 some five years before the latter took power. Kountche was an army officer. Bonkano was an officer in the National Police. Their professional paths might have crossed for any number of reasons. At some point Bonkano, who claimed to be a knowledgeable and powerful *zima*, offered to look at what his cowery shells might say about Kountche's future.[36]

In Songhay, the *zima* is a major intermediary between the social and spirit worlds. He or she organizes spirit-possession ceremonies, treats people for spirit illnesses and witchcraft, and prepares potions and magic cake (*kusu*) to protect and energize those who seek (political) power. A few *zima* receive the gift of vision. They are given cowery shells over which sacrifices to the spirit Wambata have been made. Once these shells have lived in a termite hill for seven years, they are ready to speak to their "owners." The shells uncover the past, describe the present, and predict the future. Bonkano may well have possessed such shells, for in 1969 he "observed" Kountche's future path and predicted that the young army officer would become president of Niger in April of 1974.

It is difficult to know if Kountche made use of Bonkano's divinatory skills at other times during their association. I do know of three Songhay sorcerers and diviners who claim to have done "work" for Kountche. It is admittedly difficult to state unequivocally that Seyni Kountche used sorcerers and diviners to help him make decisions, though the example of Ronald Reagan's use of astrology to set the dates of summit meetings suggests strongly that these practices are not limited to Africa. By the same token, it is incontestable that Bonkano's influence grew steadily until he became the second most powerful man in Niger.

How did Bonkano manage this remarkable rise to power? One can only speculate. We do know that at the beginning of the Kountche regime, Bonkano was merely a lieutenant in the National Police. Gradually, Kountche promoted him until he became the head of the secret police (Bureau de Coordination et de Liason (BCL).

> Kountche relied on the BCL to disorganize and repress potential opponents, and he also relied on Bonkano for spiritual advice and to help protect his personal 'fortune,' since Bonkano was from an important family of Zarma 'seers' or *zima*. As a result, Bonkano was in an ideal position to gain power, and many military officers resented his privileged access and position. On Bonkano's advice, Kountche countered that resentment by excluding virtually all military officials from top decision-making roles. In 1983 Kountche and Bonkano confirmed their ascendancy by changing all the commanders of the Republican Guard and the National Police.[37]

By September of 1983 the BCL had amassed great power and Bonkano, its director, had tapped into the National Treasury, becoming an exceedingly wealthy man. Meanwhile, the military ministers had been replaced. In their specially equipped Peugeot 505s or Renault 18s the secret police cruised about Niamey, suppressing any and all political opposition. Kountche's regime had become menacingly oppressive; he had become, to borrow from the apt Songhay expression, a "mean chief."

But the shadow cast by *zamba koy* is a long one indeed. In the spring of 1983 Bonkano warned Kountche of a potential plot against the regime. At the end of August "some strange visitors whom Kountche would not identify, landed in Niamey. Through Bonkano, they asked to meet with the President. . . . "[38] Their request, however, was refused. In September of 1983 Bonkano flew to Paris for reasons still unknown. In Paris, he encountered Mamane Sidikou, the deputy of Prime Minister Oumarou Mamane. Sidikou had flown to Paris for medical reasons. Following their meeting, Bonkano and Sidikou decided to overthrow Kountche.[39]

> In Niamey, Kountche still knew nothing . . . Bonkano, the man of whom he is least wary, was preparing to overthrow him. The Nigerien President, however, recognized danger, having had a premonition. His collaborators did not want him to participate in the Vitel Summit (October 3-4). 'I don't know exactly why,' he said himself. 'But I couldn't decide to leave. I was waiting for something. What? I knew nothing.'[40]

Bonkano reassured the President and Kountche left for the Franco-African Summit on September 29, 1983. Bonkano continued to reassure his President by telling him by telephone that all was well.

Meanwhile Bonkano, Mamane Sidikou and Amadou Seydou, the chief of Niamey's army battalion, put the finishing touches on their putsch. Bonkano invited Army Chief of Staff Ali Seybou to an annual "ceremony" at his villa. Seybou at first refused to go. But Bonkano telephoned Kountche beseeching him to ask Seybou to attend the ceremony. Kountche telephoned Seybou on October 5. Unable to refuse his superior, Seybou and several other senior military officers went to Bonkano's villa, where they were arrested and sequestered.[41] The same evening Bonkano ordered the National Guard and the National Police to surround the Presidential Palace. He also sent the National Police to secure the airport. These troop movements surprised Toumba Boubakar who tried without success to reach Ali Seybou. Thinking that something was terribly wrong, he mobilized the army to confront the National Police at the Presidential Palace. Shots were exchanged, but the engagement resulted only in one civilian death—a passerby who refused to stop his car. By 10:00 p.m. the coup had been easily repulsed because the plotters hadn't secured the support of the Nigerien Army. Kountche first learned of these events on board his presidential jet en route from Paris to Niamey.

Mamane Sidikou and Amadou Seyni were arrested. The Army captured Amadou Seyni driving a car in which he had "piled large sums of money . . . and three changes of clothes."[42] Sidikou surrendered to his superior, Prime Minister Oumarou Mamane. Bonkano somehow escaped with vast sums of money and exiled himself in France.[43] "The coup failed only because Chief of Staff Ali Seybou, the only remaining original member of the CMS apart from Kountche, and key commanders of armored and airborne groups, failed to throw in their support."[44]

The Bonkano affair considerably weakened Kountche's domestic and international support. Domestically, the coup attempt brought into relief the fissures of Kountche's regime; it also propelled debate about the nature of Kountche's judgment and character. Internationally, the Bonkano affair undermined much of Niger's support among aid-donors.

> Revelations that Bonkano had escaped with a fortune and had left behind lavish houses and mosques built with state resources were particularly unwelcome given Niger's growing financial crisis. In 1985 additional financial scandals involving massive fraud and embezzlement in several government agencies and three major agricultural productivity projects raised further suspicion about Kountche's judgment, management ability, and even his personal integrity.[45]

The Bonkano affair also revealed the internal contradictions of Kountche's regime. In 1974 the CMS proclaimed their personal integrity, their commitment to change the "old ways of thinking."

Kountche's symbolism machine made sure to separate old from new, the corrupt from the honest; it made use of Hauka-like images. And yet, the amount of corruption in the Kountche years dwarfed that of the Diori years. Kountche also stressed his military bearing. He projected himself as a tough guy who would not tolerate insubordination. And yet, his close collaborators betrayed him in 1975, in 1976, and again in 1983—indiscipline plaguing a regime that stressed discipline.

But there is much that the press and other commentators have preferred to bypass or minimize. Why did Kountche allow a character as shady as Bonkano to amass so much power? Why did Kountche place so much of his trust in the zealous "zima"? Were the declarations of Bayere Moussa prescient? Was Seyni Kountche unstable? Few people have been willing to speak directly to these questions. But in Kountche's *Jeune Afrique* interview after the Bonkano affair, Abdelaziz Dahmani, unequivocally asked Kountche about the nature of his beliefs.

> JA: Do you believe in marabouts and in supernatural forces?
>
> SK: I am above all an African and I will remain one. That is my answer. One can hardly escape these conditions and these realities.[46]

This exchange needs to be unpacked a bit. The interviewer, a Muslim, links the supernatural with *maraboutic* practices, that is, with the practices of Muslim healers and seers. Kountche's response, however, is not about Muslim healers and practitioners; it is, I think, about *sohancis* (Songhay sorcerers) and *zimas*. Kountche's indirect response is a classic example of the discourse of sorcery.[47] For all his military directness, he is imprecise in this exchange, referring to "these conditions and realities." In the discourse of sorcery one never names a plant, a victim, or another practitioner. One's discourse is purposely nebulous—for one's own protection. From the vantage of this discourse, Kountche's statement is an indirect admission of his personal implication in "these conditions and realities." This indirect admission does not exclude Kountche's Muslim piety, but it demonstrates powerfully the heretofore unmentionable: that in postcolonial Niger, sorcery, spirit possession, and the Hauka have never been far from the surface of politics. These "conditions and realities," I would contend, are also an important part of the symbolic politics of the African postcolony.

Such connections among sorcery, spirit possession, and politics are not unique to Africa. Duvalier's Haiti is a case in point. It is widely known that Duvalier played with the symbolism of Voudoun, himself publicly wearing the costume of Baron Samedi, the Voudoun spirit of death, to frighten his people into submission.[48] In the final *Jeune Afrique* article written about his regime, Kountche spoke directly about how he attempted, like the French colonial forces of yore, to capture the bodies of Nigeriens. In that edition of *Jeune Afrique*, Siradou Diallo wrote:

> One day I dared to ask him why in his first official photo, which is hung in all official places, he is presented with a severe expression and menacing eyes . . . 'Because I am neither tall or fat, it's a thing with me, to scare Nigeriens . . . You know, Nigeriens are a people who are difficult to govern. That's why I have to beat them from time to time, especially civil servants, students and merchants in order to make them realize that I have my eye on them and that they must not play with the state.'[49]

Diallo suggests that Kountche made these remarks tongue-in-cheek. But why? Why talk about "scaring" and "beating" Nigeriens? The Hauka, too, practice what I have called horrific comedy. They make people laugh. They, too, are often tongue and cheek. But their power, like that of Kountche, also scares people.

To the very end Kountche was able to tap into the Hauka aesthetic. Using symbols of force and dynamism, he managed and manipulated the complex symbolic universe that he carefully and artfully constructed. In the end it was only death that separated this *homme de force* from the power he sought, cultivated and wielded with such truculence.

I have argued that Kountche tapped into the power circuits that the Hauka initially discovered during the colonial epoch. He reappropriated the Hauka appropriation of the aesthetics of the French Colonial Army. He used these aesthetics to establish his regime, distance himself from the practices of Diori, and construct a program for Niger's future. What he didn't realize, however, is that the path of the Hauka, however one travels on it, is fraught with dangerous betrayal. In that space of *zamba* , one never knows whom one can trust. One never knows how memories of the past will haunt the present. One never knows who might unravel carefully constructed plans and aspirations. In the end, Seyni Kountche proved himself to be a man of force. He carried himself according to the rigid strictures of the military. Like the sorcerer warriors of the Songhay past, Kountche had few friends, made many enemies, and earned much respect. He died very much alone on November 10, 1987.

Kountche's official photo: "Severe expression and menacing eyes." Courtesy, Office National de l'Edition et de Press.

Memory, Power, and Spirit Possession

• • •

Even the death of a "hard" man like Seyni Kountche engenders a sense of loss, for loss often infuses memories of the distant past. In the Republic of Niger, the griot's poetry invites people to reflect about the glories of the distant past often compelling them to remember with a sense of loss. An elder in Wanzerbe, the Songhay village famous for its sorcerers, once expressed his sense of loss to me.

"If we had only listened to our fathers. Our fathers possessed incredible knowledge and power. All of that is lost today. If we had only listened, our lives would be better today."

Many of the people, young and old, whom I've known in Niger hold similar sentiments. Walking through their barren fields, millet farmers gaze at cloudless skies and mourn the losses of the spirits that had once brought rain and record harvests. Kneeling at the gravesite of a child, mourners weep from the senseless loss of many young lives. Villagers used to protect themselves from the destructive forces of the bush. "Back then," Adamu Jenitongo, the late spirit-possession priest of Tillaberi, used to say, "we were unified. There was trust, harmony. Life was sweet. Today there is dissention and distrust."

Social memories, then, are often bittersweet. Life was sweet yesterday; it is bitter today. Social memories can also be short-sighted and romanticized. In some years the Songhay spirits provided rain for bumper crops of millet; in other years the rain they withheld caused devastating droughts. In some years ritual specialists protected Songhay communities from senseless death; in other years their offerings failed to stem the tide of deadly disease.[1]

By contrast, sometimes myopic memories can *intensify* the pain of past experience: "Life may be tough today, but it was really brutal in the past." These sentiments recall the "memories of the flesh" evoked in the novels of Toni Morrison and Gayl Jones.[2] Here the intensity of memory creates an imprint—in the mind or on the body—of past lessons, past pain, past sorrow. These memories say to groups of people: never forget what happened to us. They say that one derives strength through the remembrance of despair and pain.

In this epilogue I would like to briefly extend our discussion beyond the world of Nigerien politics to think about the enduring power of social memories. Are social memories replicable? Are they verifiable? Are they realistic recallings of the past? For me, these questions are beside the point, for in many cases, memory mimics the past, and mimicry, as we remember from Homi Bhaba, is ". . . the subject of difference that is almost the same, but not quite."[3]

Fritz Kramer's pan-African survey of mimetic possession and masquerades, *The Red Fez*, demonstrates the relevance of Bhabba's discussion of mimicry. "In mimesis . . . one conforms with some thing one is not and also should not be. Hence a generally recognized difference of some sort between the portrayer and the portrayed is an absolute prerequisite for mimetic behavior."[4] Kramer suggests that the "rational" understandings of African spirit possession and the European realist novel—both examples of the mimetic faculty—is shortsighted.

> In the realistic novel, as in African spirit possession, it is a question not of some rational understanding of systems and coherence, as is true, say, of modern ethnography, but rather of suggestive, intuitively grasped images which overwhelm the author, whether of text or of the dance.[5]

Kramer, however, does not ponder the more fascinating question of why mimetic behaviors, which so often evoke social memories, are so overwhelmingly powerful?

In his *Mimesis and Alterity* Taussig confronts head-on the question of mimesis and power. His text weaves a patchwork that conjoins mimesis, mechanical reproduction, (state) power and social memory. Between the lines of the text, Taussig's prose, like the talk of the Songhay elder in Wanzerbe, evokes a sense of loss. As Francis Yates once remarked, "We moderns have no memory at all."[6] The epistemological forces of modernism, Taussig among others argues, have diminished the mimetic faculty, which, in part, accounts for the loss of what Edward Casey calls "body memory."[7] Ironically, it is through modernism's mechanical reproduction, Taussig suggests, that the mimetic faculty—and body memory—has been rediscovered and intensified.

Mechanical reproduction, of course, can heighten the senses.[8] Herein lies Taussig's take on the power of the mimetic faculty. If we accept that perception is physiognomic, then that which we perceive through mechanical production can jolt us into a new embodied awareness. Such physiognomic comprehension sometimes produces what Benjamin termed the "flash of recognition." In the end, Taussig is suggesting, I think, that the power of mimesis derives from its multisensorial affecting presence.[9] The body of the spirit medium is invaded by her or his spirit; the body of the spectator is invaded by mechanically reproduced images. In both cases bodies are physiognomically transformed which heightens possibilities for sociocultural and political change.

This argument is quite apposite as far as it goes. Although mechanical reproduction sensuously intensifies magical moments of mimesis—as in Rouch's *Les maitres fous*, it also extends the distance between observers and observed. The images in *Les maitres fous* that make Taussig and other people in North American university audiences gasp convey other messages to Songhay audiences in the Republic of Niger. The images of the horrific, dog-devouring Hauka, from whose mouths saliva bubbles like shaving cream, is a shock to anyone, anywhere. But Songhay spectators, as we have seen, are not so much concerned with the rebirth of mimesis in Euro-america; rather, they continuously worry about their precarious fate in the world. There is something in the sensuous images of the Hauka that affects Nigeriens physiognomically, so much so that the Hauka, as we have seen, have become a model for affective/effective behavior on dusty dunes and in presidential palaces.

I have argued that the Hauka have mimicked the white man to "master" him, to tap into his extraordinary power so that it might be recircuited for local uses. In Niger, people used the power of mimetic excess to oppose and come to grips with French colonial rule in the 1920s. During the first regime of Niger's postcolony, peasants used it as a kind of sedative to deaden the pain of their growing alienation. During the postcolony's second regime, the President, himself a Hauka medium, transformed mimetic excess into state policy, forging a link between mimesis and the will to power. What appeared so promising and forceful at the beginning of Seyni Kountche's regime soon turned sour. Mendacity and duplicity (*zamba*)—the underside of the Hauka's mimetic excess— sapped the regime's vitality. Blind ambition and greed snuffed out hopes for a better life in Niger. People became cynical as state power became an end in itself. Once the emptiness of his regime's simulacra had been exposed, Kountche's only goal was to hold on to power. Alas, he died a defeated man and Nigeriens greeted his passing with a huge sigh of relief.

Embodied Memories and the Cruel Path

The collective sigh of relief that greeted Seyni Kountche's death did not erase traces of his memory that are seared into Nigerien bodies and the Nigerien body politic. As Toni Morrison's novels powerfully demonstrate, embodied memories are felt strongly, viscerally, physiognomically. And yet, we have little theoretical comprehension of why embodied memories are so powerful. Taussig, by way of Benjamin, argues that physiognomic responses result from mechanical reproduction, a reproduction that heightens our sensory awareness. I have argued that Taussig's reflections on mimetic excess may account for the gasps of North American university students and faculty viewing *Les maitres fous*, but don't explain the physiognomic responses of West Africans participating in Hauka spirit possession rituals, let alone Seyni Kountche's politically adept appropriation of an already reappropriated Hauka aesthetics to legitimate the brutality of his regime.

To understand better the far-reaching effects of embodied memories— colonial or otherwise—we need to step, however precariously, beyond Taussig's world of sparkling surfaces and briefly enter Antonin Artaud's universe of embodied cruelty. Throughout his fragmented oeuvre, Artaud wrote eloquently about the physiognomics of embodied memories. Artaud believed that the power of these memories emerges from a space beyond socially asphyxiating language. For Artaud the solution to social asphyxiation was the Theater of Cruelty which means,

> a theater difficult and cruel for myself first of all. And on the level of performance, it is not the cruelty we can exercise on each other by hacking at each other's bodies, carving up our personal anatomies . . . but the much more terrible and necessary cruelty which things can exercise against us. We are not free. And the sky can still fall on our heads. And the theater has been created to teach us that first of all.[10]

In some respects Artaud yearned for the participatory theater of yore which foregrounded transformative spectacle, which reconnected spectators with their embodied memories. It is clear from Artaud's comments about myth, spectacle, and "theatrical violence" that his vision for the Theater of Cruelty was inspired by pre-theatrical rituals in which powerful symbols were employed for therapeutic ends. Indeed, the scenario Artaud outlined for the Theater of Cruelty bears striking resemblance to many West African spirit-possession rituals, including those practiced by the Songhay in the Republic of Niger.

Perhaps the vitality of Songhay spirit-possession rituals, a virtual pre-theater, compelled Jean Rouch to make such "cruel" films as *Les maitres fous.* In Rouch's films of "ethno-fiction," he pursues an Artaudian path, for he wants to transform his viewers. He wants to challenge their cultural assumptions. He wants the audience—still mostly European and North American—to confront its ethnocentrism, its repressed racism, its latent primitivism. Anyone who has been assailed by the brutal images of *Les maitres fous* has experienced Rouch's *Cinema of Cruelty.* In *Les maitres fous,* "Rouch's path is correct not only because he doesn't ignore colonialism, but because leaving constantly his own environs and exhibiting nature through the massive effects she produces elsewhere, it at no time allows the spectator to remain indifferent, but compels him in some way if not to take a position, at least to change."[11] Rouch's *Les maitres fous* evokes the meaning of decolonization: namely, that European decolonization must begin with individual decolonization—the decolonization of a person's thinking, the decolonization of a person's "self." Such an effect is clearly an element of a Cinema of Cruelty, a cinema that uses, like Artaudian theater, unsettling juxtapositions to jolt the audience.

The key, then, to the imageric power of an Artaudian Theater of Cruelty or the presence of a Hauka spirit in the body of a Nigerien medium stems less from the contours of the image than from the way, to use Bachelard's language, the image "reverberates." For Bachelard the impact of a poem lies not in its referential content, but in how referential content carries a message that strikes a resonant chord ("reverberates") in the reader. Put another way, artistic power establishes a pulsating link between poet and reader, filmmaker and audience, spirit medium and spectator. This embodied link lies somewhere beyond Benjamin's "flash of recognition"; it is more like an electric current that jolts bodies as they are charged and recharged by the social memories that define and redefine our being-in-the-world. Ever the brilliant politician, Seyni Kountche understood well the political implications of the lesson that the Hauka branded into him as a teenager. It is a lesson more of us must struggle to grasp if we are to do anything more than stare dumbfounded at the dazzling complexities that comprise contemporary life in Africa. We have much to learn from the likes of Benjamin, Bachelard and Taussig. But we must also listen very carefully to the Hauka. They know that the sky is lower than we think. They know that it may soon come crashing down on our heads.

The golden glow of the late afternoon sun illuminated the path that terror had furrowed over the man's forehead. By now the stillness of fear had overtaken the man's frail body, though his brow twitched and his eyes darted at the two Hauka who had come that day to Tillaberi. The Hauka groaned and foamed at the mouth as they inspected the man's hollow eyes. His motionless arms hung limply at his side, and his sweat-soaked shirt stuck to his body in wet patches.

Istambula, chief of the Hauka, and Major Mugu, the wicked major of colonial fame, had been beckoned to determine what or who had blocked the man's path. The man's people came from Wanzerbe, the Songhay village of sorcerers, though he hadn't visited his ancestral home in more than fifteen years. He had long left the life of the Songhay countryside, having studied in a secondary school, a lycee in Niamey, and at several European and American universities. After much hard work he earned a doctorate in soil science and returned triumphantly to Niger.

He became a government civil servant in the Ministry of Agriculture, but the ministry assigned him a menial post: agricultural extension agent in Mehanna. Terribly unhappy with this twist of fate, he asked for a new assignment, preferably a post at the agricultural research center. The minister personally turned down the request. After seven years in Mehanna, the Ministry of Agriculture demoted him to Tillakaina, a "suburb" of Tillaberi. Once in Tillakaina, the man began to consult with spirit-possession priests and sponsor spirit-possession ceremonies. At each ceremony the spirits unsucessfully attempted to unblock the man's path. Finally, Adamu Jenitongo determined that only the Hauka could help him, and so the soil scientist made offerings to them. Even so, the man's situation worsened. He remained stuck in Tillakaina. He could not sleep.

"Why did you beckon us?" Istambula asked the man.

"Because my path is blocked. I am defeated. I am tired."

"Do you know why you are tired and defeated?" Major Mugu shouted.

The man responded with silence and darting eyes.

"Do you know why?" Istambula boomed.

More silence and darting eyes.

Istambula got in the man's face and screamed. Major Mugu jabbed his finger into the man's shoulder sending jolts through the soil scientist's body.

"Your path is blocked because you have betrayed us," Istambula stated. "Your path is blocked because you speak to us with two mouths and two hearts. You have betrayed us and now you must pay for your betrayal." Istambula spat in the man's face. Major Mugu electro-jabbed him in the shoulder.

Adamu Jenitongo tried to pull the spent man away from the revenge-seeking Hauka. At last the Hauka left and the dazed man's body twitched in the dusky light. Slowly, several people from Tillakaina led him away.

And everyone knew what the Hauka knew; everyone knew which path had to be followed.

Notes

◆   ◆   ◆

Prologue

1. See P. Stoller (1992a, 1992b); A. Artaud (1958) for background on the Theater of Cruelty.
2. See J-C. Muller (1971) and P. Stoller (1992a) for critical assessments of *Les maitres fous.*
3. See J. Rouch (1956)
4. F. Fugelstad (1975, 1983)
5. See Stoller (1984, 1989a, 1992a, 1992b)
6. M. Lambek (1981) and J. Boddy (1989) are two exemplary studies of spirit possession.
7. A radically empirical, multisensorial anthropology is proposed in Stoller (1989b) and M. Jackson (1989).
8. Discussions with R. J. Coombe helped to develop this point.

Part I: Introduction

1. This position is articulated forcefully by David Howes (1991).

See also Stoller (1989b).
2. D. Howes (1991, 3).

Chapter 1: Spirit Possession

1. The functionalist take on spirit possession is best represented by I.M. Lewis (1971, 1986), E. Bourguignon (1976), and F. Goodman (1988, 1989).
2. See R.J. Coombe (1991).
3. For psychoanalytic studies of possession in West Africa, see J. Monfouga-Nicholas (1972) and A. Zempleni (1968).
4. G. Harris (1957) gives an early account of spirit possession as hysteria.
5. Monfouga-Nicholas (1972)
6. One of the best studies of spirit possession from a psychoanalytic perspective is Obeysekere (1981).
7. C. Pidoux (1955).
8. See A. Jackson (1968); W. Sturtevant (1968).

9. A. Gell (1980).

10. A. Kehoe and D. Giletti (1981).

11. G. Balandier (1971).

12. M. Lambek (1981) and J. Boddy (1989).

13. See A. Schaeffner (1965), M. Leiris (1980), G. Rouget (1980), and J-M. Gibbal (1988).

14. See Olivier de Sardan (1990), I.M. Lewis (1990), and L. Brenner (1990).

15. This criticism is provided by literary critics and philosophers. See Trinh T. Minh-ha (1988), V. Mudimbe (1988) and C. Miller (1990).

16. Stoller (1989a, 210).

17. For detailed analyses of physiognomic perception see M. Taussig (1993), S. Buck-Morss (1989), and W. Benjamin (1969).

18. A. Jagger and S. Bordo (1989), S. Suleiman (1986), E. Martin (1987).

19. P. Bourdieu (1984, 210).

20. B. Turner (1991, 11).

21. R. J. Coombe pointed this out to me.

22. Stoller (1992b).

23. J. Rouch (1989, 339).

24. Ibid., 340.

25. J. Boddy (1989, 5).

26. See L. Abu-Lughod (1986), C. Lutz and L. Abu-Lughod (1990), and P. Connerton (1989).

27. P. Schmoll (1991, 248).

28. See Comaroff and Comaroff (1992).

29. Schmoll (1991, 249).

30. Ibid., 255.

31. Ibid., 255.

Chapter 2: Cultural Memory

1. P. Connerton (1989, 5).

2. M. Halbwachs (1992, 182).

3. Ibid., 188.

4. Connerton (1989, 22).

5. Ibid., 59.

6. Ibid., 61.

7. Ibid., 71.

8. Ibid., 72.

9. Ibid., 96.

10. R. J. Coombe provided this insight.

11. See G. Lipsitz (1990) and R. Terdiman (1985, 1993).

12. T. Morrison (1987, 119).

13. See the special issue of *Cultural Critique* (Fall 1993) devoted to the works of Toni Morrison.

14. G. Jones (1986, 22).

15. Ibid., 101-02.

16. Ibid., 103.

17. Ibid., 103.

18. J-P Olivier de Sardan (1982, 1984).

19. These are histories of the Songhay Empire written in the fifteenth and sixteenth centuries. French Arabists found the manuscripts, and translated and published them in 1900 (es-Saadi) and 1912 (Kati). The texts have been useful in reconstructing the Songhay imperial past, but some scholars, notably Hale (1990), Ba (1977) and Rouch (1953, 1989) have criticized the texts for their Muslim bias against pre-Islamic practices and personages.

20. For material on the West African griotic tradition, see C. Bird (1971), A.N. Niani (1965), J. Johnson (1986), C. Miller (1990) and Stoller (1992, 1994).

21. See T. Hale (1990).

22. Histories from below articulate the historical visions of the socially

dispossessed: women, peasants, captives. For histories from below on Songhay see J-P. Olivier de Sardan (1976, 1984).

Chapter 3:Embodied Memories: Mimesis and Spirit Possession

1. A. Schaeffner (1965).
2. M. Leiris (1980) details the muddied ethics of one of the grandest, if not most controversial expeditions to collect museum artifacts. The artifacts are still on display in Paris at the Musée del' Homme.
3. J–M. Gibbal (1988).
4. Ibid., 286.
5. See M. Merleau-Ponty (1964) and B Kapferer (1992, 846).
6. M. Merleau-Ponty (1964, 151).
7. M. Taussig (1993, 2).
8. Ibid., 8.
9. Ibid., 8.
10. Ibid., 8.
11. Ibid., 19.
12. See Jackson (1989) and Stoller (1989, 1992, 1994b).
13. W. Benjamin as quoted in M. Taussig (1993, 39).
14. See Taussig (1993).
15. Ibid., 247.
16. Ibid., 242.
17. Ibid., 242.

Part II: Introduction

1. N. Dirks (1992, 3).
2. N. Thomas (1994, 3). The notion of colonial culture, however refreshing to cultural anthropologists has a long currency in Africanist historiography. Curtin (1964) is one of many examples.

3. J. Scott (1987).
4. A. Mbembe (1992, 3).
5. Ibid., 4.
6. I have chosen to use the term opposition rather than resistance for some of the reasons articulated by Mbembe. Definitions of armed resistance are clear enough, even though the bulk of the literature focuses upon large-scale armed rebellions. In contradistinction to the military resistance of El Haji 'Umar or Samory Toure, the military rebellions in Niger were small scale and sporadic. Much more care, however, must be given to our definition of the much used and abused term, cultural resistance, which I chose to call "embodied oppositions" to highlight their contested and cultural nature.
7. See Comaroff and Comaroff (1991, 1992.

Chapter 4: From First Contacts to Military Partition

1. See W. Rodney (1971), I. Hancock (1985), Mann (1985).
2. See Rodney (1971), Hancock (1985), Stoller (1985), Mann (1985), Curtin (1964, 1969), Law (1977), and Brooks (1992).
3. Rodney (1971), Mann (1985). See also Issacman (198?).
4. M. Crowder (1968, 23).
5. Some of the best ethnography of West African societies is that written by late eighteenth- and early nineteenth-century natural historians. The writings of Mungo Park (1801) Rene Caillie (1821) and

Heinrich Barth (1855-57) are cases in point. See also Curtin (1964) and Pratt (1992) on Mungo Park.

6. Crowder (1968, 26-27). Lovejoy (1981) and Curtin (1969) present a more nuanced and critical assessment of the slave trade.

7. See Crowder (1968, 26-27). A more detailed account is presented in Hopkins (1973).

8. Ibid., 27.

9. See J.L. Flint in Ajayi and Crowder (1974, 392).

10. Other historians have noted, however, that local populations demonstrated great initiative and skill in developing an overseas economy. See Brooks (1992) and Rodney (1970, 1981).

11. See J. L. Flint in Ajayi and Crowder (1974, 392). Robin Law's materials on Dahomey offer a different perspective on this question. See Law (1977).

12. Crowder (1968, 45). See also Kanya-Forstner (1969).

13. Ibid., 45.

14. See Hopkins (1973) on local British policy.

15. See Kanya-Forstner (1969); Andrew and Kanya-Forstner(1981).

16. Ibid., 56.

17. Ibid., 59.

18. The political rationale for African colonization is a hotly debated arena among Africanist historians.
    See Ronald Robinson's *Africa and the Victorians* among other titles.

19. Crowder (1968, 63).

20. Ibid., 63.

21. Flint in Ajayi and Crowder (1974, 401).

22. A.E. Hopkins (1973, 165).

23. Ibid., 165.

24. Crowder (1968, 3-4).

Chapter 5: Colonizing West Africa

1. Flint in Ajayi and Crowder (1974, 401).

2. I. Wallerstein (1961, 31). See also R. Robinson (1967).

3. Crowder (1968, 335).

4. See Olivier de Sardan (1984), C. Meillassoux (1991) and Roberts (1984) for texts on slavery in West Africa.

5. Crowder (1968, 182–83).

6. S. Roberts and M. Klein (1980, 383).

7. See Olivier de Sardan (1984) and Chapter 7 for the case in Niger.

8. Crowder (1968, 210, citing Lugard's Dual Mandate, p. 369).

9. Ibid., 210.

10. See T. Painter (1988), Crowder (1968), and Cooper (1977). Colonial governments did recognize the political importance of domestic slavery; its continued existence compelled the commitment and support of local elites. Officials argued for a gradual policy on slavery to avoid social disruption and economic collapse (R. Waller, personal communication).

11. Crowder (1968, 184).

12. R. Mercier (1933), Crowder (1968).

13. R. Mercier as cited by Crowder (1968, 184).

14. Ibid., 206.

15. Ibid., 187. The description of the

chief in Ferdiand Oyono's novel, *Houseboy*, is particularly apposite.

16. See Crowder's *Revolt in Bussa*. Indeed, the French did practice indirect rule among the emirates of northern Cameroon.

17. Crowder (1968).

18. Although British colonial administrations putatively practiced indirect rule, there are many instances of the British governing African polities more or less directly. Governing practices in the Gold Coast differed markedly from those in Northern Nigeria. See P. Hill (1970) and S. Berry (1992).

19. Crowder (1968, 378–79).

20. Mumford and Orde-Brown (1935, 96).

21. Crowder (1968, 396, citing The Advisory Committee on Native Education, 1925, 4).

22. T. Mitchell (1990, 71).

23. Mumford and Orde-Brown (1935, 92) reproduced an English translation of Jules Brevie's December 1930 statement on French colonial policy.

24. Ibid., 102, which is the English translation of Albert Charton's paper, "The social Function of Education in French West Africa."

25. T. Mitchell (1990, 84).

26. Ibid., 93-94.

27. T. J. Jones (1925, 12).

28. Comaroff and Comaroff (1992, 70).

29. Ibid., 70-71.

30. Crowder (1968, 74).

31. S. Roberts (1963, 312-13).

32. A. Kiev (1972). Liberal colonizers articulated these ideas a generation before Kiev published his book.

33. Comaroff and Comaroff (1992, 70).

34. Crowder and Ajayi (1974, 535).

Chapter 6: Embodied Oppositions

1. See Kanya-Forstner (1969), Crowder (1968), Crowder and Ajayi (1974), I. Kimba (1981), T. Weiskel (1980).

2. Most of the examples of embodied oppositions presented here come from the French colonial sphere. These cases, of course, are analogous to the colonial context in Niger and have been chosen for this reason.

3. The Quadir and Tijani constitute two Sufi brotherhoods. In both cases, members of sects pledge their allegiance to a Sufi Saint. Some members will travel to the Saint's village and serve the master. Others will make yearly pilgrimages to the Saint's village to pay homage and present gifts to the man blessed with sacred *baraka*. Each member of the brotherhood will recite a *widr* which varies with the brotherhood. See O'Brien (1974).

4. See Oloruntimehin in Crowder and Ajayi (1974). See also J. Suret-Canal (1964).

5. See Oloruntimehin in Crowder and Ajayi (1974).

6. Mitchell (1990); Crowder (1968, 72-75).

7. Crowder (1968, 83). For the most detailed on the life of Samory, see Person (1975).

8. Kouroubari as cited by Crowder (1968, 86-87).

9. Crowder (1968, 87).

10. Ibid., 72. A more detailed analysis can be found in Kanya-Forstner (1969) in which he fleshes out local rationales for ferocious resistance to the French military.
11. See N. Thomas (1994).
12. Weiskel (1980, 236). Recent studies of resistance movements detail the complexity of local situations, all of which belies, the simple distinction of collaboration/resistance.
13. Ibid., 238.
14. Ibid., 227.
15. Ibid., 229-30.
16. J. Lips (1967, 14).
17. P. Ravenhill (1980, 2); Weiskel (nd).
18. Ravenhill (1980, 2).
19. Weiskel (nd, 2).
20. C. Steiner (1987, 95-96). There is much contention about whether Baule used "colons" to warn villages of European presences or as "fetishes" to drive away Europeans. Whatever their "ritual" use in the past, the "colons" have become valuable commodities during the last 25 years. Steiner underscores the irony of this reversal. "Once created in the spirit of repulsing the invasion of Western colonizers, colonial statues are now produced in the hope of attracting an invasion of Western consumers." This last point in brilliantly analyzed in Steiner's recent book, *African Art in Transit*.
21. Another apt example is the reproduction of "string" that the Asante used to imitate British telegraph wires. Such mimicry, of course, was, like the case of the Hauka, pregnant with cultural and political meaning. Thanks to R. Waller for pointing out this example.
22. See Beier (1964).
23. Ibid., 191.
24. Ibid., 197.
25. Thanks to Herbert Cole for refining my interpretation of these plastic forms.
26. See H. Cole (1983, 3).
27. See Cole (1983, 206–07). F. Kramer describes a similar plastic phenomenon among the Fanti in Ghana, where *asafo* companies built *posuban* shrines:

> The first *posuban* were built towards the end of the nineteenth century, although their models were warships or European forts of earlier centuries; surmounting a one-or-more-storey building were rows of arches, having neither doors, walls nor vaults, and no architectonic function; standing within were naturalistic statues of horse men, animals and fabulous creatures, which are reminiscent of the adornments on European fair booths. Many of these figures were based on European models, such as the mermaid which may have been copied from the figurehead of an old sailing ship; beside indigenous animals and cultural artifacts there were dragons and unicorns, angels and devils, as well as modern instruments, clocks, cannon, machine-guns and aeroplanes (1993, 206).

28. Cole (1983, 207). Cole's passage here is conditional. That is, the Owerri Igbo may or *may not* have considered *mbari* as a way of mastering and

ridding themselves of the white man. Personal Communication January 3, 1994.

29. J. Clifford (1988, 207).
30. See Cole and Aniakor (1983)
31. Taussig (1993, 238).
32. Ibid., 238.
33. Cole (personal communication, January 3, 1994) suggests that *mbari* may not be interpreted in this manner.

Chapter 7: Colonizing Niger

1. R. Charlick (1991, 33).
2. Ibid., 34.
3. See Olivier de Sardan (1976, 1982, 1984), Kimba (1981).
4. N. Thomas (nd, 4).
5. Charlick (1991, 34).
6. Archives de Afrique Occidental Francais (AAOF), Afrique III, Dossier 26, 38 bis.
7. W. Ponty, Rapport au Governeur General de l'A.O.F. AAOF (1906).
8. Olivier de Sardan (1984, 151).
9. From a report written by Cornu, AAOF as quoted in Olivier de Sardan (1984, 151).
10. Olivier de Sardan (1984, 152).
11. See Kimba (1981), Olivier de Sardan (1984).
12. See Olivier de Sardan (1984, 153).
13. From a report written by Sol (1932). Archives National, Section Outre Mer (ANOM); see also Olivier de Sardan (1984, 166).
14. Olivier de Sardan (1984, 166).
15. See Charlick (1991); Scholl (1991).
16. Charlick (1991, 34).
17. Olivier de Sardan (1984, 163).

18. See Fugelstad (1983, 83); Schmoll (1991, 88).
19. Olivier de Sardan (1984, 168). See also Celine's *Voyage au bout de la nuit* for a literary depiction of colonial terror.
20. See Egg (1975, 28), Olivier de Sardan (1984, 167).
21. Olivier de Sardan (1984, 168).
22. Scholl (1991, 86).
23. Fugelstad (1983, 81-83).
24. See Spittler (1979).
25. See Graby's 1928 report in the Archives Nationals de Niger (ANN); see also Oliver de Sardan (1984, 174).
26. Rapport au Commandant du Cercle de Dosso, 1902. Cited in Kimba (1981, 176).
27. Kimba (1981); Olivier de Sarda (1984).
28. See J. Rouch (1989). Rouch also emphasized the same point during an interview in Paris, March 3, 1990.
29. See Stoller and Olkes (1987) and Stoller (1989b).
30. N. Leca (1939). Rapport politique du 1927, cercle de Tillaberi, ANN.
31. See Roberts and Klein (1980).
32. See Rouch (1956). The best filmic representation of Songhay migration is Rouch's remarkable *Jaguar* (1964), which follows the adventures of three young men who migrate from Niger to the Gold Coast.
33. Fugelstad (1983, 87); See also Diarra (1973).
34. See N. Leca (1939); see also Oliver de Sardan (1984, 176).

35. Schmitt, (1929) ANN. See also Olivier de Sardan (1984, 176).
36. See Painter (1988).
37. Olivier de Sardan (1984, 176-77).
38. Ibid., 177. Migration may have been also "indispensable" to young men who sought freedom from the "tyranny" of elders. R. Waller pointed this out to me.
39. Fugelstad (1983), Schmoll (1991).
40. Olivier de Sardan (1984).
41. See Charlick (1992), Schmoll (1991), Fugelstad (1983).
42. See Schmoll (1991).
43. The rather dated notion of rupture, which Olivier de Sardan has himself recently repudiated (1993) may have marked a fundamental difference between Anglophone and Francophone hysterographies. R. Waller pointed this out to me.
44. See Iliffe (1991).
45. See Schmoll (1991), Fugelstad (1983), Olivier de Sardan (1984).
46. Venel AAOF, (1908).
47. Anon (1912-16). Monographie de la subdivision de Dosso, Archives des Etudes Nigeriennes (AEN). See also Olivier de Sardan (1984, 280).
48. P. Manning (1988, 99).
49. P. Alexandre (1970, 497–98).
50. Ibid., 511.
51. Tierno Bokar and, especially, Ahmadou Hampate Ba published their religiously-inspired reflections. Ahmadou Hampate Ba became an especially distinguished historian of West Africa. Hamani Diori became the first president of the Republic of Niger. Yacouba Sylla, a Sonnike living in Senegal, established a village-based militant social order based upon Hammalist principles.
52. Ibid., 506–08.
53. V. Monteil (1964) as cited in Olivier de Sardan (1984, 280).
54. P. Alexandre (1970, 512).

Chapter 8: The Birth of the Hauka Movement

1. N. Echard (1992, 97).
2. Ibid., 97
3. Anon. Affair des Baboule, Rapport politique annuel de cercle de Niamey, (1925). Dossier 5, pieces 5, Archives de service historique d'Armee (ASHA), Vincennes, France.
4. Scherer, Rapport du tournee dans le canton de Kourtey, ANN; see also Olivier de Sardan (1984, 282).
5. Anon. Rapport politique annuel du cercle de Niamey, 1926, ANN; see also Olivier de Sardan (1984, 282).
6. Anon. Rapport politique annuel du cercle de Niamey, (1927), ANN; see also Olivier de Sardan (1984, 282).
7. Reported in J. Rouch (1989, 73–74).
8. Fugelstad (1975, 205).
9. Ibid., 205.
10. Echard prepared an unpublished manuscript on bori and Shibbo.
11. See J-C. Muller (1971), Stoller (1992).
12. See Fugelstad (1975).
13. Fugelstad (1982, 129-31).
14. P. Schmoll (1991, 95).
15. Olivier de Sardan (1984, 276-77)
16. Ibid., 284.
17. Ibid., 284.
18. Ibid., 285
19. See Olivier de Sardan (1984). More

recently Olivier de Sardan (1993) has criticized the ethnographic and historical scholarship on the Hauka—including his own—as "over-interpreted." He suggests that the Hauka is one religious phenomenon among many others in the Zarma/Songhay world, and that it has had little to do with politics, movements of resistance and the like. His article is a call for scholars of religion and politics to take a perspective from which one can "better speak of facts, leaving them the last word."(1993, 210). Olivier de Sardan's "facts" are gleaned exclusively from texts: transcribed and translated field interviews, ethnographic monographs and the archival record. He ignores the dimension of memory suggested in Part 1 of this book: what Toni Morrison calls "memories of the flesh." These cultural memories and the power they evoke are, like almost all social scientific evidence, two to three degrees removed from the scenes of their expression. Given the contingency of all scientific data, it is somewhat anachronistic to speak of putative "facts" having the last word. "Facts," too, are mere interpretations that are shaped by historical, political and social conditions. The "last" word, which is never the *last* word because of the word's ephemeral nature, is usually given to scholars who mount the most compelling arguments. Olivier de Sardan's interpretation of the Hauka is that it is a simple religious phenomenon. Such a conclusion does not explain the popularity of the Hauka today, let alone why the Hauka have played such an important role in postcolonial Niger. These are questions that I attempt to explore in Part 3 of this book.

20. See Fugelstad (1975, 1983).

21. See Stoller (1989b), M. Jackson (1989), Merleau-Ponty (1962), Taussig (1993).

Chapter 9: Transgressing to the Gold Coast

1. See Rouch (1956, 1990), Stoller (1992); see also Bourdier and Trinh (1985) on the Gurunsi's negative memories of their nineteenth-century oppressors.

2. Rouch (1956).

3. Ibid.

4. Ibid., 177.

5. Ibid., 177.

6. Ibid.

7. See Rouch's film, *Jaguar*.

8. Brachet, Historique de Filingue; carnet monographique de Filingue. Dossier 8, sous-dossier 6-c (1903-44). ASHA.

9. See J. Rouch's interview with N. Echard on France Culture in July, 1988.

10. See Rouch's film, *Les maitres fous*; see also Echard and Rouch (1988).

11. For a contextual analysis of *Les maitres fous*, see Echard and Rouch (1988), Stoller (1992); for its impact on the French New Wave, see Eaton (1979); for its surrealist tendencies, see DeBouzek (1989).

12. Echard and Rouch (1988), Stoller (1992).

13. See G. Devos in R. Predal (1982).

14. See R. Bensmaia in Predal (1982).

15. Taussig (1993, 242).

16. See T. A. Volkman (1982) as cited in Taussig (1993, 241).

17. Rouch (1978, 1009).

18. Mbembe (1992).

19. There is still much harsh reaction to the film today in North America, especially if it is presented without ethnographic contextualization.

Chapter 10: Independence and the Postcolony of Niger

1. Mbembe (1992, 2), J. Gleick (1987).

2. Mbembe (1992, 2)

3. Ibid., 3.

4. Ibid., 5.

5. Ibid., 5.

6. Charlick (1991, 41-42).

7. See Charlick (1991).

8. Ibid., 50.

9. Ibid., 51.

10. Mbembe (1992, 2).

11. Ibid., 2

12. Charlick (1992, 54).

13. Ibid., 56-57.

14. Ibid., 58.

15. Ibid., 60.

16. Jeune Afrique #1235 (1984, 35).

17. Ibid., 36.

Chapter 11: Expanding the Hauka Movement During Independence

1. When I first went to the Republic of Niger in 1969 as a Peace Corps Volunteer, the Government housed me and three other future secondary school teachers in a spacious villa. They also provided us a chef who had been trained at Cordon Bleu in Paris. He was one of many such chefs during the Diori years.

2. Soumana Yacouba, interview on December 29, 1985 in Tillaberi, Niger.

3. See A. Sidikou (1974). Indeed, the land in western Niger is dry and rocky. In the south of Songhay there are vast plains broken by rocky mesas. Here rainfall levels are usually adequate (600-800 millimeters per year). Farther north, the rainfall dwindles and the soil becomes quite sandy. Dunes extend in ranges running north-south. In the Tillaberi region, where Soumana has farmed his two fields, rainfall has for some time dropped to well under 400 millimeters per annum, a level that imperils a rain-fed millet and sorghum crop. Farther north in Gao and Timbuktu, rainfall is consistently under 300 millimeters per year which is insufficient for millet and sorghum cultivation.

   Rainfall levels are only part of Soumana Yacouba's story. Even if rain falls abundantly in a given year, it must fall in the right amounts and at the right moments in the growing cycle. Too much rain too early—say in June—means that the freshly sowed seeds will be washed away. Too little rain too early means that young millet shoots will shrivel and die. If the rains are "right" in June and July (perhaps four downpours during the month), the millet will grow well. In August, the month of greatest rainfall, there should be seven to ten downpours, which enable the millet to grow tall and strong. September requires four to five more downpours until the millet bears its green seeds. In October, farmers like Soumana pray for a hot sun that will transform green seeds into brown ones—ready for harvest. Too much rain late in the growing season, of course, will rot the millet.

The success of the millet crop also depends upon the absence of pestilence. Worms may well eat the young roots of millet shoots early in the growing season. And when the millet ripens, birds, rats, and/or locust sometimes ravage it. Given the ecological fragility of rain-fed agriculture in the Sahel, it is no wonder that farmers like Soumana Yacouba worry incessantly about the weather and the fate of their crops. In a land well known for droughts and famine, farmers have a respectful fear of hunger. Will they be able to feed their families this year?

4. Although this story was recounted in 1985, it well represents the rigors and frustrations of the peasant's life in the Nigerien postcolony.

5. Soumana Yacouba, interview on December 29, 1985, Tillaberi, Niger.

6. See Sidikou (1974).

7. Soumana Yacouba, interview on December 29, 1985, Tillaberi, Niger.

8. See Charlick (1991).

9. See Stoller (1989a, 170–71).

10. Richard Waller, personal communication, points out that there have been many "zombie" states throughout Africa. A particularly striking case was Malawi under Hastings Banda.

11. See Shildekrout (1974).

12. Echard and Rouch (1988), Stoller (1992).

13. See Rouch (1989), Stoller (1989a).

14. Stoller (1989a).

15. Fugelstad (1975, 1983).

16. I spent 1969-70 in Tera, Niger, living in the town's secondary school compound.

17. Stoller (1989a, 155-57).

18. See A. Artaud (1958), Stoller (1992b).

19. Stoller (1989a).

20. Ibid.

21. Mbembe (1992, 5).

22. See Artaud (1958), Stoller (1992b).

Chapter 12: The Hauka and the Government of General Seyni Kountche

1. Hauka aesthetics constitute a symbolic language that mimics the behaviors of the French colonial army. In terms of body movement, it highlights upright posture, stiff leg and arm movements, military salutes and stutter-steps. In addition, the Hauka's body is impervious to intense heat (fire and boiling water) as well as to pain. Facial expressions are rigid, penetrating, tough. Language use is direct and terse—no nonsense. The image of fire is important to Hauka aesthetics. Fire is nature's weapon which powerful beings (Dongo, the French military, and the Hauka) use to demonstrate their force. These are

the aesthetic contours that Seyni Kountche used to promote his program and reinforce his personal power.

2. *Le Sahel,* (April 29, 1972, 1).
3. Ibid, 4.
4. Jeune Afrique (JA) (695, 21).
5. Ibid., 22.
6. JA (669, 20).
7. JA (1235, 32-37).
8. A. Mbembe (1992, 3).
9. JA (702, 25).
10. JA (713 18).
11. It is ironic that Seyni Kountche would use the term "commanda-ment" to describe the major admin-istrators of his government. The term was employed during the colo-nial era to denote a tough and merciless local administration. In Songhay, the term "commando," is still used today to refer to *sous-prefets* of Songhay districts. With reason, Kountche wanted to disas-sociate himself from practices of the past, the "commandemant" of the Diori regime. He expelled from Niger the last vestiges of the French commandemant—the French Army garrison that had been lodged in Niamey. And yet, he refers to his own cadre as "commandemant," stressing the new power role of the military in administrative affairs. On the one hand, it was perhaps good politics to distance oneself from some aspects of the "comman-demant." On the other hand, it was equally good politics to underscore other aspects (military bearing, decisiveness, toughness) of the "commandemant."
12. JA (1402, 18).
13. *Le Sahel,* (August 6, 1975, 1, 8).
14. R. Charlick (1991, 63).
15. Quoted in JA (1402, 67).
16. *Le Sahel* (September 4, 1975 1).
17. *Le Sahel* (July 7, 1975, 1).
18. *Le Sahel* (March 9, 1976, 1).
19. *Le Sahel* (March 17, 1976, 3).
20. Ibid., p.3.
21. Charlick (1991, 63).
22. JA 795, p. 23.
23. JA 796, pp. 30-31.
24. *Le Sahel* (March 22, 1976, 1).
25. Charlick (1991, 64).
26. *Le Sahel* (March 17, 1976, 3).
27. The exception to this pattern was General Ali Seybou, Kountche's immediate successor. Seybou concealed neither his consumption of alcohol nor his martial infideli-ties. He did not go out of his way to deny his family's long and involved association with spirit possession.
28. Charlick (1991, 64).
29. Ibid., 65.
30. Ibid., 65.
31. Ibid., 65.
32. Ibid., 66.
33. Ibid., 69.
34. Stoller (1989b).
35. Interviews with Amadou Harouna, December 23, 1985 in Mehanna, Republic of Niger and Adamu Jeni-tongo, December 27, 1985 in Till-aberi, Republic of Niger.
36. JA (1192, 29).
37. Charlick (1991, 70).
38. JA (1192, 29).
39. Ibid., 29.
40. Ibid., 29.

41. Ibid., 30.

42. Ibid., 28.

43. Ibid., 30.

44. Charlick (1991, 70).

45. Ibid., 71.

46. JA (1229, 41).

47. See J. Favret-Saada (1981), Stoller (1989b).

48. See A. Metraax (1960).

49. JA 1402, p.67.

Epilogue: Memory, Power, and Spirit Possession

1. See A. H. Sidikou (1974); R. MacIntosh (1993); J-P. Olivier de Sardan (1969).

2. One thinks here of Morrison's *Beloved* (1987) and Jones's *Corregedora* (1986).

3. H. Bhabba (1985, 126)

4. F. Kramer (1993, 250).

5. Ibid, 254.

6. Cited in E. Casey (1987, 2).

7. Ibid, 2.

8. See Benjamin 1969, Buck-Morss 1994).

9. See Benjamin 1969, Buck-Morss 1994).

10. This term is derived from Robert Plant Armstrong's magisterial study of Yoruba plastic arts (1971).

11. Artaud (1958, 79).

12. Bensmaia quoted in Predal (1982, 55).

References

Films Cited

Rouch, Jean. 1956. *Les maitres fous.* Paris: Films de la Pleiade.

Archival Sources

Anonymous. 1925. Affaire des Baboule: Rapport Politique Annuel. Dossier 9, piece 5. Vincennes: Archives du Service Historique des Armees.

Anonymous. 1912–16. Monographie de la Subdivision de Dosso. Niamey: Archives des Etudes Nigeriennes.

Anonymous. 1925. Rapport Politique Annuel de Cercle de Niamey. Niamey: Archives Nationales de Niger.

Anonymous. 1927. Rapport Politique Annuel de Cercle de Niamey. Niamey: Archives Nationales de Niger.

Buck. 1903–1944. Religion, Situation Islamique des Songhay. Dossier 8, sous-dossier 6–a. Vincennes: Archives du Service Historique des Armees.

Brachet. 1903–1944. Historique de Fil-ingue: Carnet Monographique de Filingue. Dossier 8, sous-dossier 6–c. Vincennes: Archives du Service Historiques des Armees.

Cornu. 1899. Notice Sur le Pays Zaberma et son occupation par le Dahomey. Aix-en-Provence: Archives de Afrique Occidentale Francaise

Leca, N. 1939. Rapport Politique de 1927: Cercle de Tillaberi. Niamey: Archives Nationales de Niger.

Loffler. 1906. Rapport Politique de Cercle de Djerma, Monographie de l'Ancien Cercle de Djerma (version dactylographee recennet et sans references). Niamey: Archives Nationale de Niger

Ponty, W. 1906. Rapport au Governeur General de l'A.O.F. Aix-en-Provence: Archives de l'Afrique Occidentale Francaise.

Schmitt. 1929. Untitled. Niamey. Archives Nationales de Niger.

Schuerer n.d. Rapport de Tourne dans le Canton de Kurfey. Niamey: Archives Nationales de Niger.

Sol. 1932c. Rapport alimentaire dans la colonie de Niger. Paris: Archives Nationales, Section Outre Mer.

Venel. 1908. Commandant de Territoire Militaire du Niger. Aix-en-Provence: Archives de l'Afrique Occidentale Francaise.

Other Sources

Abu-Lughod, Lila. 1986 *Veiled Sentiments*. Berkeley: University of California Press.

Ajayi, J.F.A. and Michael Crowder, eds. 1972. *History of West Africa, Volume One*. London: Longman.

Alexandre, Pierre. 1970. "A West African Islamic Movement: Hammalism in French West Africa." In R.I. Rotberg and A.A. Mazrui, eds. *Protest and Power in Black Africa*. New York: Oxford University Press, 497–513.

Andrew, Christopher and A.S. Kanya-Forstner. 1981. *The Climax of French Imperial Expansion*. Palo Alto: Stanford University Press.

Armstrong, Robert Plant. 1971. *The Affecting Presence*. Champaign-Urbana: University of Illinois Press.

Ba, Adam Konare. 1977. "Sonni Ali Ber." Etudes Nigeriennes #40. Niamey: Universite de Niamey.

Barthe, Heinrich. 1857–58. *Travels and Discoveries in North and Central Africa in the Years 1849–1855*. 3 Vols. New York: Harper.

Bastide, Roger. 1978. *The African Religions of Brazil*. Baltimore: The Johns Hopkins University Press.

Beier, Ulli. 1964. "The Agbegijo Masqueraders." *Nigeriea Magazine* 182: 189–99.

Bensmaia, Rena. 1982. "Jean Rouch ou le cinema de la cruaute." In R. Predal, ed. *Jean Rouch, un griot gallois*. Paris: Harmattan, 50–59.

Berry, Sara. 1992. "Hegemony on a Shoestring: Indirect Rule and Access to Agricultural Land." *Africa* 62(3): 327–57.

Bird, Charles. 1971. "The Mande Bard." In C. Hodge, ed. *The Oral Tradition in Mande*. Bloomington, IN: Indiana University Press.

Bhabba, Homi. 1994. *The Location of Culture*. New York: Routledge.

Boddy, Janice. 1989. *Wombs and Alien Spirits*. Madison, WI: University of Wisconsin Press.

Bourdieu, Pierre. 1984. *Distinction*. Cambridge, MA: Harvard University Press.

Bourdier, Jean-Paul and Trinh T. Minh-ha. 1985. *African Spaces: Designs for Living in Upper Volta*. New York: Africana Publishing Co.

Bourguignon, Erica. 1976. *Possession*. San Francisco: Chandler.

Brooks, George. 1992. *Landlords and Strangers: Ecology, Society and Trade in Western Africa*. Boulder: Westview.

Caille, Rene. [1930] 1965. *Journal d'un voyage a Tembouctou et a Jenne dans l'Afrique centrale*. 3 Vols. Paris: Anthropos.

Casey, Edward. 1987. *Remembering: A Phenomenological Study*. Bloomington, IN: Indiana University Press.

Celine. 1953. *Voyage au bout de la nuit.* Paris: Gallimard.

Charlick, Robert. 1991. *Niger: Personal Rule and Survival in the Sahel.* Boulder: Westview Press.

Cole, Herbert. 1982. *Mbari.* Bloomington, IN: Indiana University Press.

Cole, Herbert and Chike Aniakor, eds. 1983. *Igbo Arts: Community and Cosmos.* Los Angeles: Museum of Cultural History (UCLA).

Cooper, Frederick. 1977. *Plantation Slavery on the East Coast of Africa.* New Haven: Yale University Press.

Comaroff, Jean. 1985. *Body of Power, Spirit of Resistance.* Chicago: University of Chicago Press.

Comaroff, Jean and John Comaroff. 1990. "Goodly Beasts, Beastly Goods: Cattle and Commodities in a South African Context." *American Ethnologist* 17(2): 195–217.

Comaroff, John and Jean. 1991. *Of Revelation and Revolution: Christianity, Colonialism and Consciousness in South Africa, Volume One.* Chicago: University of Chicago Press.

Comaroff, Jean and John. 1992. *Ethnography and the Historical Imagination.* Boulder: Westview Press.

Connerton, Paul. 1989. *How Societies Remember.* Cambridge: Cambridge University Press.

Coombe, Rosemary. J 1991. "Encountering the Postmodern: New Directions in Cultural Anthropology." *Canadian Review of Sociology and Anthropology* 28: 188–205.

Crowder, Michael. 1968. *West Africa Under Colonial Rule.* Evanston, IL: Northwestern University Press.

Crowder, Michael, ed. 1971. *West African Resistance: the Military Response to Colonial Occupation.* New York: Africana Press.

Curtin, Phillip. 1964. *Image of Africa* Vols 1. and 2. Madison: University of Wisconsin Press.

Curtin, Phillip. 1969. *The Atlantic Slave Trade.* Madison: University of Wisconsin Press.

DeBouzek, Jenny. 1989. "The Ethnographic Surrealism of Jean Rouch." *Visual Anthropology* 2(3–4): 301–17

DeVos, George. 1982. "Les maitres fous et anthropologie americaine." In R. Predal, ed. *Jean Rouch, un griot gaullois.* Paris: Harmattan, 59–62.

Diarra, A. 1973. *Femmes Africaines en devenir: Les femmes Zarma du Niger.* Paris: Editions Anthropos.

Dirks, N. 1992. *Colonialism and Culture.* Ann Arbor: University of Michigan Press.

Eaton, Mick, ed. 1979. *Anthropology-Reality-Cinema: The Films of Jean Rouch* London: British Film Institute.

Echard, Nicole. 1992. "Cultes de possession et changement social. L'exemple du bori hausa de l'Ader et du Kurfey (Niger)." *Archives de Sciences Sociales des Religions* 79(2): 87–101.

Egg, Lerin and Venin. 1975. *Analyse Descriptive de la Famine des Annees 1931 au Niger, et Implication Methodologiques.* Paris: INRA

Favret-Saada, Jeanne. 1981. *Deadly Words: Sorcery in the Bocage.* London: Cambridge University Press.

Featherstone, Mike, Mike Hepworth

and Bryan Turner, eds. 1991. *The Body: Social Process and Cultural Theory*. San Francisco: Sage.

Fugelstad, Finn. 1975. "Les Haaka: Une interpreation historique." *Cahieus d'Etades Africainer* 58: 203–16.

Fugelstad, Finn. 1983. *A history of Niger: 1850–1960*. Cambridge: Cambridge University Press.

Gell, Alfred. 1980. "The Gods at Play: Vertigo and Possession in Muria Religion." *Man*, n.s. 15: 219–49.

Gibbal, Jean-Marie. 1988. *Les Genies du Fleuve*. Paris: Presses de la Renaissance.

Gleick, James. 1987. *Chaos*. New York: Viking.

Goodman, Felicitas. 1988. *How About Demons*. Bloomington, IN: Indiana University Press.

Goodman, Felicitas. 1990. *When the Spirits the Ride Wind*. Bloomington, IN: Indiana University Press.

Hale, Thomas. 1990. *Scribe, Griot and Novelist*. Gainesville, FL: Univeristy of Florida Press.

Harris, Grace. 1957. "Possession 'Hysteria' in a Kenyan Tribe." *American Anthropologist* 59: 1046–66.

Henderson, Mae. 1991. "Toni Morrison's Beloved: Re-membering the Body as Historical Text." In H.J. Spillers, ed. *Comparative American Identities: Race, Sex, and Nationality in the Modern Text*. New York: Routledge, 62–87

Hill, Polly. 1970. *Studies in Rural Capitalism in West Africa*. London: Cambridge University Press.

Hopkins, Anthony. G 1973. *An Economic History of West Africa*. New York: Columbia University Press.

Howes, David (ed.). 1991. *Varietis of Sensory Experience*. Toronto: University of Toronto Press.

Iliffe, John. 1991. *The African Poor*. London: Cambridge University Press.

Isaacman, Alan and Betty Isaacman. 1983. *Mozambique: From Colonialism to Revolution*. Boulder: Westview.

Jackson, Alfred. 1968. "Sound and Ritual" *Man*, n.s. 3: 293–300.

Jackson, Michael. 1989. *Paths Toward a Clearing*. Bloomington, IN: Indiana University Press.

Jagger, Alison and Susan Bordo. 1989. *Gender/Body/Knowledge*. New Brunswick, NJ: Rutgers University Press.

Jones, Gagl 1987. *Corregidora*. New York: Grove Press.

Johnson, John W. 1986. *The Epic of Son-Jata*. Bloomington, IN: Indiana University Press.

Jones, Thomas Jesse. 1925. *Education in East Africa*. New York: Phelps-Stokes Fund.

Kapferer, Bruce. 1992. "Review of Fusion of the Worlds." *American Ethnologist* 19(3):846–47.

Kehoe, Alice and Dody H. Giletti. 1981. "Women's Preponderance in Possession Cults: The Calcium-Deficiency Hypothesis Extended." *American Anthropologist* 83: 549–62.

Kimba, Idrissa. 1981. *Guerres et Sociétés*. Niamey: University de Niamey.

Kramer, Fritz. [1987] 1993. *The Red Fez: Art and Spirit Possession in Africa*. London: Verso Press.

Lambek, Michael. 1981. *Human Spirits*.

Cambridge: Cambridge University Press.

Lash, Scott. 1991. "Genealogy and the Body: Foucault/ Deleuze/ Nietzsche." In M. Featherstone, et. al, eds. *The Body: Social Process and Cultural Theory.* San Francisco: Sage, 256–81.

Law, Robin. 1977. *The Oyo Empire: 1600–1836.* Oxford: Clarendon Press.

Leiris, Michel [1958] 1980. *La Possession et ses Aspects Theatraux Chez Les Ethopiens de Gondar.* Paris: Le Sycomore.

Lewis, I.M. 1971. *Ecstatic Religion.* Harmondsworth, England: Penguin Books.

Lewis, I.M. 1986. *Religion in Context.* Cambridge: Cambridge University Press.

Lipsitz, George. 1991. *Time Passages.* Minneapolis: University of Minnesota Press.

Lips, Julius E. 1966. *The Savage Strikes Back.* New York: University Books.

Lovejoy, Paul ed. 1981. *The Ideology of Slavery.* Beverley Hills: Sage.

Lutz, Catherine A. and Lila Abu-Lughod eds. 1990. *Language and the Politics of Emotion.* Cambridge: Cambridge University Press.

MacIntosh, Roderick. 1993. "The Pulse Model: Genesis and Accommodation of Specialization in the Middle Niger." *Journal of African History* 34(2): 184–220

Mann, Kristin. 1985. *Marrying Well: Marriage, Status and Social Change among the Educated Elite in Colonial Lagos.* Cambridge and London: Cambridge University Press.

Manning, Patrick. 1988. *Francophone Sub-Saharan Africa, 1880–1985.* Cambridge: Cambridge University Press.

Martin, Emily. 1987. *The Woman in the Body.* Boston: Beacon Press.

Mbembe, Achille. 1992. "The Banality of Power." *Public Culture* 4(2): 1–30.

Meillassoux, Claude. 1991. *The Anthropology of Slavery.* Chicago: University of Chicago Press.

Mercier, Rene. 1933. *Le travail obligatoire dans les colonies africaines.* Paris: Larose.

Merleau-Ponty, Mauric.e 1964. *L'Oeil et L'Esprit.* Paris: Gallimard.

Meyer, Morris. 1989. "Review of Fusion of the Worlds." *High Performance* 12(4):32.

Metraux, Alfred. 1960. Haiti: Blacks Peasants and Voodoo. New York: Universe Books.

Meyer, Morris. 1991. "Review of Fusion of the Worlds and Hausa Medicine." *Text and Performance Quarterly.* October: 336–40.

Miller, Christopher. 1990. Theories of Africans. Chicago: University of Chicago Press.

Mitchell, Timothy. 1988. *Colonizing Egypt.* Berkeley: University of California Press.

Monfouga-Nicholas, Jacqueline. 1972. *Ambivalence et Culte de Possession.* Paris: Editions Anthropos.

Morrison, Toni. 1987a. *Beloved.* New York: Knopf.

Morrison, Toni. 1987b. "The Site of the Truth." In W. Zinsner ed. *The Art and Craft of Memoir.* Boston: Houghton Mifflin, 109–132.

Monteil, Vincent. 1964. *L'Islam noir.* Paris: Seuil.

Mudimbe, Valentin Y. 1988. *The Invention of Africa.* Bloomington, IN: Indiana University Press.

Muller, Jean Claude. 1971. Revie of *Les maitres fouds. American Anthropologist.*

Niani, D.T. 1965. *Sunjata: An Epic of Old Mali.* London: Longman.

Obeysekere, Gananath. 1981. *Medusa's Hair.* Chicago: University of Chicago Press.

O'Brien, Donal B. Cruise. 1971. *The Mourides.* Oxford: Clarendon Press.

Olivier de Sardan, Jean-Pierre 1969. *Les Voleurs d'Hommes.* Etudes Nigeriennes No. 25. Niamey: Universite de Niamey.

Olivier de Sardan, Jean-Pierre. 1976. *Quand Nos Peres Etaient Captifs.* Paris: Nubia.

Olivier de Sardan, Jean-Pierre. 1982. *Concepts et Conceptions Sonay-Zarma.* Paris: Nubia.

Olivier de Sardan, Jean-Pierre. 1984. *Sociétés Sonay-Zarma.* Paris: Karthala.

Olivier de Sardan, Jean-Pierre. 1993. "La surinterpretation politique: Les cultes de possession hawka du Niger." In J-F Bayart, ed. *Religion et Modernite Politique En Afrique Noire.* Paris: Karthala, 163–213.

Oloruntimehin, B. D. 1974. "The Western Sudan and the Coming of the French 1800, 1893." In Ajayi and M. Crowder, eds. *History of West Africa I.* Evanston, IL: Northwestern University Press, 344, 380.

Oyomo, Ferdinand. 1966. *Houseboy.* London: Heineman

Painter, Thomas. 1988. "From Warriors to Migrants: Critical Perspectives on Early Migrations Among the Zarma of Niger." *Africa* 58(1): 87–100.

Park, Mungo. [1801]1960. *Travels* London: Dent and Sons.

Person, Yves. 1968–75. *Samori, une revolution dyula.* Dakar: IFAN, Memoire # 80. 3 Vols.

Pratt, Mary Louise. 1992. *Imperial Eyes: Travel Writing and Transculturation.* New York: Routledge.

Predal, Rene, ed. 1982. "Jean Rouch, un griot gallois." *CinemAction* 17. Paris: Harmattan.

Pidoux, Charles. 1955. "Les Etats de Possession Rituelle Chez les Melanos—Africains." *Evolution Psyciatrique,* Fasc. II.

Ravenhill, Philip. 1981. *Baule Statuary Art: Meaning and Modernization.* Philadelphia: ISHI.

Roberts, Steven. 1963. *The History of French Colonial Policy 1870–1925.* London: Archon Books.

Roberts, Richard. 1984. *Warriors and Merchants.* Palo Alto: Stanford University Press.

Roberts, Richard and Martin Klein. 1980. "The Bamana Slave Exodus in 1905 and the Decline of Slavery in the Western Soundan." *Journal of African History* 21(3): 375–95

Robinson, Ronald. 1967. *Africa and the Victorians: The Official Mind of Imperialism.* New York: St Martins Press.

Rodney, Walter. 1970. *A History of the Upper Guinea Coast.* London: Oxford

University Press.

Rodney, Walter. 1981. *How Europe Underdeveloped Africa.* Washington,D.C.: Howard University Press.

Rouch, Jean. 1956. "Migrations au Ghana." *Journal de la Société des Africanistes* 26 (1–2): 33–196.

Rouch, Jean. 1978. "Jean Rouch Talks About His Films to John Marshall and John W. Adams." *American Anthropologist* 80(8): 1005–20.

Rouch, Jean. 1989. *La Religion et la Magie Songhay,* (2nd ed.). Brussels: Free University.

Rouget, Gilbert. 1980. *La Musique et La Transe.* Paris: Gallimard.

Scarry, Elaine. 1985. *The Body in Pain.* London: Oxford University Press.

Schaeffner, Andre. 1965. "Rituel et Pre-theater." In *Histoire des Spectacles.* Paris: Gallimard: 21–54.

Schmoll, Pamela. 1991. *Searching for Health in a World of Disease* (Ph.D. Dissertation). Dept. of Anthropology, University of Chicago.

Sikidou, Arouna Hamidou. 1974. *Sédéntarité et Mobilité Entre Niger et Zagret.* Etudes Nigeriennes #34. Niamey: Université de Niamey.

Spittler, George. 1979. "Peasants and the State in Niger." *Peasant Studies* 8(1): 30–47.

Steiner, Christopher. 1987. "Review of Statues Colons." *African Arts* 22(1): 95–96

Steiner, Christopher 1994. *African Art in Transit.* New York and London: Cambridge University Press.

Stoller, Paul 1985. "A Phenomenological Approach to Pidgin and Creole Languages." In I. Hancock ed., *Diversity and Development in Pidgin and Creole Languages.* Ann Arbor: Karona Press, 1–15.

Stoller, Paul. 1989a. *Fusion of the Worlds.* Chicago: University of Chicago Press.

Stoller, Paul 1989b. *The Taste of Ethnographic Things.* Philadelphia: University of Pennsylvania Press.

Stoller, Paul. 1992. *The Cinematic Griot: The Ethnography of Jean Rouch.* Chicago: University of Chicago Press.

Stoller, Paul. 1994a "Conciousness Ain't Conscious." In C. Nadia Sermetakis ed., *The Senses Still.* Boulder: Westview Press, 109–23.

Stoller, Paul. 1994b. "Ethnographies as Texts/Ethnographers as Griots." *American Ethnologist* 20(2).

Stoller, Paul and Cheryl Olkes. 1987. *In Sorcery's Shadow.* Chicago: University of Chicago Press.

Suret-Canal, Jean. 1964. *L'Afrique noire: L'ere colonial 1900–1945.* Paris: Editions Sociales.

Sturtevant, William. 1968. "Categories, Percussion and Physiology." *Man,* n.s. 3: 133–34.

Suleiman, Susan R. 1986. *The Female Body in Western Culture.* Cambridge, MA: Harvard University Press.

Taussig, Michael. 1993. *Mimesis and Alterity: A Particular History of the Senses.* New York: Routledge.

Terdiman, Richard. 1985. *Discourse/Counter-Discourse.* Ithaca: Cornell University Press.

Terdiman, Richard.1993. *Present Past. Modernity and the Memory Crisis.* Ithaca: Cornell University Press.

Thomas, Nicholas. 1994. *Colonialism's Culture: Anthropology, Travel, and Government.* Princeton: Princeton University Press.

Trinh T. Min-ha. 1988. *Woman, Native, Other.* Bloomington, IN: Indiana University Press.

Turner, Byran S. 1991. "Recent Developments in the Theory of the Body." In Mike Featherstone et. al., *The Body: Social Process and Cultural Theory.* San Francisco: Sage: 1–36.

Wallerstein, Immanuel. 1961. *Africa: The Politics of Independence.* New York: Vintage Press.

Weiskel, Timothy. 1980. *French Colonial Rule and the Baule Peoples: Resistance and Collaboration, 1889–1911.* Oxford: Clarendon Press.

Zempleni, Andras. 1968. *L'Interpretation et La Therapie: Traditionelle du Desordre Mental Chez Les Wolof et Les Lebou (Senegal).* Paris: Institut d'Ethnologie.

Index

◆　　◆　　◆